Multiliteracies and e-learning2.0

FOREIGN LANGUAGE PEDAGOGY

CONTENT- AND LEARNER-ORIENTED

Edited by Gabriele Blell and Rita Kupetz
Co-founded by Karlheinz Hellwig

VOLUME 28

Zu Qualitätssicherung und Peer Review der vorliegenden Publikation

Die Qualität der in dieser Reihe erscheinenden Arbeiten wird vor der Publikation durch beide Herausgeberinnen der Reihe geprüft.

Notes on the quality assurance and peer review of this publication

Prior to publication, the quality of the work published in this series is reviewed by both editors of the series.

Ivana Marenzi

Multiliteracies and e-learning2.0

PETER LANG
EDITION

Bibliographic Information published by the Deutsche Nationalbibliothek
The Deutsche Nationalbibliothek lists this publication in the Deutsche Nationalbibliografie; detailed bibliographic data is available in the internet at http://dnb.d-nb.de.

Zugl.: Hannover, Univ., Diss., 2014

Library of Congress Cataloging-in-Publication Data
Marenzi, Ivana.
Multiliteracies and e-learning 2.0 / Ivana Marenzi.
pages cm
Includes bibliographical references.
ISBN 978-3-631-65652-5
1. Language and languages—Computer-assisted instruction. 2. Language and languages—Computer-assisted instruction—Research. 3. Language and languages—Study and teaching—Computer network resources. 4. Computers and literacy. 5. Literacy—Social aspects. 6. Educational technology. I. Title.
P53.28.M37 2014
418.0078'5—dc23

2014038899

Cover Image:
Title : The LearnWeb2.0 design framework – a multi-tier model
Source: The circle was adapted by author from Yelland et al., 2008, p.200

D 89
ISSN 1430-8150
ISBN 978-3-631-65652-5 (Print)
E-ISBN 978-3-653-04937-4 (E-Book)
DOI 10.3726/978-3-653-04937-4

Peter Lang Edition is an Imprint of Peter Lang GmbH.

Peter Lang – Frankfurt am Main · Bern · Bruxelles · New York · Oxford · Warszawa · Wien

This publication has been peer reviewed.

www.peterlang.com

Preface

Modern society brings with it a multiplicity of changes both at a local and a global level. They constitute a fundamental challenge for everyone involved in education – administrators, teachers, parents, and students – which is to teach and learn in such a way as to cope with an unpredictable future. Students are thus required not only to be literate, but also to self-teach and be able to adapt their skills to the environment in which they live in order to be successful both now and in the future. The challenge for educators is to support students in emphasizing skills that address the present social requirements but which reflect future ones as much as possible.

My own experience has involved a rather variegated educational route. My initial goal after finishing school was to become a fresco restorer. Instead, I earned a university degree in Modern Languages and Literature, attended a Master's degree in Media Science and Technology, worked as an ICT technician at the University of Pavia in Italy, and, finally, obtained a position as a researcher at the L3S Research Center in Hannover, Germany. When I started my PhD, about six years ago, my interest was focused on e-learning and online collaboration. The task I set myself was to bring educational research closer to the learning scenario. The results of 5 years research as an educational technologist, described in this volume, would not have been possible without the contribution of various people who have, directly or indirectly, influenced both my professional, as well as my personal life.

First, I would like to thank Prof. Wolfgang Nejdl for giving me the opportunity to work at the L3S Research Center, an ideal work environment. Without his unfailing enthusiasm and encouragement from the early stages of my work, this thesis would never have been written. Collaboration and discussion with my colleagues at the L3S Research Center has been an essential source of information and enrichment for both my professional and personal development.

I owe a great debt of gratitude to my supervisor Prof. Rita Kupetz for her professional support, patience, and insightful advice that were crucial for the initial set-up of my research on multiliteracies and for the development of this work. I am also indebted to my second supervisor, Prof. Anthony Baldry, for the many fruitful discussions we have had throughout my PhD, and for all the things I have learned from him.

My warm thanks to all colleagues of the LearnWeb team, in particular Sergej, Philipp, Jaspreet, and the various students who helped us improve the LearnWeb system as it went through many stages of implementation: Mounika,

Armin, Maximilian, Olex, Jaspreet, Ankit, Rahil, Sanyia, Trevor. Many thanks to the L3S technicians and project assistants who have always been very supportive, whenever I have approached them with minor or major requests. It is immensely helpful to work in such a relaxed and friendly environment.

I wish to thank all professors, teachers and students who collaborated with us in the evaluation of the functionalities and pedagogical affordances of the LearnWeb Framework providing their feedback over the years in various scenarios in both Germany and Italy. In particular, Prof. Rita Kupetz, Eva Holdack-Janssen, Deirdre Kantz, and Francesca Bianchi helped out, by co-designing the learning activities for their courses. Special thanks go to Maria Bortoluzzi for starting up the YELL professional online community and for her close and invaluable collaboration in involving other teachers and researchers with her enthusiasm and professional initiative.

I would also like to thank all members of the English Department, Faculty of Philosophy, Leibniz Universität Hannover for their insightful remarks and comments during the PhD seminars I attended. I would like to distinctly mention Prof. Gabriele Blell who was also Head of my thesis commission, as well as Hannah Ruhm and Carmen Becker who helped me prepare some of the documentation as requested by the Faculty.

I'm very grateful to Deirdre Kantz for her last-minute proofreading of my thesis. It goes without saying that any errors and slip-ups are entirely my own responsibility.

I would like to thank all my friends and especially my office mate Marco who welcomed me each working day with his warm and joyful greeting "un solare buongiorno".

Finally, I wish to thank all my family who have always encouraged me, and, in particular, Giada who accompanied these years of work with her inexhaustible cheerful playfulness. Without all the love, understanding and support I got from all of you I would not have made it.

Table of contents

"Working together we can help build a world where our children learn, in many languages, not only how to surf the net, but also how to make waves (Shneiderman, 1997)". Quoted in Graddol (2001, AILA Review 14, p. 58).

Courtesy of[1]

1 http://2.bp.blogspot.com/-YZbjHVqLs9Q/UPKd5LgF0mI/AAAAAAAAAEg/4jZ_o_OGkZ4/s320/waves+in+a+pan.jpg

Zusammenfassung: multiliteracies und e-learning2.0

Durch neue Technologien und insbesondere soziale Netzwerke ändern sich Interaktion und Kommunikation, Suche und Austausch von Informationen, und dadurch die Möglichkeiten für Bildung und Lernen. Emails ermöglichen einfache Kommunikation zwischen Personen unterschiedlicher Länder und Kontinente, Nachrichten werden online verbreitet und gelesen, so gut wie jede Zeitung und jedes Magazin ist im Web präsent und ermöglicht die Diskussion von Beiträgen und die Verbreitung weiterer Informationen. Web 2.0-Technologien unterstützen die Kolloboration in Gruppen, den einfachen Austausch von Informationen, und die gemeinsame Arbeit an Dokumenten.

In diesem Kontext sind die üblichen Sprach-, Lese- und Schreibfähigkeiten zwar notwendig, aber nicht mehr hinreichend für die moderne Wissensgesellschaft. Neue Technologien und neue Arten der Kommunikation und Interaktion fanden und finden Eingang in Bildung und Lernen, zuerst mit abgeschlossenen Einheiten zu Lerninhalten (CBT – *Computer Based Training*), zwischenzeitlich auch mit Einbeziehung des Web 2.0. In neuen Lernkontexten müssen Lernumgebungen über Kurs- und Lehrplan-zentrierte Modelle hinausgehen, und Lerner-zentrierte und selbstorganisierende Lernnetzwerke unterstützen. Sie müssen die Verbindung mit Online-Räumen und -Netzwerken unterstützen, und effektive Möglichkeiten für den Austausch und die gemeinsame Arbeit an Lerninhalten bieten.

Vor diesem Hintergrund zielt diese Promotionsstudie darauf ab, einen für dieses neue Lernen geeigneten pädagogischen Ansatz (*Multiliteracies*) mit einer neuartigen Lernumgebung (LearnWeb2.0) zu unterstützen und zu integrieren, um auf diese Weise die Potenziale sozialer Netzwerke für das Lernen auszuschöpfen. Statt Werkzeuge für kollaboratives Lernen in traditionelle Lernplattformen einzubauen, untersuchte diese Arbeit die Möglichkeiten eines Bottom-Up-Ansatzes, in dessen Rahmen Web 2.0 Services als Bausteine für eine neue Art von kollaborativer Lernumgebung genutzt wurden.

Im Rahmen des Forschungszentrums L3S, in Zusammenarbeit mit Kollegen, erarbeitete und evaluierte die Autorin dieser Arbeit neue Ansätze zur Weiterentwicklung der LearnWeb2.0 Plattform, als Such- und Kollaborationsplattform aufbauend auf verschiedenen Web 2.0 Systemen. Sie verfolgte dabei einen iterativen evaluationsgetriebenen designbasierten Forschungsansatz, mit enger Verzahnung von Forschung, Entwicklung, Evaluation und Nutzung der Plattform.

Dabei war eine enge interdisziplinäre Zusammenarbeit unabdingbar, um sowohl informatische als auch pädagogische Aspekte zu erforschen und zu verknüpfen, ebenso wie die Einbeziehung von Lehrenden und Lernenden, um deren Anforderungen zu berücksichtigen. Die Zusammenarbeit fand auch mit Kollegen und Lehrenden anderer Universitäten, exemplarisch im Kontext von Content and Language Integrated Learning (CLIL) statt. Die Evaluationen brachten wichtigen Input für die Entwicklung entsprechender Funktionalitäten und der Benutzeroberfläche der Plattform, sowie des pädagogischen Rahmens für diese CLIL-Kurse und für den Einsatz der Plattform. Dabei wurden die folgenden Forschungsarbeiten durchgeführt:

1. Design und Implementierung der ersten Version von LearnWeb2.0;
2. Analyse und Evaluation von Design und Usability von LearnWeb2.0 in unterschiedlichen Szenarios: Identifikation und Sammeln der Benutzeranforderungen in diesen Szenarien;
3. Erste Abstimmung der Anforderungen mit den bestehenden LearnWeb2.0 Funktionalitäten;
4. Evaluation des Systems in zwei Lehrveranstaltungen an zwei unterschiedlichen Universitäten, mit dem Ziel, Rückmeldungen und Anregungen von Lehrern und Studenten zu bekommen, welche Funktionalitäten hilfreich waren und was verbessert werden sollte;
5. Identifikation und Definition von Prioritäten für neue Funktionalitäten, die entwickelt werden sollten.

Die Rolle der Autorin in diesem Forschungskontext war die eines *Educational Technologist*. Dies umfasste Vorschlag und Diskussion passender pädagogischer Theorien, Identifikation der Szenarios und Phasen, die durch die Lernumgebung unterstützt werden sollten, sowie die Leitung und Moderation des Prozesses der Unterstützung von Lehrenden und Studierenden durch die Entwickler von LearnWeb2.0 und durch die Autorin. Als *Educational Designer* und Forscher ging die Arbeit deutlich über die Datenerhebung und Analyse hinaus, und umfasste die Entwicklung von Methoden zur Kommunikation und zum Informationsaustausch zwischen den Projektbeteiligten – Entwickler und Nutzer (Lehrende, Lernende und Forscher) – ebenso wie das Design der Lernumgebung, um unterschiedliche Szenarien in Lehre und Forschung zu unterstützen. Im Rahmen der Lehre basierte das pädagogische Setup auf dem Vorschlag der Lehrenden, die Autorin entwickelte das Konzept für die Unterstützung durch LearnWeb2.0.

Das Ziel des ersten Evaluationszyklus war es, Vor- und Nachteile des Systems für die ausgewählten Szenarien auszuloten, um darauf aufbauend das System weiter zu entwickeln. LearnWeb2.0 wurde hierbei im Rahmen des Sommersemesters 2010 in zwei Lehrveranstaltungen genutzt, einmal an der Leibniz Universität Hannover, einmal an der Universität Pavia in Italien.

Um die Vielfalt pädagogischer Aspekte und Perspektiven zu berücksichtigen, verfolgte die Autorin einen "Mixed Method" Forschungsansatz, der sowohl qualitative als auch quantitative Daten aus unterschiedlichsten Quellen berücksichtigte. Qualitative Befragungen waren wichtig um auch die Benutzer aktiv in die Weiterentwicklung und Nutzung der Platform einzubeziehen. Im Rahmen der Forschungsarbeiten wurden LearnWeb2.0 Activity Logs entwickelt und ausgewertet, Diskussionen zum Feedback von Nutzern – Lehrende und Lernende – moderiert und zusammengefasst, und das Skydev Logbook geführt und ausgewertet, in dem als "Research Log" System alle Software-änderungen vermerkt wurden. Daten aus Nutzerevaluierungen wurden in Excel-Dateien gesammelt und als Graphen und Charts visualisiert. Auf Basis dieser Analysen diskutierte und initiierte die Autorin entsprechende Änderungen und Erweiterungen der Lernumgebung, um die Anforderungen der Nutzer zu berücksichtigen, und die Nutzung von LearnWeb2.0 im Rahmen von CLIL zu verbessern.

Auf Basis des ersten Zyklus und entsprechender Verbesserungen und Erweiterungen von LearnWeb2.0 arbeitete die Autorin in einem zweiten Zyklus an Anforderungen und Personalisierungen für unterschiedliche Szenarien und Lernziele, und am pädagogischen Ansatz und seiner Unterstützung durch die Lernumgebung. In dieser Phase lag der Schwerpunkt auf den folgenden Forschungsarbeiten:

1. Leitung der Implementierung neuer Funktionalitäten in der zweiten LearnWeb2.0 Version, zur Unterstützung der Nutzeranforderungen und zur engeren Integration und Unterstützung der Lehre im Rahmen des universitären Fremdsprachenerwerbs;
2. Analyse und Evaluation weiterer Nutzeranforderungen zur Personalisierung von LearnWeb2.0 für unterschiedliche Szenarien;
3. Definition eines theoretisch fundierten Modells und entsprechender Struktur für LearnWeb2.0.

Grundlage für das pädogogische Design sind der *Multiliteracies*-Ansatz und das darauf aufbauende *Learning by Design* Framework, und das Ziel, eine enge Integration von Informationstechnologien und Lehr-/Lern-Kontext zu erreichen. Dies wurde durch das von der Autorin entwickelte *LearnWeb2.0 Design Framework*, ein Mehrebenenmodell, verwirklicht, das LearnWeb2.0 Funktionalitäten und Nutzung mit der *Multiliteracies*-Pädagogik verknüpft. Das

Framework unterstützt durch den theoretisch fundierten Rahmen und eine darauf basierende Anleitung für Lehrende, Forscher und Entwickler Diskussion und Design von Lehrveranstaltungen mit entsprechender Einbindung der Lernumgebung.

Abstract

The world is changing fast thanks to the pace of social and technological development. New technologies and social networks have changed the way people interact, search and share information, and how they learn. E-mails allow instant communication between people across the world. People access the news online, as most magazines, newspapers and services of all kinds have constantly-updated website and blogs where users can find information and contribute with their own comments and data. Web 2.0 technologies thus provide a means to collaborate online by editing and sharing content with other people.

In this context, traditional literacy skills, based on the ability to read, write and speak no longer satisfy the needs of today's information society. Technology and new ways of communication and interaction have been adopted in education in various forms, originally using *Computer Based Training* (CBT) units and other educational applications but more recently privileging e-learning2.0 platforms. In the contemporary learning context, there is the need for learning environments to go beyond course-centric and curriculum-centric models, and instead envision learner-centred and self-organised learning networks. These much-needed approaches connect participants and support collaborative knowledge creation.

For these reasons, this research intends to integrate a strong pedagogical foundation (*multiliteracies*) with a new kind of e-learning environment tapping the potential of social networks for learning (*LearnWeb2.0*). Instead of adding collaborative tools in traditional LMSs (*Learning Management Systems*), the research reported here has explored a bottom-up approach that adopts a combination of Web 2.0 services as way to introduce more co-operation and collaboration into online learning activities.

Working with colleagues at the *L3S Research Center* in Hannover and following an *Iterative evaluation-driven design-based research* approach, the author has carried out research designed to improve the *LearnWeb2.0* platform, developing a new version for searching distributed Web 2.0 repositories and integrating different Web 2.0 tools. This *Iterative evaluation-driven* research necessarily involved experts from different disciplines (computer scientists and educators) as well as other stakeholders, most obviously teachers and students. Collaboration with universities supporting CLIL (*Content and Language Integrated Learning*) courses was essential, as was their evaluation and feedback, when designing good e-learning supports for language learning scenarios. In particular, at the *L3S Research Center*, this involved the following steps in the first phase of this doctoral work:

1. Design and implementation of the first version of the *LearnWeb2.0* environment;
2. Analysis and evaluation of the design and usability of the *LearnWeb2.0* system in various scenarios: identification and collection of the users' requirements in different settings;
3. Preliminary matching of the requirements with existing *LearnWeb2.0* functionalities;
4. Evaluation of the system in two university courses to obtain feedback from teachers and students about what worked well and what had to be improved;
5. Identification and definition of priorities for new functionalities to be adopted and implemented.

The specific role of the author within the research was as an *educational technologist*. In particular, this involved referring to several educational theories and approaches, identifying the various scenarios that would benefit most from the support of a technological environment, and guiding the process whereby teachers and students participating in the evaluation are properly supported. Thus, as an educational designer in general, the role of the researcher was not so much to elicit data, but rather to develop methods that facilitated communication between the various project stakeholders: developers and users (*i.e.* teachers, students and researchers) and to design and provide a suitable support for different scenarios in education and research. In educational settings, the method adopted was for the teacher to suggest the pedagogical approach and for the researcher to ensure this approach was supported by technology. The methods used were designed to guide and iterate development and evaluation through the various phases (e.g. design, development, evaluation, analysis) constantly encouraging stakeholders to make suggestions that would improve the system. This process of iteration is a key point in the research, one that is detailed in the various chapters of this volume.

The goal of the first evaluation cycle was to test what functionalities worked well and what was missing in the first version of LearnWeb2.0, in an effort to improve the system in keeping with users' requirements. Accordingly, the system was used and evaluated during the summer semester 2010 in two university courses, one at the Leibniz University of Hannover in Germany, the second at the University of Pavia in Italy.

With a view to taking a variety of educational aspects and perspectives into consideration, the author adopted a "mixed method" approach to the research that was designed to collect both qualitative and quantitative data from a variety of sources. Qualitative phases were important to involve users actively and improve the platform's usage. The research involved taking *LearnWeb2.0* activity logs into account, keeping the minutes of periodic meetings (teachers' and students' feedback) and analysing the records of the *Skydev Logbook*, which was used as a "research log" system tracking software changes (both those requested and those implemented). Data deriving from users' evaluations was collected in Excel files and used to record the results and visualise them in the form of graphs and charts. Analysing these data together with the developers, the researcher checked what functionalities worked well and what was missing and improved the system in keeping with users' emergent requirements, before relating the findings to CLIL methodology.

Armed with these initial appraisals of the second version of the *LearnWeb2.0* system, the author undertook a second evaluation cycle, this time less focused on the design and usability of the system, and concerned rather more with collecting users' requirements and customising the system to support different scenarios and learning goals. During the winter semester of 2011 *LearnWeb2.0* was used in a German course at the *Leibnizschule High School* in Hannover, in a case study involving pupils from 8th and 12th grades who set about collecting and discussing materials from the Web on the theme of Postwar Literature. During the winter semester of 2012, the system was evaluated as a sharing platform by a community of teachers and researchers at the University of Udine, Italy, within the YELL project (*Young English Language Learners*).

In order to define the main framework and the functionalities to be implemented in support of various virtual communities, the following activities were carried out in the second phase:

1. Implementation of new functionalities in the second version responding to users' feedback and better supporting language teaching and learning scenarios;
2. Analysis and evaluation of other user requirements vis-à-vis the customisation of the *LearnWeb2.0* system in different scenarios;
3. Definition of a theoretical model and a basic educational structure for the system.

Regarding the pedagogical setup, the researcher built on the *multiliteracies* approach and the *Learning by Design Framework* so as to improve the integration of information technology and educational context. The result was a *multi-tier model,* called the *LearnWeb2.0 Design Framework*, which connects *LearnWeb2.0* functionalities with *multiliteracies* pedagogy, providing a common theoretical reference and guide for teachers, researchers and developers when discussing how to design course activities and how to support the learning process.

1 Introduction and motivation

> "When all men, wherever they may be, have equal access to the same vast communications network, they will inevitably become Citizens of the World."
>
> (Clarke, 1962, p. 183)

Modern society brings with it a multiplicity of changes both at a local and global level. New social practices have been developing and we have to face up to transformed kinds of employment, new ways of participating as citizens in public spaces, and new ways of interacting with others. In everyday life, we experience an increasing diversity of discourses and are constantly involved in negotiations over meanings. The development of communication technologies has given rise to an array of different communication channels that provide us with various representations of information and various possible interpretations of the meanings associated with this information. Similarly, communication and interactions with others are changing. In a global environment, the phenomenon of multilingualism requires careful attention not just because of the pluralism of languages, but rather because of a growing variety of "social languages" in professional, national, ethnic and sub-cultural contexts (Gee, 1996). To live well in this world "people must be able to recognize such diversities and be flexible enough to negotiate with others unlike themselves" (Kellner, 1998, p. 103).

In the modern knowledge society, where competitiveness is an increasingly important factor, education plays a strategic role towards personal achievement and social integration and equality. Schools have a very important role in preparing people to face up to this changing reality, and in creating the learning conditions which support them when interacting in familiar, as well as in unfamiliar contexts. Traditional *literacy* teaching, based on the ability to read, write, listen and speak a language is no longer enough to ensure that all students benefit from education in ways that allow them to participate fully and equally in public, community, and economic life. In their Manifesto *A Pedagogy of Multiliteracies* (1996), the New London Group (NLG) authors identified a multiplicity of social and cultural aspects that call for a broader view of literacy. They suggested "a new kind of pedagogy in which language and other modes of meaning are dynamic representational resources, constantly being remade by their users as they work to achieve their various cultural purposes" (NLG, Cazden et al., 1996, p. 64) as well as the renovation of pedagogy relating to literacy where learners are no longer considered passive recipients of contents, nor simply expected to reproduce what they learned from the teacher. Instead, they must become active participants of the learning process transforming available resources (*Available Designs*) into innovative and creative new meanings (*the Redesigned*). In their idea of Design, we are both inheritors of patterns and conventions of meanings and at the same time active designers of meaning. In accordance with this idea, in the researcher's opinion the role of technology is to support teachers in designing learning activities in different contexts and to facilitate the monitoring of the learning process.

This doctoral work intends to investigate different scenarios in which technology can support the learning process in new ways of meaning-making. The focus is on online interaction and collaboration from the standpoint of *Educational Technology*: the field of research which studies the design and implementation of educational environments using a systematic approach. With this approach, various issues are analysed in relation to more general frameworks (such as theoretical models, analysis of the overall context etc.) (Calvani, 2004, p. 12; author's translation).

As Scanlon points out:

> "Research in this area has a variety of goals: determining the mechanisms of collaborative learning, gaining evidence to improve software design and the provision of educational guidelines as well as the design of good tasks for collaborative learning. Various communities are involved in the enactment of this research, ranging from computer scientists involved in Technology Enhanced Learning (TEL), psychologists studying thinking and learning mechanisms, and educationalists trying to design effective collaborative learning settings." (Scanlon, 2011, p. 321)

In the following sections three important issues in the field of research are described, namely Web 2.0, the *multiliteracies* framework and CLIL (*Content and Language Integrated Learning*). The motivations and the directions of the present work are sketched so as to address these issues. Section 1.4 gives an overview of the structure of the thesis.

1.1 Web 2.0

In 2005 Tim O'Reilly defined Web 2.0 as an "architecture of participation", going beyond the page metaphor of Web 1.0 to deliver rich user experiences (O'Reilly, 2007).

The term *Web 2.0* refers to a second phase of the Web which developed from being a predominantly read-only medium to one where users contribute and share contents. Even if many inequalities still exist in access to digital technology, the use of Web services is becoming an increasingly central aspect of most people's lives at any age. People increasingly communicate with each other and participate online in social and cultural life manipulating and sharing various types of contents, from text (Blogs and Wikis) to images in Flickr, audio, podcasting and videos in YouTube. Other tools help categorising and organising information (social bookmarking and RSS feeds), or share it through social networks such as Facebook (Marenzi et al., 2008b). The use of these services provides new means through which knowledge is propagated, ideas are exchanged and work is published (Abel et al., 2009a). In comparison with Web 1.0, the novelty lies in the different role played by users who not only find information but become authors at the same time.

Social software works bottom-up: people with similar interests use a system to spontaneously form communities and interact with others to achieve their personal goals. This is in contrasts with more traditional situations where people are placed into groups defined within a specific organisation (Marenzi et al., 2008b). Examples of social software include wikis, blogs, social tagging, podcasting or video-casting, that provide an opportunity for social interaction. Creativity, sharing and collaboration are encouraged; users create content (for example Wikipedia, the largest online encyclopedia created by readers) and make it available to others who may in turn intervene and contribute to it adding their own comments or materials. In this way a huge amount of data is provided and available on the Web, but at the same time there is the risk of "information overload". It is more and more difficult to find the information needed and trust reliable resources.

"Typically different Web 2.0 infrastructures focus only on particular media types, videos in YouTube, pictures in Flickr, or bookmarks in Delicious, even though these resources belong to one and the same context" (Abel et al., 2009c, p. 1). Thus, despite the variety of available resource sharing systems, finding and linking distributed resources related to the same context is still difficult. In addition to this, most of the available tools support people in their search activity and search items in different tools, "but do not support joint searching and resource sharing in a group working on a common task" (Abel et al., 2009a).

To address these issues, one of the main objectives underpinning this doctoral work was to design and improve an integrated environment that combines different multimedia resources from several Web 2.0 systems, and provides functionalities to support collaborative search.

1.2 Multiliteracies framework

Due to the development of communication technologies, a number of different communication channels provide us with various representations of information and various possible interpretations of meanings. In several situations such as at work, as citizens or in our personal life, new social practices have been developing and we have to reckon with transformed kinds of employment, new ways of participating as citizens in public spaces, and new ways of interaction with others.

In the modern knowledge society, education plays a strategic role towards personal achievement and social integration and equality. Schools have a very important role in preparing people to engage with this changing reality, and in creating the learning conditions which support them to interact in familiar, as well as unfamiliar contexts. Traditional *literacy* teaching, based on the ability to read, write, listen and speak a language is no longer enough to ensure that all students benefit from education in ways that allow them to participate fully and equally in public, community, and economic life.

In 1996 the New London Group authors suggested the urgent need to renovate *literacy* pedagogy (NLG, Cadzen et al., 1996). In their manifesto they pointed out the need for "A Pedagogy of Multiliteracies" which goes beyond the traditional curriculum focused on teaching grammar and standard forms of a language. *Literacy* is not a matter of correct usage, rather it is a way of communicating; we should teach how a language is used in a specific context or in a variety of discourse occurrences. This approach is very close to the constructivist concepts of *scaffolding* and *zone of proximal development* (Vygotsky, 1978), where the basic idea is that cognitive development is directly linked to social development and that the way a student thinks and what s/he learns derive from the environment in which he or she lives, and from the teacher's guidance or the collaboration with more capable peers. Standard education and immersion in the context are not enough to provide comprehensive knowledge. We also need to involve learners more actively and let them express their subjectivity and participate with creativity in the transformation of new meanings (Kalantzis et al., 2010). Learners are no longer considered passive recipients of contents, nor are they simply expected to reproduce what they learned from the teacher; they must become active participants of the learning process transforming available resources (*Available Designs*) into innovative and creative meanings (*the Redesigned*).

In this context the present research investigates how Web 2.0 technologies and multimedia resources can be used in the classroom "to provide students with a wider range of *learning skills*" (Mehisto et al., 2008, p. 11).

1.3 CLIL

CLIL (*Content and Language Integrated Learning*) is one of the most promising approaches to foreign language teaching and learning to emerge in the last twenty years that attempts to take into consideration the needs of students in the changing society.

Internet and new technologies have changed contemporary society's interaction and meaning-making practices considerably: dealing with linguistic and cultural differences is a central part of our working, social, and private lives. In a globalised world, interaction with others requires a shared language for communication, and language learning and teaching are increasingly important. Knowing a language today is not important simply for personal knowledge, but "is crucial to the way we live in modern society" (Warschauer, 2001, p. 55).

New challenges for traditional school-based teaching, pedagogies and curricula are emerging. As reported in the CLIL/EMILE report (Marsh, 2002), to be effective in a society where developing communication skills and building intercultural knowledge is important, "language teaching needs to diversify classroom methodology, provide opportunities to study content through different perspectives, and increase learners' motivation and confidence in both the language and the subject being taught". "The promise of integrating both content and language learning is challenging, and to be successful, good resources, a clearly defined set of objectives, and good task design are essential" (Marenzi et al., 2010). "Exposure to foreign language in real-life contexts as well as the use of authentic subject-specific materials can be more effective than foreign language textbooks" (Wolff, 2003, p. 220). But it is still difficult to find good and authentic materials for CLIL because many resources are localised and teachers spend much time in preparing suitable materials for their classrooms. According to Mehisto (2012, p. 16), "Quality learning materials guide students in seeking out and using other resources (sources) for learning". Good search strategies and tools that support teachers and students in finding useful resources for CLIL are needed.

In this context new search strategies are investigated and better tools for collaborative searching are provided which can help teachers and students to find reliable and authentic material for their classrooms.

1.4 Overview and structure of the thesis

This section provides an overview of the structure of the thesis, and the reasoning behind the different chapters. Different steps in the research are described in the various chapters as well as the results already collected in papers accepted and presented in various international conferences and workshops during the past four years. The researcher argues that CSCL (*Computer Supported Collaborative Learning*) and *Educational Technology* can play an important role in promoting and supporting learning in different scenarios.

Chapter 1 gives the introduction and motivation for the doctoral work describing the three main topics involved in the research, such as Web 2.0 (Section 1.1), the Multiliteracies Framework (Section 1.2) and CLIL in Section 1.3.

Part I (Theoretical Background) provides a theoretical basis for the thesis.

Chapter 2, *Pedagogy and Technology Enhanced Learning (TEL)*, gives an overview of the most relevant pedagogical frameworks such as Behaviourism, Cognitivism (Section 2.1) and Constructivism (Section 2.2) as the fundamental basis for the development of e-learning (Section 2.3), *Computer Supported Collaborative Learning* (Section 2.4) and e-learning2.0 strategies (Section 2.5). Section 2.6 describes in greater detail what *Educational Technology* is, and what the role of the educational technologist is, making the connection between *literacy*, collaboration and organisational skills in education. Finally Section 2.7 provides a summary discussion of the various topics. Chapter 2 includes the contributions taken from the following published works:

Marenzi Ivana (2012): Designer genres: social, interactional, technological and multimodal aspects of Web 2.0. In: Cambria Mariavita, Arizzi Cristina, Coccetta Francesca (eds.): *Web Genres and Web Tools*. Como: Ibis, 174–214.

Marenzi Ivana & Zerr Sergej (2012): Multiliteracies and active learning in CLIL: the development of LearnWeb2.0. *IEEE Transactions on Learning Technologies* (TLT). Los Alamitos, CA, USA, 5(4), 336–348. DOI:10.1109/TLT.2012.14

Part II (Empirical Research) focuses on the development and the empirical evaluation of the LearnWeb2.0 platform with the pedagogical goal of supporting collaborative searching and sharing activities in different learning scenarios.

Chapter 3, *Search, collaboration and sharing in the Web*, gives an overview on the available Web 2.0 platforms that allow social searching and sharing of resources on the Web, and provides a short discussion on open issues such as availability, aggregation and storage of educational resources. Section 3.1 addresses some of these issues, describing the TENCompetence project and the LearnWeb2.0 prototype system as a collaborative search-and-sharing platform. Section 3.2 describes the LearnWeb2.0 system design and architecture (version 1) in more detail, and provides a short comparison with other existing solutions. Chapter 3 is built upon the work published in:

Abel Fabian, Marenzi Ivana, Nejdl Wolfgang & Zerr Sergej (2009b): Sharing distributed resources in LearnWeb2.0. In: Ulrike Cress, Vania Dimitrova, & Marcus Specht (eds.): *Learning in the Synergy of Multiple Disciplines*, Proceedings of the 4th European Conference on Technology Enhanced Learning (EC-TEL 2009). Springer, (5794), 154–159.

Abel Fabian, Marenzi Ivana, Nejdl Wolfgang & Zerr Sergej (2009c): LearnWeb2.0: resource sharing in social media. In: *Proceedings of Workshop on Social Information Retrieval for Technology-Enhanced Learning (SIRTEL'09)*. Aachen, Germany, (535), 1–63.

Marenzi Ivana, Demidova Elena, Nejdl Wolfgang & Zerr Sergej (2008b): Social software for lifelong competence development: challenges and infrastructure. *International Journal of Emerging Technologies in Learning (iJET)*, 3(2008), 18–23. ISSN: 1863–0383.

Marenzi Ivana, Demidova Elena & Nejdl Wolfgang (2008c): LearnWeb2.0: Integrating social software for lifelong learning. In: *Proceedings of the World Conference on Educational Multimedia, Hypermedia and Telecommunications (ED-Media 2008).* Chesapeake, VA: AACE, 1793–1802.

Marenzi Ivana, Zerr Sergej & Nejdl Wolfgang (2008d): Providing social sharing functionalities in LearnWeb2.0. In: Koper Rob, Stefanov Krasses and Dicheva Darina (eds.): *Stimulating Personal Development and Knowledge Sharing.* Proceedings of the 5th TENCompetence Open Workshop. Sofia: Faleza Office, 9–14. ISBN 978-954-92146-5-9. <http://dspace.learningnetworks.org/bitstream/1820/1961/1/proceedings%20Sofia.pdf> [accessed August 2013]

Marenzi Ivana, Zerr Sergej, Abel Fabian & Nejdl Wolfgang (2009): Social sharing in LearnWeb2.0. *International Journal of Continuing Engineering Education and Life-Long Learning* (IJCEELL), 19(4-5-6), 276–290. DOI: 10.1504/IJCEELL.2009.028826.

Marenzi Ivana (2012): Designer genres: social, interactional, technological and multimodal aspects of Web 2.0. In: Cambria Mariavita, Arizzi Cristina, Coccetta Francesca (eds.): *Web Genres and Web Tools.* Como: Ibis, 174–214.

Chapter 4, *Design-based research and evaluation methodology*, describes the fundamental methodology adopted through the thesis for the evaluation and development of the LearnWeb2.0 system. The notion of *Iterative evaluation-driven design-based research* is defined and further details about the empirical research (such as the course setup and the data elicitation methods) are given in Section 4.2.

Chapter 4 includes contributions from:

Marenzi Ivana & Zerr Sergej (2012): Multiliteracies and active learning in CLIL: the development of LearnWeb2.0. *IEEE Transactions on Learning Technologies* (TLT). Los Alamitos, CA, USA, 5(4), 336–348. DOI:10.1109/TLT.2012.14

Chapter 5, *First evaluation cycle: system design and usability*, includes the description of the first evaluation cycle focused on the LearnWeb2.0 system design and usability to collect feedback from users and improve the functionalities of the tool. In addition to the team-work within the L3S Research Center, this chapter describes collaboration with the Faculty of Philosophy (English Department) in Hannover, as well as with the Faculty of Medicine in Pavia, Italy. In particular, it presents the preliminary research questions addressed in the first phase of the research (Marenzi et al., 2010), such as:

- *How can a platform for collaborative work and collaborative searching be appropriately used and adapted in different university contexts so that it helps in the process of*

learning how to teach English in a CLIL context and in the process of learning how to improve English as a foreign language?
- *What pedagogical and project design should be used to support teaching and learning CLIL concepts at university level and to foster student reflection on methods and materials appropriate for CLIL?*

In answer to the first research question Sections 5.1 and 5.2 discuss in detail the pedagogical design of the two CLIL and ESP (*English for Specific Purposes*) courses which were supported by LearnWeb2.0 during the summer semester of 2010. The former was held at the Leibniz University of Hannover in Germany, the latter was carried out in the University of Pavia, in Italy. After the description of the first course, in Section 5.1.5 the researcher provides the LearnWeb 2.0 integrative framework as a specific contribution for CLIL. In Section 5.2.5 the integration of LearnWeb2.0 with MWS (*Multimodal Web Search*) is described in the context of an English for Specific Purposes learning scenario. Section 5.3 gives a summary of LearnWeb2.0's evolution towards the second release, together with a short description of the main functionalities of this second release of the system. In answer to the second research question the evaluation design and promising preliminary evaluation results are described. Chapter 5 includes the research presented in:

Marenzi Ivana, Kupetz Rita, Nejdl Wolfgang & Zerr Sergej (2010): Supporting active learning in CLIL through collaborative search. In: X. Luo et al. (eds.): *Advances in Web based learning - ICWL 2010*, Proceedings of the 9th International Conference on Web-based Learning. Berlin-Hidelberg: Springer, LNCS 6483, 200–209.

Marenzi Ivana & Nejdl Wolfgang (2012): I search therefore I learn. Supporting active and collaborative learning in language teaching. In: Okada, A., Connolly, T. and Scott, P. (eds.): *Collaborative Learning 2.0: Open Educational Resources*. IGI Global, 103–125.

Marenzi Ivana & Kupetz Rita (2012): CLIL teacher training and Web 2.0. Symposium on language learning beyond the classroom. In: Tania Pattison, *IATEFL 2011 Brighton Conference Selections*. Eynsham: Information Press, 126–129.

Marenzi Ivana (2014): Interactive and collaborative supports for CLIL: towards a formal model based on digital literacy. In: Rita Kupetz & Carmen Becker (eds.): Content and Language Integrated Learning (CLIL) by Interaction. Frankfurt am Main: Peter Lang.

Chapter 6, *Second evaluation cycle: Users requirements and customisation.* The second evaluation cycle started in September 2011, in order to assess and evaluate the second release of LearnWeb2.0, more focused on collecting users' requirements and customising the system to support different scenarios and learning goals. Section 6.1 describes a case study during the winter semester 2011 involving pupils from 8th and 12th grade classes in a German course at the Leibnizschule high school in Hannover using LearnWeb2.0 to collect and discuss materials from the Web relating to postwar literature. Section 6.2 sketches the evaluation of LearnWeb2.0 by a community of teachers and researchers within the YELL (*Young English Language Learners*) project. Section 6.3 summarises the new functionalities introduced in the latest release of the LearnWeb2.0 system according to the users' requirements and its customisation for different scenarios. In Section 6.4 a short comparison of the four scenarios and directions for further developments are given. Chapter 6 includes the research presented in:

Holdack-Janssen Eva & Marenzi Ivana (2012a): Learning about literature on the Web in a German school. In: P. Vittorini, R. Gennari, I. Marenzi, F. De La Prieta Pintado, J. M. Corchado Rodriguez (eds.): *Proceedings of the International Workshop on Evidence-based Technology Enhanced Learning* (EbTEL 12), Advances in Intelligent and Soft Computing. Springer-Verlag GmbH, (152), 57–65. ISSN 1867–5662.

Holdack-Janssen Eva & Marenzi Ivana (2012b): LearnWeb2.0 im Deutschunterricht. Informationssuche und -auswertung im Deutschunterricht mit LearnWeb2.0. In: Schlobinski Peter & Torsten Siever (eds.): *Sprache und Kommunikation im Web 2.0.* Seelze (Der Deutschunterricht 6), 64–73.

Bortoluzzi Maria & Marenzi Ivana (2013): YELLing for Partnership: a social platform for sharing practice and reflection in teacher training for language learning. In: Antonella Riem Natale, Maria Renata Dolce, Stefano Mercanti, Caterina Colomba (eds.): *The Tapestry of the Creative Word in Anglophone Literatures.* Udine: Forum editrice, 249–262.

Bortoluzzi Maria & Marenzi Ivana (2014): YELLing for collaborative learning in teacher education: users' voices in the social platform LearnWeb2.0. Submitted for review at *International Journal of Social Media and Interactive Learning Environments (IJSMILE)*, 2(2), 182–198.

Part III (New Research Framework) summarises the research contributions resulting into the *LearnWeb2.0 multi-tier* framework. The previous research experience is revisited with more experienced eyes and a final reflection and practical suggestions are given to improve the co-design of pedagogical course design, technological support, and research data evaluation.

Chapter 7, *New research framework and refined research questions*, looks more deeply into the *multiliteracies* approach to better embed and improve LearnWeb2.0 in the educational context. At this stage of the research, there was a need to re-route the basic research questions towards a new pedagogical framework.

The refined research questions investigate:

- *How can the LearnWeb2.0 functionalities be integrated with the pedagogical notion of the multiliteracies approach, and how can this integration be represented through an appropriate model?*
- *What course design should be used? How should LearnWeb2.0 be used in various learning scenarios?*

To answer these questions, the researcher studied the *multiliteracies* approach and the *Learning by Design* framework to reinforce the pedagogical setup of the doctoral research work and to support the application of LearnWeb2.0 in various scenarios.

The goal of Chapter 8, *The LearnWeb2.0 design framework – a multi-tier model*, is to enhance the *multiliteracies* approach and the *Learning by Design* framework with the Web 2.0 features provided by the LearnWeb2.0 collaborative search-and-sharing system. Section 8.1 describes an ESP case study revisited from a *multiliteracies* perspective. In Section 8.2 the new *LearnWeb2.0 multi-tier* framework is introduced which provides a common theoretical reference and a guide for teachers, researchers and developers when discussing how to design and support course activities as well as to make the learning process more explicit for students. A reflection on the LearnWeb2.0 contribution to *multiliteracies* education is given in Section 8.3, to explain the researcher's motivation for connecting it with the educational context and information technology.

Chapter 8 reports on the work published in:

Marenzi Ivana & Zerr Sergej (2012): Multiliteracies and active learning in CLIL: the development of LearnWeb2.0. In: *IEEE Transactions on Learning Technologies* (TLT), Los Alamitos, CA, USA, 5(4), 336–348. DOI:10.1109/TLT.2012.14

Marenzi Ivana, Baldry Anthony & Nejdl Wolfgang (2012): Towards an integrative approach for CLIL: the LearnWeb2.0 model. In: Gabriele Blell & Christiane Lütge (eds.): *Fremdsprachendidaktik und Lehrerbildung: Konzepte, Impulse, Perspektiven.* Berlin: Münster et al: LIT, 95–112.

Marenzi Ivana (2013): A multiliteracies approach for supporting language learning courses at university level. In: J. Jovanovic and R. Chiong (eds.): *Technological and Social Environments for Interactive Learning*, Santa Rosa, CA: Informing Science Press, 249–276.

Marenzi Ivana & Kantz Deirdre (2013): ESP course design – a multiliteracies approach. In: *Reshaping Learning: Transforming Education through the Fusion of Learning and Technology*, Proceedings of the 13th IEEE International Conference on Advanced Learning Technologies (ICALT 2013). Beijing, China.

Chapter 9, *Conclusions and future work*, provides a summary of the research carried out in the doctoral work and sketches future directions in the chosen research field.

I
Theoretical Background

2 Pedagogy and Technology Enhanced Learning (TEL)

> "Learning must be a way of being – an ongoing set of attitudes and actions by individuals and groups that they employ to try to keep abreast of the surprising, novel, messy, obtrusive, recurring events." (Vaill, 1996, p. 42)

This chapter provides a theoretical basis for the thesis. It gives an overview of the most relevant pedagogical frameworks such as Behaviourism, Cognitivism (Section 2.1) and Constructivism (Section 2.2) as the fundamental basis for the development of e-learning (Section 2.3), *Computer Supported Collaborative Learning* (Section 2.4) and the e-learning2.0 strategies (Section 2.5). Section 2.6 describes what *Educational Technology* is in greater detail, together with an investigation into the role of an educational technologist, in particular as regards the work of making connections between *literacy*, collaboration and organisational skills in education. Section 2.7 provides a summary and discussion.

2.1 Behaviorism and Cognitivism

We can take 1954 as the starting date for the technology of education, when Skinner published his article *The science of learning and the art of teaching*. Skinner is the most representative author of *Behaviorism*, developed during the first half of the 20th century in the United States. One of the premises of Skinner's *radical behaviourism* is that the study of behaviour should not be based on hypotheses about the inner self stated as causes of behaviour, but should rather be based on observational descriptions. According to Skinner (1968), it is impossible to determine what happens in the human mind. To improve teaching and learning *programmed instruction* is a possible application in education as it allows students to carry out learning activities at their own rate, to check their own answers and to advance only after they give a correct answer. Some principles of this methodology are the breaking down of learning contents into small learning units, active learner participation in answering the intermediate questions, and immediate feedback about the learning unit. This idea was later adapted by Gagné (1965), who invented *programmed learning* for school teaching. Unlike *programmed instruction* which is intended to modify students' behaviour, *programmed learning* is used to teach facts and skills. Authors such as Tyler (1949), Gagné (1965) and Bloom (1984) drew up criteria for curricular design and taxonomies to classify educational goals and objectives. In the 1960s the detailed planning of the curriculum became important as well as did customisation of learning pathways according to students' needs and specificities (Calvani, 2004, p. 18).

As a response to *Behaviourism*, at the end of the 1950s *Cognitivism* suggested a new theoretical framework for the understanding of the human mind. In 1960 Bruner created the Harvard Centre for Cognitive Studies; in the same period Chomsky (1965) created his approach to linguistic transformations and Newell and Herbert (1972) initiated artificial intelligence by proving a theorem using a computer. At that time the metaphor of the human being as "a processor of information" emerged. In educational contexts, one of the most important contributions of *this movement was* the role of previous-knowledge in the learning process. Brown, Collins and Duguid (1989) argued that it was important for students to find significant and authentic activities in the context of their personal experiences. Cognitive science thus holds that learning skills detached from the user's experience will not allow users to apply information received to concrete cases: a passive learner, viewing learning as something to which one is subjected, will not be motivated (Rizzo, 2009). Learning develops from the connections between the previous knowledge of the individual and the external information arising from the external world. Any informative support such as schemas, synthesis or questionnaires can be used as an *advance organiser* to stimulate the learner's knowledge and anticipate the major learning subjects. Meta-cognition thus becomes a very important process in education.

Both *Behaviourism* and *Cognitivism* stressed the importance of a linear and rational structure for learning paths characterised by feedback and additional supports, but avoiding causal events. During the 1980s this objective and the rationalistic approach adopted in the use of hierarchical and sequential models became increasingly weaker, as did trust in artificial intelligence. Scientists increasingly agreed that knowledge is situated and depends on context.

2.2 Constructivism

At the beginning of the 1990s most scientists from the cognitive area, educational designers and technologist followed a new theory called *Constructivism*.

The shift from *Behaviorism* and *Cognitivism* to *Constructivism* was rather dramatic. Whereas *Behaviorism* and *Cognitivism* suggested the need to analyse a task by breaking it down into manageable chunks, and measuring performance based on previously established objectives, *Constructivism* on the other hand, came to promote more open-ended learning experiences based on the premises that learning methods may not be efficacious for each learner in the same way.

The term *Constructivism* has been used as an umbrella term for a diversity of views. It is beyond the purposes of this section to detail similarities and differences across various constructivist theories. In general, all constructivist theories committed to the general view that (1) the learning process should consist in active knowledge *construction* rather than simple acquisition of knowledge, and (2) instruction should *support* that construction rather than simply communicate knowledge. As Rizzo suggests, "*Constructivism* may be seen as a set of strategies designed to make students aware of their learning" (Rizzo, 2009, p. 49).

The educational expert, following a constructivist theory, pays more attention to the new concept of *learning environment* than to the sequence of short learning tasks. A learning environment is a specific space (real or virtual) where different kinds of information, resources and tools are available to support and facilitate collaboration and problem solving. Vygotsky's concepts of *scaffolding* and *zone of proximal development* supported constructivist approaches at interpersonal level. Vygotsky's (1978) basic idea was that cognitive development is directly linked to social development and that the way a student thinks and what s/he learns derive from the environment in which s/he lives. In general socially oriented constructivist theories, consider *scaffolding* as "a comfortable environment where the learner can find good tips and supporting materials such as compelling tasks, templates and guides, designed to help the development of his/her cognitive and social skills" (Yelland & Masters, 2007, p. 365). On the other hand, cognitively oriented constructivist theories such as discovery learning (Bruner, 1967), and microworlds (Papert, 1980) emphasise exploration and discovery.

In the 1980s emphasis came to be placed on giving greater weight to problem solving skills, information-finding and critical analysis of information presented in one way or another to students. There was thus a "refocusing on the process of *how to learn* rather than on learning specific contents" (Rizzo, 2009, p. 35). The advent of hypertext at the end of the 1980s represented the collapse of the linear approach. Hypertext technology has had a crucial role in influencing educational design by showing that it must be recursive and open to continuous integrations. It is not possible to solve all problems organising all the educational activities in advance, but the design must be modular, with the direct involvement of the user to create tentative prototypes and adopt incremental integrations in the learning process. "Anyone, teacher or student, wanting to use technology needs to learn to integrate directed teaching with constructivist approaches and must thus choose the technological resources and methods of integration which optimise the chosen strategy, in other words scaffolding and building on what pre-exists" (Rizzo, 2009, p. 44).

Only a few years later, the Internet became popular and the attention of scientists was driven by the virtual interconnection of computers throughout the world and the growth of virtual communities. At the beginning of the 1990s the *personal computer* developed into *interpersonal computing* and technology started to be an environment to support the social creation of knowledge (Barret, 1994). The new concept of *Collaborative Learning-Work* appeared, as well as CSCW (*Computer Supported Collaborative Work*) as a term referring to people working in groups with the aid of computers. Human intelligence and knowledge were recognised as distributed and situated (Brown, et al., 1989; Norman, 1993) and the world of information was considered as a huge database where we can find the details we are looking for. This idea of distributed resources becomes a metaphor to describe how both the human mind, as well as the Web, work. Knowledge is no longer considered to be objective and measurable but acquires new peculiarities such as multidimensionality, and negotiated and creative acquisition.

"In *Constructivism*, control over the learning process shifts from the teacher to the student, with the learner playing an active role in the learning process" (Ullrich et al. 2008). The teacher focuses mainly on preparatory activities, provides support where assistance is needed and is thus an initiator of, and adviser in, the learning process. Knowledge is actively produced by the individual, it is situated in a concrete context, and develops within social collaboration and negotiation activities (Jonassen, 1994). Schools do not have the goal of making all their students achieve the same level, but become more similar to "*knowledge building communities*, with the awareness that every learner is different and knowledge will be spread in different ways and degrees among learners" (Merrill, 2000, p. 4).

Constructivism challenges traditional teaching and proposes an innovative approach arguing that students, armed with suitable skills that help them resolve practical, daily problems must *construct* their knowledge, rather than obtain it passively from the teacher. The teacher's role is to "orchestrate all the resources deemed necessary, and to guide students in the choice of objectives and learning goals" (Rizzo, 2009, p. 52).

Several socio-constructivist theories grew as variants of constructivist learning theory. In general, these approaches hold that individual knowledge relies on its social construction (Piaget and his colleagues Doise and Mugny). Especially relevant in this respect is the social world of a learner where communication takes place with people who directly affect that person, including family, friends, teachers, peer-students, but who also engage other actors (e.g. domain experts or unknown users in social networks) to participate in the dialogue. Socio-constructivist educational contexts are strongly student-centred and action-oriented. They are characterised by collaborative and co-operative models, but at the same time incorporate strategies and provide students with tools to organise their knowledge so that they become more autonomous. Teachers and curricula have to become flexible and to adapt to the diversity of contexts and to students' expectations. Examples of teaching strategies include teaching in contexts that might be personally meaningful to students, or designing small-group collaboration tasks and class discussions to negotiate shared meanings with students (Wood et al., 1995).

At the same time, constructivist teaching makes the management of the learning process much more complex and unpredictable than traditional teacher-directed instruction. New technologies foster actions and inclusive learning environments. However integrating education with technology is not always a smooth procedure. While *Constructivism* is fully applicable to computer-mediated learning where individuals have an active role in the construction of knowledge by exploring materials and using resources to meet their learning needs, social constructivism becomes instead the theoretical foundation for web-based collaborative learning, in which individuals interact and learn through a process of adaptation and negotiation of meanings in formal and/or informal situations. Computers, in fact, are not just means to retrieve information but are also an important means of communication and information sharing that have enacted the shift "(…) from a logic of interaction *with* the computer to people's interaction *via* the computer. Emphasis is placed on interaction, through dialogue within real, albeit virtual, communities" (Kern & Warschauer, 2000, p. 11). Developments in new technologies have therefore enabled the change from computers as aids that support learning to computers as tools to be embedded in learning environments where all dimensions of time, space and interaction are included. This entails the need to draw up and define *blended learning* models where technologies are integrated with face-to-face teaching and facilitate students' access to materials and sharing of content, so as to allow them to participate in interactive, collaborative tasks.

2.3 E-learning

> "The best way for teachers to learn how to be an effective online facilitator is for them to experience the process first-hand; undertake an online course themselves and experience what it's like from a student perspective."
>
> (Effective Online Facilitation, Australian Flexible Learning Framework[2], 2003, p. 5)

2 http://gtuc.edu.gh/colt/Effective_Online_Facilitation.php

The Use of Media and Technology in Education

Human beings have always worked to develop tools to extend their cognitive and communicative capacities. For a long time, well before the use of personal computers in educational contexts, several media technologies such as radio, television, video-recorders and projectors were used in classrooms. Modern communication media make it possible for interaction to take place among large numbers of people (e.g. via e-mail, Internet forums, or social networks) as well as intense long-distance exchanges.

The propagation of new media in education is characterised by different phases and different uses. At the beginning of the 1980s *programmed instruction* started in the United States. *Tutorials* were used as a substitute for the teacher to manage the students' learning path (computer *tutor*). By the middle of the 1980s, the computer was considered as a *working tool* with the growth of general purpose software (such as electronic writing, databases, spreadsheets).

Web 1.0 – Hypertext

At the beginning of the 1990s the computer started to be considered as a tool for multimedia and interpersonal communication. With the diffusion of the Internet, people started to use *e-mails, web forums* and *chats* to communicate with other people by typing text or using audio and video-conferencing for instant communications; different *browsers* appeared to search for information and for resources on the Web.

The term *Hypertext* was coined by Ted Nelson around 1965 to indicate a text which is not linear but which contains links to other texts, thus enabling an easy and flexible connection of information over the Internet.

Web 2.0 – Social Web

At the end of the 20th century the computer increasingly became an effective communication and collaboration tool both at work and in learning environments. Social sharing tools such as Flickr and YouTube, or social networks such as Facebook, allow people to connect and create new online communities. Today, children are expected to know the various technologies available and are encouraged to use media tools in school. Communication and interaction are not only internal to the classroom but allow for example children to reach children in other countries and from other cultures.

At the end of the 1990s, the expansion of the Web and the use of technology in education generated a new area of study called *e-learning* (electronic learning). The term comprises all forms of electronically-supported learning and teaching that use computers and the Web to transfer knowledge (ITTC[3]). The field of *Technology Enhanced Learning* (TEL) describes the support of any learning activity through technology (the focus is more on the technological support). The term *e-learning* instead, refers more specifically to a particular pedagogical approach that uses technology.

Two major forms of electronic learning can be identified. The earlier type, based on *Computer Based Training* (CBT) or *Computer Based Learning* (CBL), were mainly focused on the interaction between the student and the computer providing exercises, tutorials or simulations. With the advent of the WWW (*WorldWideWeb*), the prevailing paradigm in the regular school system became *Computer Mediated Communication* (CMC), where the focus was on interaction between students and their instructors using the computer as a mediator for their communication. CBT/CBL required more individualized (self-study) learning, while CMC involves more flexible learning activities as well as teacher/tutor facilitation.

In addition, the emergence of multiple mobile and ubiquitous technologies provides tools for sustaining learning communities, enabling collaborative tasks, and favoring learning-in-context scenarios. Dillenbourg and Jermann (2007, p. 286) describe *blended learning* scenarios that integrate both school and authentic settings (e.g. workplace or user-generated contents) as "integrated learning". In general, in e-learning spatial-temporal restrictions are reduced and the learning process is centered on the learner who can decide what, how, when and where s/he wants to study. The expert assumes the role of "*tutor* and *facilitator* of the process" (Calvani & Rotta, 2003, p. 222), technologies are considered as a support for learning and communication, and learning goals are re-negotiated during the process. The designer of e-learning environments has the difficult task of choosing the most suitable composition between contents, support and interactivity.

Significantly, the Web offers a new environment as compared to traditional educational settings and so it is necessary to promote a new didactic methodology, not reusing the traditional procedures. Educators need to take advantage of the specific *affordances* of online learning which are different from the face-to-face experiences, such as for example:

Digitality: learning resources can be found on the Internet in addition to materials provided by the teacher; the learning process can be based mainly on the

3 ITTC (International Trade Training Center), http://international-trade-training.net/E-learning

collaborative group-work of the students; the results can be readapted and reused in other courses. The learning materials, if correctly structured and annotated, can become *learning objects* (small units of content easily recognizable and transferable) and be shared in Open Educational Resources (OER) repositories to be reused.

Spatial and relational ubiquity: individuals or groups of people can interact online even if they are physically in different places. If there is no psychological distance (feeling of loneliness or abandonment), online distance can be viewed as "*virtual proximity* which allows new types of communication and collaboration on the Web" (Moore 1993, p. 31).

Temporality: the possibility of asynchronous communication allows amplification and diversification of the rhythms of learning. More flexibility is possible when people need different time spans in which to reflect, internalise and revise learning material or tasks. The *e-learning designer* must be careful to distinguish between openness and dispersion: too much freedom and autonomy may lead to a feeling of abandonment. The educational expert must "support the learner's autonomy and make his/her learning progresses explicit" (Calvani, 2004, p. 77).

Presence and virtuality: an important decision the *e-learning designer* has to take is the level of virtuality to be adopted in the course. Presence seems to be still essential for some activities and cannot be left out. *Blended* solutions make it possible to bring together the potentialities of both face-to-face and online solutions (Driscoll, 2002; Bonk & Graham, 2006), but sometimes it is difficult to find the right balance.

Interaction and interactivity: interaction and interactivity are, of course, important concepts for learning, but they must be analysed and adopted in accordance with specific educational requirements (Puntambekar et al., 2011). Not always it is true that the more interaction is present, the better it is for the learning process. Sometimes the lack of interaction can be bad, but also an excess of interactivity can be negative and distracting, reducing the time needed for reflection (Norman, 1993). Even more, *instructional interaction* does not happen spontaneously just because of the tool, but must be carefully planned and designed. There must be a loop (question, answer, reply/feedback) between the actors so that the interaction takes place and continues in a meaningful and productive way to avoid boredom, overload or frustration (Marenzi, 2010).

The problem of good interaction is visible in particular in the design of courses on the Web where different types of interactions can be distinguished: interaction with content, interaction between peers, interaction with experts etc. Online social interaction is important to overcome the individual's online isolation and to facilitate new ways of social participation in online learning (Prinsen et al., 2008). The type of interaction and how it is used are often two of the main elements that make a qualitative difference in online courses. Not all attempts at collaborative learning make it possible to achieve satisfying results, because "in some circumstances, this type of approach may lead to conformity of results and loss of process, lack of initiative, misunderstandings, conflicts and compromises" (Rizzo, 2009, p. 78). It is also true, however, that these circumstances can be found in traditional learning environments as well. It must be clarified whether these difficulties are due to the use of an online system, or technical problems, or whether it denotes the existence of questions of a social nature such as a lack of willingness to co-operate at a distance, laziness or simply optionality. Interactivity in e-learning can only be successful if positive attitudes and initiatives are shown by the participants. Social learning does not take place in a constructive way without co-operation between participants or proper knowledge of the potential of the online system.

Technological innovation: attention must shift from technology itself to the design and introduction of *technological innovation* that must pursue different phases such as: "preparation, evolution of the users' perception of the tool, technical support during the project, consolidation of the methodology" (Calvani, 2004, p. 63). Kaye (1992, p. 2) points out that "to use an e-learning system to the best advantage, every application requires the teacher to provide correct programming and organisation of the learning process, as well as the active and staged involvement of students within a context that provides objectives, interests and work commitments". A basic assumption is that the technical skills of e-learning systems have been acquired by both parties. Technical skills are secondary, but, nevertheless, essential for appropriate use. This aspect cannot be overlooked, as "the boundaries between technical and learning are sometimes hard to define" (Rizzo, 2009, p. 79).

Professional profiles: e-learning also needs new professional profiles to take care of the different aspects of design and learning management, for example *ICT technicians, content managers, tutors, evaluation experts*, and *educational technologists*. There are even different types of tutors: in the classroom the role of the tutor is to be a *facilitator* and a *mentor* to support the learning path; the online tutor must help, guide, and motivate students who are distant in space and could otherwise lose contact with the learning process (Rotta, 2002). In online learning, the instructor's role is even more critical, as s/he has to help learners overcome potential barriers caused by technology such as time management, and distance interactions between learners and instructors. Online instructors need to develop specific competencies in different areas such as: technical competence, administration, design, facilitation of the interactions, evaluation. There is some overlap between them: some contexts may require additional or different actions (Pampaloni, 2006).

Evaluation: evaluation is always a crucial activity in educational settings and it is even more difficult in online courses. On the one hand, online systems allow constant monitoring and quick responses, but to be efficient, the data must be stored carefully, visualised and represented in a meaningful way. Beside monitoring activities, online educational environments should allow *formative evaluation*, that is, not only a *summative evaluation* of the final results during the official exams, but also feedback "in itinere" that students can obtain from the teacher (or from their peers) during the learning process to correct or simply give advice to the learner. This kind of *formative evaluation* does not give judgments or marks, but has a dynamic and indicative character to help the learner in developing additional awareness in the project and in his/her learning progress and achievements (Schuitemaker-King, 2013). Even if the material and the learning environment has been carefully designed and prepared, a new online approach could disorient the learner who would gain from prompt feedback or encouragement from the teacher or the tutor. "The right information at the right time, or the lack of it, can play a crucial role in the success of the whole experience" (Calvani, 2004, p. 83; author's translation).

Quality: for *e-learning* courses, a few quality standards and criteria have been suggested by international organisations such as the *International Standard Organization* (ISO - www.iso.org/) or the British *Quality Assurance Agency for Higher Education* (www.qaa.ac.uk/). A few tips for quality are:

- Pay attention to formative planning and design in addition to the technological approach;
- Design good quality material but also allow the learners to access other kinds of information and make it part of their personal knowledge;
- Learn and adopt specific techniques for online teaching (which is not the same as in the classroom);
- Include peripheral support from different professional roles such as developers, technicians, tutors, experts, and peers.

While early e-learning systems, based on CBL or CBT were often used to transfer knowledge adopting an autocratic teaching style, the systems that were developed later based on *Computer Supported Collaborative Learning* (CSCL), encouraged the shared development of knowledge.

2.4 Computer Supported Collaborative Learning

> "A culture in which young people don't listen to each other, or discuss fairly the merits of each other's contributions, or one in which their ideas are routinely rejected, will prevent collaboration from occurring at all."
>
> (Facer & Williamson, 2004, p. 18)

"*Computer-Supported Collaborative Learning* (CSCL) is an emerging branch of the learning sciences concerned with studying how people can learn together with the help of computers" (Stahl et al., 2006, p. 409). Much progress has been made in the field over the past twenty years, thanks to growing research on collaborative learning and the development of communication capabilities through computers. Participants use technology to communicate, interact with each other, share knowledge, and construct knowledge as a group. In this respect, CSCL inherently takes much from constructivist and socio-constructivist learning theories. Since the general focus of CSCL is on supporting socially mediated learning, this approach brings together several disciplines such as cognitive psychology, computer science and education and provides a multidisciplinary and interdisciplinary challenge for discourse between them (Fischer et al., 2007b).

Collaborative learning

The two terms *collaboration* and *cooperation* are often used as synonyms in the literature. It is useful to make a distinction though, as regards structuring group interactions and task organisation. *Collaboration* implies working in a group where two or more people work interdependently on the same problem to achieve a common goal, respecting each individual contribution and depending on each other results at the same time. *Cooperation,* as described by Ingram (2009, p. 2537), "is a structured way of sharing the work and delegate parts of it to each member of the group". Cooperation often involves separate activities with little interdependence between the participants and the different tasks.

The basic idea of collaboration can be found in Vygotsky's *Social Learning Theory* with the notion of *zone of proximal development* (Vygotsky et al., 1978) according to which, "knowledge is developed by the interaction of the individual with his/her surrounding culture and society" and tasks that can be too difficult for a single learner are made possible with the assistance of a more skilled individual or a teacher. These ideas feed into Stahl's *Collaboration theory* which suggests that "knowledge is constructed in social interactions with others, and collaborative learning is a process of constructing meaning that most often takes place in group interactions" (Stahl, 2004, p. 60). The goal of *collaboration theory* is to understand how meaning is constructed and re-learned through group interaction. It has been shown that when learners collaborate with peers, "they may come to externalize their knowledge, monitor each other's learning, and jointly negotiate meaning" (Fisher et al., 2007a, p. 1; Swain, 1993). These joint activities may stimulate "significant individual cognitive processes (induced in interactions with others) that help construct new knowledge" (King, 2007, p. 18).

For a long time though, collaboration in learning activities faced a cultural resistance and has been largely overlooked by educators. The premises of social Darwinism, and Skinner's work on programmed learning and behavioural modification were the basis of competitive and individualistic learning. In contrast to these approaches, collaborative learning is now "widely accepted as a pedagogical practice that can be employed in classrooms to stimulate students' interest in learning through involvement with peers" (Gillies, 2008, p. 244). When students interact collaboratively they learn to listen to one another, share information, discuss differing perspectives and, in so doing, develop mutual understandings of the topic and of the contents.

According to Brett (1996) *collaborative learning* corresponds to "the acquisition of knowledge by individuals, skills or attitudes arising as the result of group interaction". It is not easy to find a comprehensive definition for collaborative learning though. According to Dillenbourg:

> "The broadest (but unsatisfactory) definition of 'collaborative learning' is that it is a *situation* in which *two or more* people *learn* or attempt to learn something *together*, but there is no guarantee that the expected interactions will actually occur. Hence, a general concern is to develop ways to increase the probability that some types of interaction occur."
>
> (Dillenbourg, 1999, p. 5)

Huber and Huber (2008, p. 113) describe "collaborative learning as a product-oriented approach" compared to cooperative learning as a "process-centred approach". In both cases the activity is carried out with common goals and leads to a common final result but, while collaborative groups are usually given only general advice or guidelines on how to proceed and try to solve the learning task as a whole, cooperating groups divide the common task into several sub-tasks and merge their result later.

At the end of the 20th century the Web has become an important infrastructure for e-learning and *lifelong-learning*. New challenges for the expert are related to the following issues: *How do people collaborate online? How can we support knowledge building in online communities? What type of blended learning (a mixture of presence and virtuality) is more efficient in what scenarios?* (Calvani, 2004, p. 28; author's translation). Online *collaboration* is a dialectic process of argumentation which can start casually (social networks) or in a systematic way, in a *community of practice* (CoP) or *community of learning* (CoL) (Herring, 2004). An example is a community of teachers, who create online groups to share documents and experiences with their colleagues, to discuss and compare different points of view, get to know new colleagues and collaborate in new research projects.

When collaboration is mediated by computers though, some problems may be further augmented. For example, some research has demonstrated that students often do not collaborate well online, "they often do not build well-grounded arguments, or they may have problems in effectively coordinating their joint efforts" (Fischer et al., 2007b, p. 1). "Computer-mediated collaboration might be an extra task and cause extra cognitive load for the students" (Hesse, 2007, p. 92). Learners may put less effort into common work because they feel overloaded by dealing with the computer interface, or because fewer and different communication channels are available than in natural face-to-face settings. To balance the additional task of managing interactions via computer-mediated communication, adequate scripts can be used as scaffolds to provide guidance on how to collaborate (Rummel & Spada, 2007).

The teacher's role

The introduction of technology in different environments has changed both the role of the teacher and the role of the learner. Even if the focus in CSCL is on individuals collaborating with their peers, the teacher's role is vital in choosing among different collaborative techniques and in facilitating learning (Pozzi et al., 2010). The teacher has to carefully design the learning tasks and decide the complexity of the problem to be solved by the students. The problem must be of sufficient complexity to warrant team work. It is important that instructors introduce the CSCL tasks to the students in the broader context of the course design, to clearly define the learning goals and the learning outcomes of the activity. In this way learners are made aware of the objectives and they are more motivated and actively involved in the learning process. Though the task may be collaborative in nature, students may need training on how to work in a truly cooperative process. Once the activity has begun, the teachers' role is to kick-start and to monitor the discussion so as to facilitate interaction and learning (Prinsen et al., 2008). Teachers' discourse for example should change and adapt to the collaborative learning situation becoming more encouraging, facilitating communication among students, providing feedback on task performance, and "provide students with environments where they feel supported and emotionally secure" (Johnson & Johnson, 2003, p. 150). Gillies discusses the additive benefits derived from "training teachers in the specific communication skills that are designed to enhance teacher-student interactions during cooperative learning" (Gillies, 2008, p. 248).

An important consideration for educators who implement online learning environments is that without a proper structure, any CSCL strategy can lose its effectiveness. Support might also be required to mitigate technical issues during the activity. Using the computer for learning requires both good motivation on the part of students and good organisation of tasks and technological support. Ideally, teachers should provide solid *scaffolding* and proper facilitation to support students in using technology to build learning foundations with their peers. "The collaborative activity can be more or less structured according to the situation" (Pozzi et al., 2010, p. 48). Instructors should carefully plan CSCL designs balancing the difficulty of the tasks presented and deciding the extent of the scaffolding needed in each scenario. Task-specific interactions for example could be very detailed using "scripted cooperation" (Hueber & Hueber, 2008, p. 118) or use a more open approach prescribing group roles to each individual members such as "listener" or "social facilitator".

Scripting in CSCL

The book *Scripting Computer-Supported Collaborative Learning: cognitive, computational and educational perspectives* (Fischer et al., 2007a) gives an extensive overview of how interactions can be regulated in learning environments. In principle, any interaction with others provides opportunities for learning, however "some forms of interaction and activity have been found to be more effective in facilitating learning than others" (King, 2007, p. 13). Unfortunately it is rare for collaborating learners to spontaneously use effective interaction procedures without some explicit form of other guidance (learners generally tend to interact with each other at a very basic level). For this reason numerous attempts have been made to promote learning by structuring and regulating interaction within collaborative groups so that learners are required to interact in ways that induce cognitive processes appropriate to their learning task. These methods of structuring interaction have generally been referred to variously as "scaffolding learning" (King, 2007, p. 14). Recently the term "scripting collaboration" has been adopted.

The term *script* has different connotations and traditions in different disciplines: for cognitive psychology, the term script describes individual memory structures that guide learners in their understanding and behaviour in particular situations; in computer science, scripts are used to create formal languages and devices to guide learners through complex work or learning processes; in education, scripts are instructional scaffolds that guide and structure collaboration processes within groups of learners "to show them how to act" (King, 2007, p. 17). For this reason, negotiation is necessary between researchers and practitioners in the three disciplines to more precisely describe their specific notions of what scripts are and find interdisciplinary approaches to scripting (Fischer et al., 2007a).

Dillenbourg and Jermann (2007, p. 276) describe *collaboration scripts* as "instructional means that aim to make collaboration processes more productive". However different researchers consider different aspects of collaboration while designing scripts. In particular two kinds of scripts can be distinguished. At "macro design level" organisational issues are specified such as the nature of the task *(What is the group's task?)*, the time schedule, and the group composition (*Who collaborates with whom?)*. On the other hand, "micro level" collaboration scripts provide support for specific processes within a given activity. In this approach "important questions are for example *What are the specific collaboration processes?* or *How should learners carry out these activities?*" (Fischer et al. 2007b, p. 2). According to Suthers, (2007, p. 178) "Macro scripts set up the conditions" while "micro scripts typically try to enforce the forms of interaction".

Besides *task division* in CSCL students also have to cope with *time constrains* of a specific schedule, and *technical coordination* for the use of the online features (Rummel et al., 2011). From this point of view, scripts can be described in terms of "tasks (to be performed by students), teams (to carry out the tasks) and time constrains according to which the task has to be accomplished" (Pozzi et al., 2010, p. 53). What differentiate the two micro and macro types of approaches is the level of structuredness of each of the three dimensions. At the macro level the structuredness can be flexible and tuned to some extent on the fly; at micro level the task is always highly structured, while team and time are strictly predetermined *a priori*. Structuring activities at macro level lets a wider margin of freedom to both students (whose interactions are not completely guided) and tutors, who may intervene and tune the micro-design of the activities if some parts of the process result to be week. Usually choosing between macro and micro level design may depend on the target population: the macro approach is more useful when students are adult and have already developed a good degree of self-regulation in their learning, as well as the ability to argue and think critically (for example the CLIL trainee teachers, Section 5.1). "Adopting a micro level approach is more advisable when students are younger and need support to improve their ability to discuss the argument" (Pozzi et al., 2010, p. 54), for example in the study at the Leibnizschule (Section 6.1). In addition to this, while micro scripts are usually meant to be internalised as cognitive strategies, macro scripts are didactic aids to learn content and are not meant to be internalised as cognitive strategies that are supposed to be already at the disposal of the individual (Demetriadis, 2013).

These are the reasons why macro scripts were adopted in most of the case studies described in this thesis. During the evaluation of the case studies in the doctoral research work CSCL scripts were adopted mainly at the macro level to describe the sequence of activities to be carried out (Sections 5.1.3 and 5.2.3). A "macro level" script was used mainly to define what was the group task, giving more freedom to the students to autonomously organise the specific collaboration processes required to conduct the activities. Different collaborative techniques were included into the macro design level such as discussion, collaborative searching and annotation of resources, classroom presentation, and collaborative creation of the teaching unit. The level of structuredness varied considerably between the various techniques and also across the various courses (at the Leibnizschule for example a structured *jigsaw* activity was used, see Section 6.1.1). This approach avoided the risk of 'overscripting' but, on the other hand, allowed less well-defined evaluation of the interactions.

Criticism and concerns

Even though CSCL gives promising perspectives for enhancing education, several barriers and challenges to achieving successful implementation still have to be overcome. First of all, "sufficient access to computer technology is required for all participants" (Warschauer, 2012, p. 130). This aspect cannot be underestimated even if access to computers has improved in the last 15 to 20 years. Furthermore, instructors' attitudes about technology are still hesitant: some teachers find that the time needed to monitor students' activities, review, comment on, and grade student products can be more demanding than for traditional face-to-face classrooms (Bannon, 1989; Redmond, 2011).

The concept of scripting could also give rise to some concerns as regards the possibility of 'over-scripting'. If learning activities are too controlled and regulated at the micro level, computers may become an obstacle to productive collaboration rather than a support and they could decrease students' motivation (Dillenbourg, 2002). Some concern also needs to be expressed about feedback and assessment. The analysis of the collaboration process is an important research topic, but defining good assessment methods for collaboration quality is not a trivial task (Meier et al., 2007). Furthermore, it is usually argued that a teacher organising a syllabus that relies heavily on the integration of computers must draw up quality control guidelines so that the effectiveness and usefulness of the syllabus can be assessed. Some scholars consider, however, that "there is a need to shift away from teacher-led quality control of students' learning to students' *own* quality control of their learning" (Rizzo, 2009, p. 59). Already in 2001 Kupetz carried out a pilot study on portfolio self-assessment in two classroom-based university courses (Kupetz, 2001b; Kiernan, 2001). More recently Pavlou and Kyza (2013) investigated the effectiveness of technological mediation in collaborative peer-feedback, while Long and Aleven (2013) suggest an intelligent tutoring system to support students' self-regulated learning (SRL).

2.5 E-learning2.0

> "A distance education system consists of all the component processes that make up distance education, including learning, teaching, communication, design and management, and even such less obvious components as history and institutional philosophy."
>
> (Moore & Kearsley, 1996, p. 5)

Today's *knowledge-based* society demands different attitudes than in the past vis-à-vis learning and working skills. "The use of blogs, wikis, media-sharing services, and other social software, has been shown to create exciting new learning opportunities for people, and to support the creation of social networks and communities of practice among company employees as well as individuals" (Marenzi et al., 2008b). The paper *Towards Web 2.0 Driven Learning Environments* focuses on building on "a new generation of user-centric, open, dynamic Web, with peer production, sharing, collaboration, distributed content and decentralized authority in the foreground. This new Web generation is often termed Web 2.0" (Chatti et al., 2008, p. 372).

People-driven approaches to learning are being implemented around Web 2.0 concepts. Downes (2005) coined the term *e-learning2.0* to refer to learning activities using Web 2.0 technologies. In conventional e-learning systems tasks were usually delivered to students using assignments which were later evaluated by the teacher. In contrast, the e-learning2.0 perspective places increased emphasis on social learning and use of social software such as blogs, wikis, podcasts and virtual worlds such as *Second Life* (http://secondlife.com/), where "the learner is seen as a participant who is actively engaged through a rich set of interactions within online communities" (Marenzi et al., 2008b). Kervin and Derewianka (2011) explore the role of various technologies in learning and provide a few examples of how new technologies can be used to support students' language development. Emergent Web 2.0 tools and social software applications facilitate connecting people to other people, sharing content and ideas, getting support, and learn from others (Marenzi & Zerr, 2012).

A few examples of Web 2.0 tools are:

Flickr (http://www.flickr.com/) – a popular website for users to share and embed personal photographs. The service is widely used as an image-hosting and video-hosting website, as well as an online community. Bloggers for example use Flickr to host images that they embed in blogs and social media.

YouTube (http://www.youtube.com/) is a video-sharing website on which users can upload, view and share a wide variety of video content, including movie clips, TV clips, and music videos, as well as amateur user-generated content such as video blogging and short original videos. YouTube's big social impact is due to the new concept that "anyone can upload content that everyone else can view" while in previous video-hosting websites the owner of the website provided the content.

SlideShare (http://www.slideshare.net/) is a Web-based service for sharing presentations in various formats such as PowerPoint, PDF, Keynote or Open Office. Users can upload files privately or publicly, presentations can then be viewed on the site itself, downloaded, or embedded on other sites. The service was originally addressed in particular to businesses employees, but it was expanded to host and share a large number of documents in various formats including videos and webinars. SlideShare users can also rate, comment on, and share the uploaded content.

The increased collaboration and networking facilities made possible by the rise of Web 2.0 technologies provides new opportunities to overcome many of the failings of traditional Technology Enhanced Learning solutions. A substantial difference between traditional e-learning and *social networks* environments is that the second are open and can be organised and customised by students: courses are not designed (such as materials to be delivered and learning path) but only the general tasks and the learning goals are given. Since socio-constructivism views learning as an activity which takes place in a social rather than individual context, Web 2.0 would appear to be beneficial for such learning as it encourages the active contribution of participants (Marenzi & Zerr, 2012). However schools are not ready for the social networking trends yet, and Web 2.0 tools have made minimal penetration in Higher Education (HE). Most frequently, single tools are adopted to carry out specific tasks. For example:

- Social bookmarking sites such as *Del.icio.us* are used to facilitate collaborative research;
- Social writing platforms such as Wikis and *GoogleDocs*, are integrated into writing-intensive courses where two or more participants edit a document in real time on the Internet;
- Blogs are used to expand course activities beyond the classroom, motivating students who write for a wider audience.

With such a diverse use, the potential for Web 2.0 applications in HE is vast but its reach is still potentially undetermined. Instructors gather these tools using them separately in their lessons, but the majority does not yet embrace and integrate various social networking sites as teaching or learning tools. An insufficient number of universities, and university organisations, have, as yet, invested in Web 2.0 applications, either in terms of a systematic examination of their potential use or in terms of customising or redeveloping them to comply with HE needs. Web 2.0 seems beneficial because it stresses knowledge sharing and creativity, but is a potentially disruptive technology because of the potential organisational, institutional and cultural changes it brings to established models of HE. A quick and tentative survey of examples of Web 2.0 technologies carried out in 2007 relating to their use in universities (LEAD project[4]) revealed that in most cases, innovations are still hesitant and unsteady. Even so, within the educational environment, and HE in particular, there are signs that Web 2.0 is in the first stages of an evolution characterised by a process towards specialised functions that will lead HE institutions, universities in particular, to develop and invest in specialised but shared Web 2.0 services. In Marenzi (2012) the social, interactional, technological aspects of Web 2.0 tools are discussed in terms of general uses as well as specialised uses in academia focusing on Web 2.0 tools as potentially emergent educational genres. The intuition is that after a period of rapid development in which numerous social networking genres and subgenres have mushroomed, a phase of rationalisation, characterised by integration and interoperability, is likely to ensue. A process is envisioned in which Web 2.0 macrogenres will emerge, as a result of a fairly conscious process of genre design. Genres thus created will be superordinate vis-à-vis current Web 2.0 genres but will provide a framework in which the process of cross-fertilisation between lower-order genre types (genres, subgenres and mini-genres) can develop (Baldry & Thibault, 2006b).

4 http://www2.epcc.ed.ac.uk/~lead/

Established educational methods may need to be reshaped to incorporate the benefits of Web 2.0 tools advantageously and engage students in extended collaborative learning opportunities (Thompson, 2007). Research into student expectations reveals significant changes in the way people communicate and expect to communicate which need to be anticipated by educators (Kvavik & Caruso, 2005). Current school curricula are still heavily focused on traditional print-based materials and often do not cover the range of skills adolescents acquire out-of-school experiences. On the other hand, participation in online worlds and other forms of digital culture transform students' expectations and needs for their future lives. Integrating Web resources into teaching could help reduce the gap between "young people's use of technology outside of school" (Hague & Payton, 2010, p. 11), and increasing learning opportunities that accommodate different learning styles and needs. The results of the Futurelab[5] research on digital literacy published in the *Digital literacies across the curriculum* handbook show that "over the past twenty years there has been a significant increase in the difference between young people's digital technology use outside and inside school" (Hague & Payton, 2010, p. 11). Whereas till the 1990s, most children learned to use technology only in the classroom, recently more and more children arrive at school already with some experience of digital media. For this reason, their previous personal experience and knowledge should be considered and taken as a starting point for learning in the classroom. The teacher's role is to help students in using technology for learning providing good scenarios and tasks which help them enhance their knowledge. According to Mayall (2007, p. 22), "this would increase students' motivation and active participation in learning activities". Nonetheless, success is neither automatic nor guaranteed. As Mehisto et al. remark:

> "For new technologies to be truly relevant in educational contexts, they need to be used to support young learners in taking their thinking another step forward. It is by using these technologies in new ways, by accessing new information, by connecting with others and by building something new that is connected to the students' lives, their community and the world at large that the new technologies become effective, relevant, educational tools."
>
> (Mehisto et al., 2008, p. 192)

The challenge for practitioners is to adapt the curriculum to learners' changing needs. To succeed in this, a better understanding of young people and their changing behavior is required. The Web offers teachers numerous opportunities

5 http://www.futurelab.org.uk

to create materials and collaborative tasks that implement these principles. Web 2.0, in particular, includes resources that engage students in co-construction of knowledge and skill development. However these technologies must be used with specific purposes and functions, and students should feel strong motivation as regards what they are doing. Available materials and communicative tools need to be aligned with pedagogical purposes and integrated into meaningful learning situations (Sharples et al., 2013). Teachers have to create authentic learning situations, design relevant tasks that involve students in problem-solving and negotiation of meaning: this contributes to giving added value to the content that Internet mediation makes more sustainable and closer to everyday reality.

2.6 Educational technology

"It's not just the tool, but the educational rationale that counts."

(Prof. Gavriel Salomon, Invited keynote at *Ed-Media2000*)

"*Educational technology* is the study and ethical practice of facilitating learning and improving performance by designing, creating and applying appropriate learning systems and resources using educational as well as technological processes" (Richey, 2008, p. 24). It investigates the use of technology in education from a range of perspectives: the learner's, the teacher's and the researcher's.

Educational technology is often associated with instructional and learning theories, so that the term may include the techniques used by educators in a broader sense. According to the AECT Committee[6] (*Association for Educational Communications and Technology Definitions and Terminology Committee*), there is a difference between *instructional technology* and *educational technology*. While the former is defined as "the theory and practice of design, development, utilization, management, and evaluation of processes and resources for learning", the latter includes other approaches used in the process of developing human capabilities. The areas in which these approaches can be used are really broad, including, for example, the design of online courses (*What are the characteristics of online courses? What critical aspects are there?*), teacher training (*How should courses for educators be organized? What should educators know about the use of technology?*), introduction of new technologies in education (*What quality criteria should backup technological innovation? How can the results be evaluated?*) (Calvani, 2004, p. 7; author's translation).

6 http://www.aect.org/about/div_.asp?DivisionID=18

Besides supporting the correct introduction of media at school, an important task for the *educational technologist* is to understand the best way of introducing innovation and to suggest criteria and guidelines to increase the quality of education supported by technology. In an educational context the following questions are frequently asked: *Is technology useful for learning? What happens when media are introduced in education? If the learning process is influenced by the media, is this influence helpful?* Technology in general can refer to specific objects, such as machines or hardware, but can also encompass broader themes including systems, organisational methods or techniques. The technological aspect is not represented in the tools that can be used, but in the planning and systematic approach to learning requirements which must be analysed and made explicit on the basis of theoretical models. The attitude of the educational technologist regarding the introduction of the media in educational contexts is detached and the tendency is to use critical evaluations and historical analysis to approach the problem in a rational way. The media do not influence learning directly but there are many other factors, personal and social, which come into play. Educational technologists do not apply technology in a deterministic way, but instead try to apply ICTs (*Information and Communication Technologies*) to basic educational models that comply with current social requirements. They adopt a critical stance towards the use of technology rejecting the mere delivery of content, and stressing the need instead to adopt a critical approach that highlights learner motivation and involvement, the danger of information overload, different ways of supporting and evaluating the learning process (Calvani, 2004, p. 12; author's translation). Technology is not effective by itself but its potentiality must be included and evaluated as one resource in a complex setting. Too strong a guidance conflicts with the idea that learners should learn to plan and develop their own learning strategies. A good question to ask in this respect is: *What are the learning goals*? Educators need to be able to detect the right cognitive potential to be applied to the right context. Similarly educational technologists need to be able to find and suggest the right interface (liaise) to allow expressiveness, as well as individual or social knowledge building. For this reason, it is important to define and understand what the competences and tasks of the educational technologist are compared to other professional profiles.

Who is the Educational Technologist

The *educational technologist* is an expert who uses theoretical models and established research criteria to design and create appropriate learning environments for different learning scenarios. To better understand the learning scenario and to design appropriate learning environments, the educational technologist must refer to previous theoretical models and methodologies, selecting and adopting the most suitable for the current conditions (social and cultural conditions as well as the specific project work).

Figure 1: The Educational technologists http://Kellykvk.files.wordpress.com

It is important to distinguish this role from other occupational profiles in the learning scenario, such as the *educator* who is particularly skilled in using tools and systems with students or the *ICT technologist*, who is more concerned in verifying the accessibility and the usability of tools. The educational technologist is more concerned with a careful evaluation of the different types of learning and the potential cognitive dynamics, keeping track of previous experiences and of previous evaluation results. For educational technologists the communication tool is only one part of the complete learning environment, as they pay more attention to teachers' and learners' requirements. Their task is to improve the integration of technology in course design bearing in mind other educational factors such as the learning goals or the appropriate communication and interaction strategies. The distinguishing feature of their expertise is an *interdisciplinary approach* which integrates knowledge from different fields such as pedagogy, communication, psychology, and takes advantage of a comprehensive system of theoretical models, methodologies and technological systems to support specific learning requirements in controlled settings.

Increasingly, information becomes a problem in an educational context because it can lead to overload. The educational technologist must support teachers to handle the overload of learning systems and to critically select the most useful information which becomes meaningful knowledge. A critical step for educational technologists and designers is the initial phase of a course when it is very important to clarify the learning goals to be achieved. They have to work together with the teacher to list the requirements and activities needed to achieve learning goals.

2.7 Summary and discussion

Chapter 2 gave an overview of the most recent pedagogical approaches, from Behaviourism to Constructivism, as a theoretical basis for the development of TEL a support to all learning activity through technology and for the most recent application techniques such as Educational Technology. The following paragraphs summarise the various phases discussing the key pedagogical concepts from an educational point of view.

Pedagogical approaches are becoming more and more open, flexible and social. In a similar way, the use of technology in education is extensively grounded in socio-cultural and socio-constructivist models where learning is seen as a social process, which results in knowledge construction mediated by other people. Starting from Behaviourism and Cognitivism, the most recent educational approaches are based on the constructivist idea of the learner. While Behaviourism and Cognitivism stressed the importance of a linear and rational structure of the learning path reinforced with feedback and additional supports, during the 1980s this objective and rationalistic approach of the hierarchical and sequential models became weaker and weaker and scientists increasingly agreed that knowledge is situated and depends on context.

At the beginning of the 1990s Constructivism promoted a more open-ended learning experience where the methods and the results of learning are not easily measured and might not be the same for each learner. The educational experts paid more attention to the new concept of *learning environment* rather than to the sequence of short learning tasks. "The control over the learning process shifted from the teacher to the student, with the learner playing an active role in the learning process" (Ullrich et al., 2008, p. 706). Learning has to take place in context and in collaboration with others, while the teacher focuses mainly on preparatory activities, and acts as an adviser in the learning process providing support where assistance is needed.

Towards the mid-1980s the new technologies became even more popular and, with the growth of general-purpose software, computers came to be considered as *working tools*. However, for quite a long time the integration of new technologies at school proved to be difficult. At the beginning of the 1990s the *personal computer* developed into *interpersonal computing* and technology started to be an environment to support the social creation of knowledge (Barret, 1994). Developments in new technologies have enabled the change from computers as aids that support sequential learning, to computers as tools to be embedded within learning environments to support communication and collaborative information sharing.

By the end of the 1990s, the expansion of the Internet and the use of technology in education had generated a new area of study called *e-learning*. At the beginning of the e-learning era, a strong emphasis was placed on how to centralise and standardise the learning experience. "Most learning content was created and delivered via LMSs (*Learning Management Systems*) such as *WebCT, Blackboard, Moodle, ILIAS,* as static-packaged online courses and modules" (Chatti et al., 2008, p. 371). In most cases, an initially paper-based learning resource was simply converted into a digital form and a classroom training event was transformed into an online course. However, what is important in learning, is not content or technology, but rather "the support of learning as a cognitive and constructive process" (Chatti et al., 2007, p. 410). Traditional LMSs still approach group membership in a top-down fashion (Marenzi et al., 2008b), whereas modern learners and knowledge workers resist one-size-fits-all, centrally-managed learning approaches that often fail to address what today's learners need. "Hessan and Vogt stress that courses, by definition, capture yesterday's knowledge" (Rosenberg, 2006, p. 4), whereas most learning today both at work and at school is informal, for example through games, social networks, simulations and storytelling. Learning and knowledge are more than static content, and technology is just an enabler to reach new open sources and learn from them. As Chatti remarks, "At the heart of learning lie people" (Chatti et al., 2007, p. 410).

Systems based on *Computer Supported Collaborative Learning* (CSCL) encourage the shared development of knowledge. The field of CSCL takes much from Constructivist and Socio-constructivist learning theories that emphasise knowledge as the result of learners interacting with each other, sharing and building knowledge as a group. Since collaborative learning is demanding, it needs to be supported by adequate scaffolds. Educators must be able to detect the right cognitive potential to be applied in the right context, while educational technologists must be able to find and suggest the right interface to allow expressiveness, as well as individual or social knowledge building. Educational technologists and designers have to work together with the teacher to list the requirements and activities needed to achieve learning goals. A specific benefit of CSCL is that, helped by proper teacher facilitation, students can use technology to experiment, build their learning foundations and construct their knowledge with peers. Technology should provide new types of media and create opportunities that enhance the experience for learners by supporting collaborative groups in negotiating the knowledge they are building. The rise of Web 2.0 technologies overcomes many of the failings of traditional Technology Enhanced Learning solutions providing more support for collaboration and networking. While conventional e-learning systems were basically used to deliver instructional materials and assignments to students, the new *e-learning2.0* places much emphasis on the use of open and social software such as blogs, wikis, and podcasts. Social software and social learning have been shown to create exciting new learning opportunities for people and to support the creation of networks and communities of practice among company employees. In work environments social software is changing the traditional way in which learning systems, groupware and other project-oriented collaboration tools work (Marenzi et al., 2008b). In learning contexts, social software has become a means of connecting people to other people, not only to share documents, but also "to share ideas, get effective support, and collaboratively create new content, and learn from others" (Chatti et al., 2008, p. 370). Within online communities the learner becomes more active and engaged in interactions. Web 2.0 and social networking tools and communities require explicit *will and skill* on the learner's part. Current Web 2.0 technologies support learners in searching and organising different kinds of resources and information. Learning thus becomes a peer-based but, at the same time, a more autonomous activity.

In recent decades, the new concept of *individualised learning* is taking hold. Some researchers take a more extreme position considering the need to shift away from teacher-led quality control of students' learning to students' *own* quality control of their learning (Rizzo, 2009). The idea is that, in order to become their own masters in the context of working with others, individual learners have to achieve their learning objectives both singly and collectively. Learners have to take responsibility for their own learning, but will also need to demonstrate that they do possess their own learning style and strategy. Hence, for effective learning to take place, learners need to "develop the ability to manage their own time efficiently, set achievable goals, find appropriate resources, whilst critically evaluating their own understandings as well as the ideas of others" (Rizzo, 2009, p. 26).

Established educational methods and learning beliefs might need to be reshaped in order to take advantage of the benefits of Web 2.0 and engage students in extended collaborative learning opportunities. Practitioners need to provide students with a new set of techniques which allow them to acquire the multiple skills they need in the new society. The challenge for educational institutions and teachers is no longer to provide tools and learning tasks for students to acquire pre-defined knowledge, but to provide methods and techniques to support learners in *exploring* the diversity of resources (both educational and not explicitly educational) available to them. Knowledge acquisition nowadays is no longer isolated in closed learning environments designed to match a specific learning path, but is becoming more and more based on open and experience-oriented *skills* development. Students are exposed to new forms of informal learning which require them to acquire the ability of finding good quality and reliable data, as well as critically analysing information and re-contextualising it in different settings. A recent model which is getting a foothold in educational scenarios is represented by MOOCs (*Massive Open Online Courses*) which provide a more global, open delivery and collaborative construction of knowledge contents to accommodate different learning styles (Grünewald et al., 2013).

Considering the huge amount of data available on the Web, new tools are required to make those data easily accessible, explorable, and reusable from an educational point of view. To be able to analyse and understand these newly emerging forms of informal learning, a new set of technical and pedagogical techniques are required (Sharples et al., 2013). On the other hand though, many technological challenges are still open: "rules for standardisation and interoperability of data sources should be agreed upon and adopted by practitioners and institutions" (Dietze et al., 2013, p. 62); the Web should be structured in a consistent way, mapping and interlinking the Web data so as to give learners the opportunity to better orient themselves and to become really autonomous in finding the resources they need. From the educational point of view, a way should be found to handle the diversity of subject domains, and to better assess the quality and trust of resources available on the Web. From the pedagogical point of view, a new paradigm and effective guidelines should be suggested and experimented to renovate and modernise formal education.

In the author's opinion, facilitating interaction and collaboration between experts in the various fields involved in this paradigm change (e.g. computer scientists, pedagogues and educators) can help to find joint solutions and solve some of the aforementioned open issues.

II
Empirical Research

3 Search, collaboration and sharing in the Web

> "The shift to global information-based economies has meant a dramatic increase in the need to deal with large amounts of information and to communicate across language cultures. Memorisation is less important in this information-rich time than *effective search strategies*."
>
> (Warschauer & Healey, 1998, p. 60)

The previous chapter showed how in the 21st century learning becomes increasingly 'situated in action'. To quote Seely Brown (2002, p. 72), "learning becomes as much social as cognitive, it is concrete rather than abstract, and it becomes intertwined with judgment and exploration". As such, the Web becomes not just a source of information, but rather a learning medium where knowledge is socially constructed and shared. For this reason, the development of Web 2.0 tools has reached a big success with the general public, and researchers have been studying the new Web trends to apply Web 2.0 concepts to the learning process and create new learning experiences for various kinds of online communities.

In this context the researcher, in the role of educational technologist, started the first phase of her research, studying how people search, collaborate and share resources on the Web. The initial goal was to take advantage of the new social networking trend and to see how those practices could be adopted in an educational context.

The success of Web 2.0 and specific platforms such as YouTube, Flickr, and Delicious demonstrates that people are willing to share knowledge and resources with other people. "Thanks to the growing success of Web 2.0 platforms, people share information and resources within their social community and beyond" (Abel et al., 2009b, p. 154). While the use of Web search engines has focused attention on the activity of searching, this activity is really only one part of the entire information access process: information retrieval through searching and browsing, analysis and synthesis of results. Russell et al. (1993, p. 269) discuss this process as the process of *sensemaking*. The social aspect of this process is emphasised in Evans and Chi (2008, p. 485), who discuss a model to understand social searching, where they distinguish between different phases of collaborative searching including *foraging* (Pirolli & Card, 1999, p. 644), sensemaking and organising, as important aspects of this activity. "They propose several design suggestions that enhance collaboration during searching, which mainly involve enhanced means of communication via email or instant messaging and the integration of social navigation support into the search results" (Abel et al.,

2009a, p. 1). In 2008 Amershi and Morris presented Co-Search[7] "a system developed to improve the experience of co-located collaborative Web search by leveraging readily available devices such as mobile phones and extra mice" (Amershi & Morris, 2008, p. 1647). Various research studies have shown that social searching and exploration techniques can improve the effectiveness of Web searching. "A survey[8] conducted by Morris (2008) at a large U.S. technology company showed that a large proportion of users engage in collaborative activities when they search. The study also showed that many tasks in both professional and casual settings benefit from the ability to jointly search and share resources with others" (Abel et al., 2009a, p. 1). "SearchTogether" (Morris & Horvitz, 2007) supports synchronous searching where all members of a group search simultaneously or collaborate asynchronously by reusing the result history. "The most highly rated social annotation features in the interface are query histories, ratings and comments" (Abel et al., 2009a, p. 1).

"Nonetheless, the Web is a challenging environment, in which user-generated resources are distributed among a set of heterogeneous online storage tools, each of which provides specific functionalities" (Marenzi et al., 2008d, p. 9). "On the Web, users are often forced to distribute related resources across different applications according to the type of resource, e.g., pictures in Flickr, videos in YouTube and bookmarks in Delicious, even though all these resources belong to one and the same learning context" (Marenzi et al., 2008b, p. 21). An important aspect of competence development, which cannot be supported by a single Web 2.0 application, is the desire to share findings related to common activities. Knowledge workers, in particular, need an environment, which allows the direct sharing of resources in different formats (Rosenberg, 2001). Such an environment should enable users to execute desired actions directly in one step, even if the orchestration of services provided by different Web 2.0 applications is required.

Despite the variety of the available Web 2.0 tools, linking distributed resources related to a common activity is not provided by existing applications. "Most of the Web 2.0 applications and their orchestrations focus on finding resources related to user information needs" (Zerr et al., 2011, p. 1350). Although this is a necessary first step, aggregation and usage of the retrieved information is a different matter that has received insufficient critical attention so far. On the one hand, portals like iGoogle and Netvibes help to locate information distributed

---

7 http://research.microsoft.com/en-us/um/people/merrie/papers/cosearch.pdf
8 http://research.microsoft.com/en-us/um/people/merrie/papers/collab_search_survey.pdf

across different information sources. On the other hand, such portals typically provide no facilities for integration of the information obtained from these sources as they merely support creation of a personalised desktop made up of favourite links to knowledge resources, without providing a way of actually linking them together.

Several tools and platforms have been developed to support different aspects of communication and online collaboration (e.g. *mashups*) but it is still difficult to find good interfaces suitable for educational contexts. Even if the Web is really useful to search for information, there is a big difference when dealing with educational resources. *Knowledge* is not the same as *information* and it is still difficult to find good material for learning. In particular the material is often unstructured or localised and it is still difficult to judge the reliability of some sources to be used in the educational context. "Popular resource sharing systems allow users to upload and share content, but do not focus on educational resources. Petrides et al. (2008, p. 98) point out that there is a need for platforms, which allow users to share open educational resources and inspire a culture of continuous improvement of these resources" (Marenzi et al., 2010, p. 205). The demand for platforms that allow students to share open educational resources is also discussed in Held and Cress (2009). "In addition, sharing and linking distributed educational material related to the same context requires an environment which permits the storage of resources in different formats" (Marenzi et al., 2010, p. 205).

To address these issues, the LearnWeb2.0 system[9] has been developed within the TENCompetence European project as a collaborative search and sharing platform. It integrates several popular resource sharing systems as well as social networking systems such as YouTube and Flickr and provides advanced features for organising and sharing distributed resources in a collaborative environment. The main goal was to design a new learning environment which could use the potentialities of social networks to support the requirements of different learning scenarios. In the following section the TENCompetence project is introduced and the first version of the LearnWeb2.0 system is described.

3.1 TENCompetence: the project and the prototype

The goal of the TENCompetence[10] project (running from December 2005 to December 2009) was to design and develop a technical and organisational

9 http://learnweb.l3s.uni-hannover.de/lw/
10 http://tencompetence-project.bolton.ac.uk/

infrastructure supporting lifelong-learning in Europe serving the needs of individuals, various social groups, and organisations. The spirit behind TENCompetence was to collect relevant information about different knowledge resources relating to lifelong-learning and gathering them in an integrated environment from where they can be easily accessed (Marenzi et al., 2008b).

The project's first stages implemented an infrastructure that "integrated models and tools for the creation, storage and exchange of knowledge resources[11]" (Koper et al., 2009; Marenzi et al., 2009), making information accessible to learning and enhancing the learning experience. This *Knowledge Resource Sharing and Management* (*KRSM*) infrastructure brought together information stored on institutional servers, centralised repositories, learner desktops by means of *Peer-to-Peer Technology* and online community-sharing systems such as Flickr and YouTube (Demidova et al., 2007, p. 691). The KRSM architecture is depicted in Figure 2.

Figure 2: KRSM Architecture

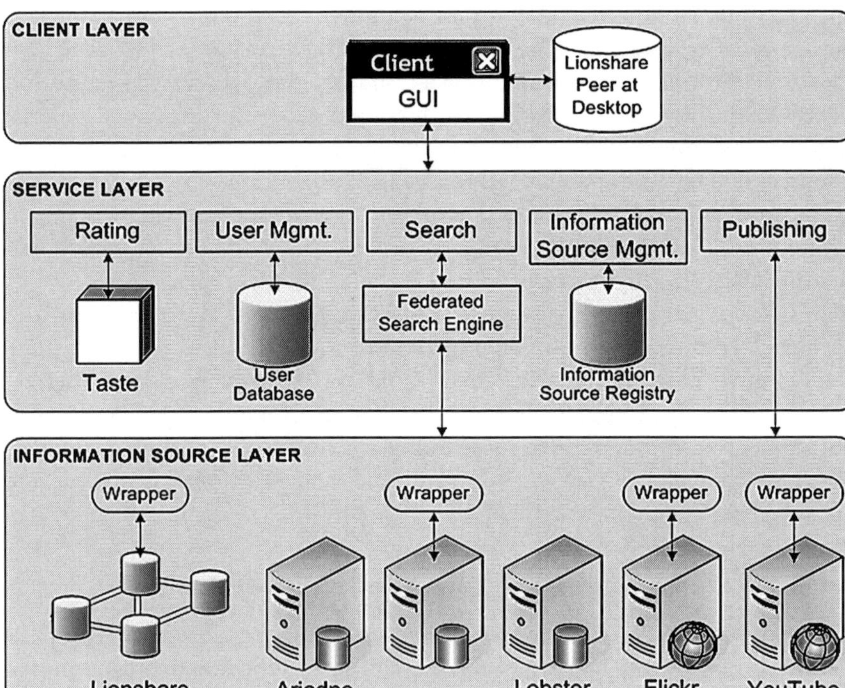

11 http://www.learningfrontiers.eu/?q=tel_project/TENCOMPETENCE

Already with current *Enterprise Resource Planning* (ERP) solutions, integration of diverse systems is a challenge. "Applications do not converse, they do not share data or reuse services or applications in a uniform and interoperable way. With Web 2.0, new types of application have to be integrated into this already complicated environment, to provide functionalities for knowledge resource sharing and exchange" (Marenzi et al., 2008b, p. 18).

The second phase of the TENCompetence project extended the integration of Web 2.0 applications to support a variety of scenarios (Marenzi et al., 2008b). The LearnWeb2.0 system was initially included as a component of the TENCompetence infrastructure as a platform for searching distributed Web 2.0 repositories. The focus was put on the *features* of existing Web 2.0 applications such as tagging, bookmarking and commenting integrated into the LearnWeb2.0 platform for sharing, discussing and creating knowledge resources for lifelong-learning and competence development (see Table 1).

The researcher had the opportunity to join the L3S Research Center, Leibniz University in Hannover, at that time, and participated in this phase of the project activities. In particular her task was to categorise various Web 2.0 tools and select what services should be integrated in the LearnWeb2.0 system. The integrated *Personal Competence Manager* (PCM) resulting from the TENCompetence project was tested in a set of pilots. LearnWeb2.0 was not at the centre of the evaluations performed though, so little feedback was obtained on how to further improve the system. The Personal Competence Manager resulting from the TENCompetence project was abandoned in December 2009 when the project ended.

The LearnWeb2.0 system - PHP prototype evaluation and improvement

After the end of the TENCompetence project, the researcher together with a group of developers at the L3S Research Center, decided to continue the work and support in particular teachers and students in collaborative search. Considering the exponential growth of content on the Web, the idea was to investigate the possibility of creating an integrated environment which supported collaborative search and organisation of open educational resources collected in several social networks and selected through annotations by a trusted community. An integrated infrastructure was envisaged in which it was possible to host a set of Web 2.0 tools which can interact as an over-arching LMSWeb2.0 macrogenre to overcome Web 2.0 weaknesses in education such as lack of reliability and information overload (Marenzi, 2012).

Since the first prototype of LearnWeb2.0 was intended as a collaborative tool for searching and sharing resources found in social networks, at the beginning

Table 1: TENCompetence infrastructure – features description

Feature	Description	Services in use: Delicious	SpreadCrumbs	Flickr	YouTube	GroupMe!	Last.fm	Wordpress	Bloggers	Facebook	Orkut	Open ID	Example benefits gained by LearnWeb2.0
3.1 Resource selection and sharing	Supported media types: bookmarks, images, videos, *GroupMe!* groups, *HTML* snippets and audio	✓	✓	✓	✓	✓	✓	✓	✓	✓	✓		Sharing of diverse media via aggregated social networks
3.2 Annotating search results	Types of annotations: tags, semantic markup and *SpreadCrumbs*	✓	✓	✓	✓	✓	✓	✓					Annotation of multiple resources in parallel
3.3 Bookmark sharing and notification	Types of notification: *RSS/ATOM* feeds and internal message notification	✓	✓			✓		✓	✓	✓	✓		Aggregation of notifications across different services
3.4 Resource aggregation and sequencing	Aggregation techniques: standing queries, grouping and clustering			✓		✓							Standing queries containing diverse media, sequencing
3.5 Resource upload	Supported actions on uploaded resources: read, write, delete	✓	✓	✓	✓	✓		✓	✓				Uniform (user) interface
3.6 Aggregation and manipulation of social networks	Social relations: friends, groups and typed relations	✓		✓			✓			✓	✓		Sharing is based on aggregated social networks
3.7 Collaborative content creation	Types of content: resource compositions, *HTML* snippets and comments					✓		✓	✓	✓	✓		Collaborative bundling of multimedia resources together with textual descriptions
3.8 Virtual Web2 working space	Resource Discovery via keyword-based (full text) search, tag-based search, explorative search, and faceted search	✓	✓	✓	✓	✓	✓	✓	✓				Central management of diverse resources
3.9 Authorization and access control	Authorization levels: public, restrictive to grounds and individuals, private or based on advanced policies	✓		✓			✓			✓	✓	✓	Fine-grained access control based on existing social networks
3.10 Single sign-on	Users and applications that act on behalf of the user are enabled to sign in											✓	Encapsulation of sign-on procedures for all involved services

of the research work, a few preliminary studies were carried out mainly concerning the potential of social software tools and the challenges involved in different working and university scenarios (Abel et al., 2009c). A preliminary evaluation of the PHP version, the architectural design and the functionalities of LearnWeb2.0 are described in Abel et al. (2009a). The paper presents the results of a user study on the usage of social annotation features such as sharing, rating, commenting and tagging, in collaborative search processes. Making use of LearnWeb2.0 as a resource sharing system, participants collaboratively searched for resources on a specific theme. The study addressed the following research questions:

1. *In what situations is searching social media more useful than regular Web searching?*
2a. *What group processes appear in collaborative searching?*
2b. *How important or prevalent are social notification services, including rating, grouping, tagging, comments?*
3. *How do people react to and take advantage of notifications of results and feedback from colleagues or collaborators?*

Motivated by these research questions, the analysis of the results was based on a questionnaire on the use of Web 2.0 tools as well as on the specific LearnWeb2.0 functionalities designed to support collaboration, and on LearnWeb2.0's log files. A first finding is that there is an imbalance between what users search for and what they actually share: users typically share files, often images, that are important for them personally, but they usually search for media, video and audio, that is of common interest. A second finding is that social annotations are only considered as secondary relevance indicators for search results: title and description are viewed as more important. When sharing, users preferred writing comments to light-weight mechanisms such as tagging. As tags are known to be useful for enhancing keyword-based searching, means for automatically tagging need to be devised. In general, the results indicated that collaborative search requires direct communication to be integrated into the system. Current social annotation techniques *do* enhance result listings, but do not support interaction between group members *sufficiently*. Moreover, as users mainly focus on the contents of the search results, it would be better if group communication were presented separately from the search results (Abel et al., 2009a).

During 2009 the LearnWeb2.0 platform was evaluated in an educational environment as well, to support collaborative project work. The papers Marenzi et al. (2008d; 2009) focused on the knowledge sharing and collaboration aspects, and described the main functionalities of LearnWeb2.0 for lifelong competence development. In Marenzi et al. (2009) a group of ICT technicians working in the information systems area motivated by a real world knowledge sharing scenario at the University of Pavia, had to design and organise *European Computer Driving License* (ECDL) courses online. After a preliminary experience with LearnWeb2.0 in various contexts and smaller case studies, the researcher, together with the team of researcher at the L3S Research Center, decided to adopt a systematic research approach to improve the current version of the system for specific user requirements. In this context, exploratory research has been conducted over four years to help determine the best research design, what data collection method should be used and what subjects should be selected. This more specific approach included the following steps:

- Design, evaluation and adaptation of the LearnWeb2.0 platform in the specific setting of a CLIL scenario (Section 3.2)
- Systematic data collection and evaluation of the results using an *Iterative evaluation-driven design-based* research approach (Section 4.1)
- Development and improvement of the system according to the users' feedback (Section 5.3)

In the following paragraphs the system design and the new functionalities of LearnWeb2.0 for CLIL are described, as well as a comparison with other existing solutions. A detailed description of the *iterative evaluation-driven design-based* research process is given in Chapters 4, 5 and 6.

3.2 LearnWeb2.0 (v.1): system design

The design of the new LearnWeb2.0 release has targeted specific user requirements to address specific learning needs, in particular the setting of CLIL learning scenarios. To be successful in the CLIL context the use of authentic subject-specific material is required, but it is still difficult to find good and authentic material since a lot of resources are localised and teachers spend a lot of time in preparing suitable material for their classrooms. The new system design was intended to provide good search strategies and better collaborative tools to support teachers and students in finding reliable and authentic material for their CLIL classroom.

In the following paragraphs the first release of the new LearnWeb2.0 system is described. More details on the CLIL scenario and evaluation can be found in Chapter 5 of this thesis.

3.2.1 Conceptual overview

One key design principle of the new release of the system in 2009 was to connect LearnWeb2.0 to the network of popular existing Web 2.0 systems frequently used by the students. In this way LearnWeb2.0 users build on their experiences with these systems. The second design goal was to support active and project-oriented learning in CLIL (Section 5.1).

In line with the findings presented in Ullrich et al. (2008), who discussed how the integration of popular Web 2.0 services into education can stimulate active participation of learners in the learning processes, and motivated by the first design goal, the new LearnWeb2.0 design integrated various resource sharing systems to provide an environment that supports learners and educators in sharing, discovering, and managing learning resources. As resources come in different formats, LearnWeb2.0 supports appropriate media types (such as images, videos, and Power Point presentations, as well as written texts), and does so in an integrated way, in contrast to *mashups* such as Netvibes or iGoogle, which provide access to various Web 2.0 services in a single environment, but keep these services separated (Thang et al., 2007). With respect to the second design goal, LearnWeb2.0 was designed as an active learning environment to support collaborative searching and project work in a CLIL context.

The specific role of the researcher in the LearnWeb2.0 system development was to connect developers and users, and to guide the improvement of the system for the chosen pedagogical contexts. Some tasks in this regard were for example: analysing scenarios and learning requirements; designing learning environments together with teachers; discussing user requirements with developers; evaluating the system performance with regard to the user expectations and learning goals; supporting teachers and learners in using the system as a tutor; and improving the system design in keeping with users' feedback.

3.2.2 LearnWeb2.0 architecture and implementation

Figure 3 depicts the LearnWeb2.0 architecture and shows the Web 2.0 services integrated into the system. The LearnWeb2.0 core and interface were implemented using the PHP (*Hypertext Preprocessor*) programming language and the open source CakePHP framework[12]. The application was built as a set of modules for various functionalities and used the MySQL database to store application related data (e.g. user details, profile settings, translations and logs).

Whereas each single Web 2.0 application was specialised in a set of specific predefined tasks, such as storing, editing or discussing specific types of resources, the integrated LearnWeb2.0 environment provided a rich set of functions and a seamless overview of the entire distributed learning space. The system provided several innovative features designed to support teachers and students in collaborative group searching and annotation of resources from various Web 2.0 services such as YouTube, SlideShare, and Flickr, including: 1) "a personal learning space offering a seamless overview of the entire set of learning resources distributed across various Web 2.0 repositories" (Abel et al., 2009c, p. 6); 2) collaborative searching, sharing and aggregation of different learning resources; 3) integration of the user's social networks and resources from different Web 2.0

12 http://cakephp.org

Figure 3: LearnWeb2.0 Architecture (v.1 – PHP)

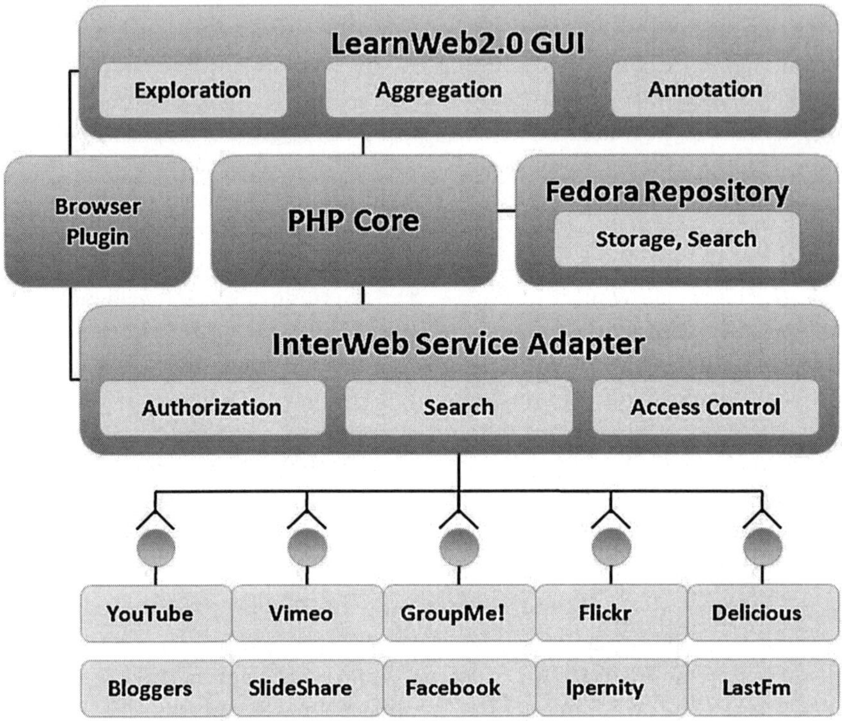

services; (4) annotation facilities such as rating, tagging and commenting that can help users to discuss and select the most relevant resources for their task (Marenzi et al., 2009). In this way LearnWeb2.0 (v1) supported (i) both kinds of users: educators and learners, as well as (ii) traditional educational resources, and resources originally not intended for education.

In the following paragraphs a short summary of the main LearnWeb2.0 functionalities is given, associated with the pedagogical principles which were the fundaments of the software development. To make LearnWeb2.0 an effective web-based collaborative learning environment, was not only a software design challenge, but it also required an effort for considering, designing and applying appropriate pedagogical principles related to software development for education. The functionalities and interfaces of existing software were taken into account (Section 3.2.4) and constituted the basis for the development of a new web-based learning environment devoted to multi-domain activities and collaborative learning.

Integration – to provide flexibility and modularity

"Web 2.0 resource sharing systems allow users to upload and share content" (Marenzi et al. 2010, p. 5), however most of these platforms only support specific media types, and are limited to specific functionalities. LearnWeb2.0 was designed to be adapted to different learning scenarios and educational contexts, as well as to be used in conjunction with other pieces of software. It provides a seamless Web service interface to access a number of popular Web 2.0 sources and social networking systems such as YouTube, Flickr, Facebook and LastFm as a storage platform, with the potential to add many more. The modularity allows users to select the Web 2.0 tools and services they need to use in the context of a specific project or learning scenario. This ensures the "correspondence between the system's design and the educational environment, situation and context in which it will be used" (Rubens et al., 2005, p. 278). The Web 2.0 service adapter InterWeb module is depicted in Figure 4. InterWeb provides Web 2.0 functionalities such as: authentication, resource searching, social network exploration and resource uploading. LearnWeb2.0 users do not login to each Web 2.0 system, but authorise InterWeb to access these services simultaneously, benefitting from LearnWeb2.0's single-sign-on functionality.

Figure 4: Integrated Web 2.0 tools through InterWeb (v.1)

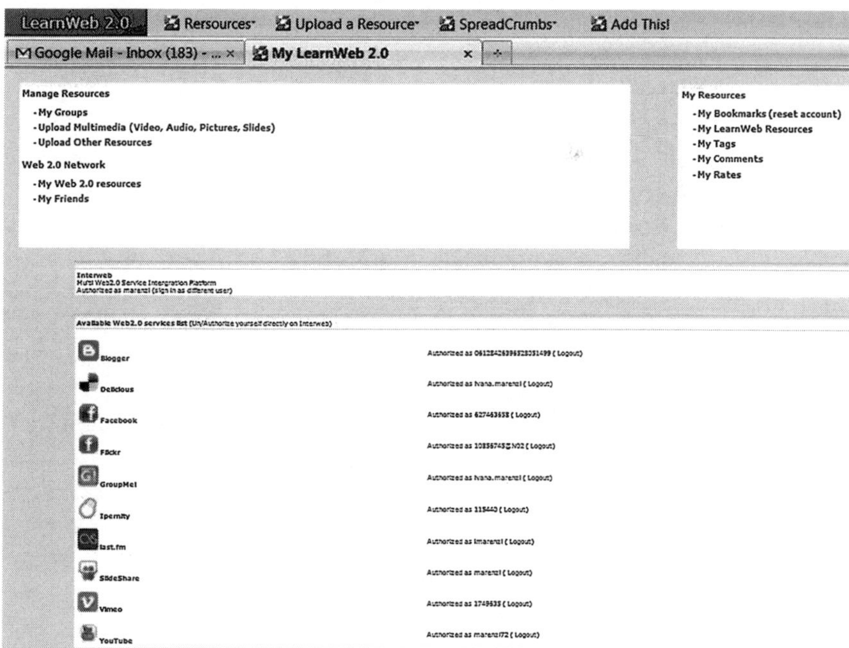

LearnWeb2.0 uses web-service calls to InterWeb, which propagates them to each of the integrated applications, aggregates all results into one result object and returns it to LearnWeb2.0. InterWeb is provided with an API (*Application Program Interface*) and is available as a web-service for all authorised applications. To use InterWeb the user requests an API key accompanied by a secret token. The authorisation component is also used when third-party applications access InterWeb services. During the registration process every LearnWeb2.0 user also obtains an InterWeb account. It is possible to create a "default user" account and copy it to other users so that a class of students can easily obtain a default set of Web 2.0 accounts and immediately start working with the system. Later on it is possible for each student to switch from the InterWeb account to their own Web 2.0 tools accounts, if they wish.

Fedora Repository. Working with digital objects requires sustainable technology for creating, managing, publishing, sharing and preserving metadata content such as titles, tags, descriptions and user comments. For this purpose, Fedora[13] has been integrated as the main resource annotation and storage facility. The Fedora Repository manages digital objects, organised in hierarchical structures, and stored in XML (*Extensible Markup Language*) format. In this repository, digital objects from different Web 2.0 sources can be annotated with metadata.

Search and exploration

LearnWeb2.0 provides an integrated view on the search results obtained from all integrated Web 2.0 services. It provides users with a generic search interface for several kinds of resources such as images, video clips, social network contacts, including LearnWeb2.0 itself. The search interface (Figure 5), contains a text field in which the user types in a keyword, and a search button to start the searching process. LearnWeb2.0 searches both locally in its own repository and in external Web 2.0 platforms (Marenzi et al., 2010, p. 6).

"The aggregated search results are presented as a list and accompanied by meta-information (snippets) and preview images. Typically a search result contains a title, a preview image and optionally a more detailed description. The user can interactively refine the results, e.g. sort the result list by attributes such as title, description, date or tag. Using the advanced search functionality, the user can specify properties of the desired resources and select a set

13 Fedora: open source software developed by Fedora Common (http://fedora-commons.org/)

Figure 5: Search interface – search results view (v.1)

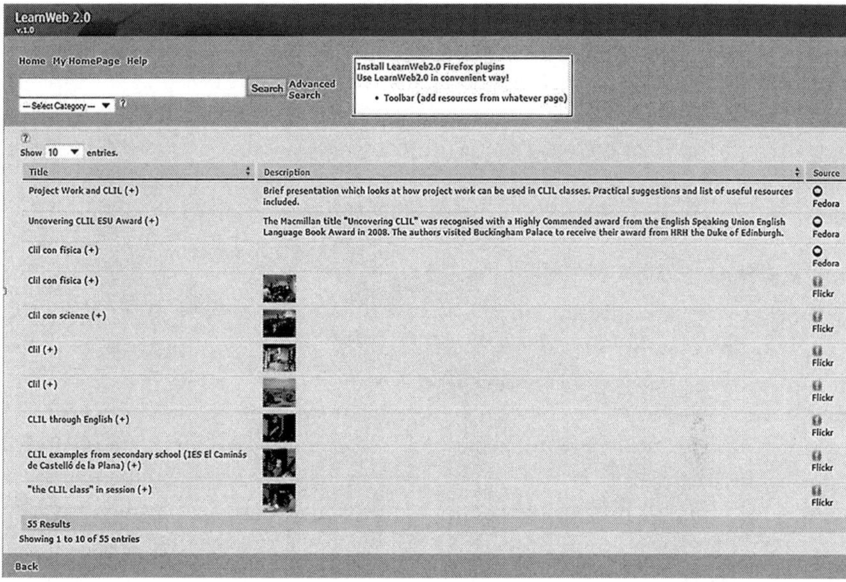

of resources based on a common property like a tag, a file type, a timestamp in case the user is only interested in particular media types such as videos or audios, or combinations thereof. The user can browse through the result list and select resources that suit his/her learning task best" (Marenzi et al., 2010, p. 6). On the server side, search requests for integrated services are generated from the user's query so that they correspond to search functionalities supported by a particular service. Responses from different services are combined into a single RSS (*Rich Site Summary*) atom feed made available to users along with a rendered list of search results.

Typically a search result contains a title, a preview image and optionally a more detailed description. The feed can be used as a standing query in any RSS reader, monitoring the appearance of new resources for that query. These capabilities provide a seamless view on all resources stored in the various Web 2.0 accounts of the users, creating their personal Web 2.0 learning space.

In order to support collaborative searching, LearnWeb2.0 provides automatic resource annotation. Once a search result is displayed in LearnWeb2.0, it is automatically tagged with the corresponding query terms (the original keywords). These keywords can later be used by other users to search and explore the learning resource spaces available in LearnWeb2.0.

Upload and Sharing

The Web is not the only place where users can find relevant materials. Useful resources can also be located on the users' computer or are acquired through other devices such as a photo camera. Using LearnWeb2.0 users can directly upload a resource from their computer or from an external source to a suitable Web 2.0 tool and enrich it with useful annotations (Marenzi et al., 2008d). These functionalities support the need to deal with the content and collaboration aspects relevant for successful CLIL material design in relation to formal models.

Aggregation -organisation of information

To support resource aggregation, the first version of LearnWeb2.0 provided the grouping functionality based on the integrated GroupMe! component (Abel et al., 2007). Users can create groups of learning resources to bundle resources that belong to the same learning context (Figure 6). By naming folders users may create their own categorisation and organisation of information, and different categories may include materials from different courses and classes. Users can be members of the same group so that several users can contribute resources. Groups are fully visualised (i.e. images include previews) and videos can be watched directly.

Figure 6: GroupMe! groups (v.1)

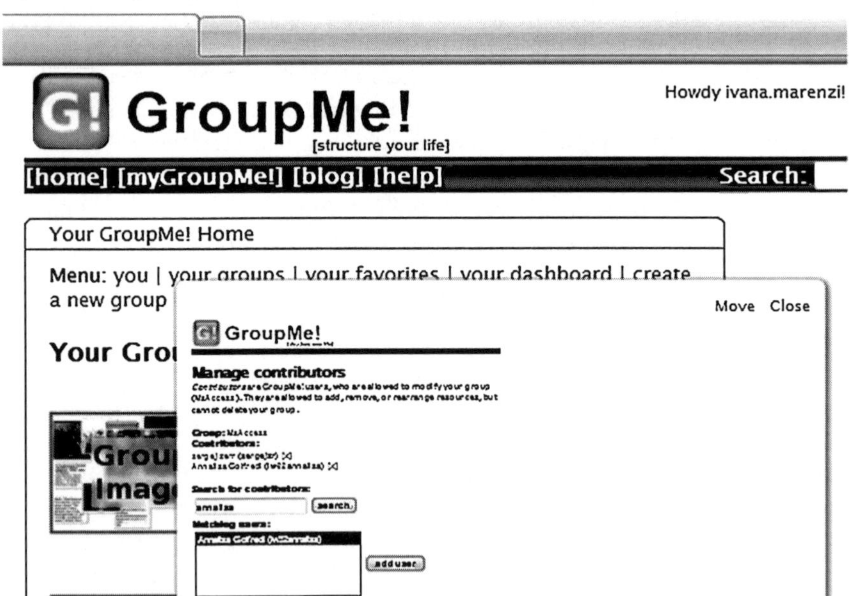

The integration of GroupMe! is not yet optimal though: groups of resources are not directly integrated in the LearnWeb2.0 environment and the interface is different; no communication is provided between different groups; there is no opportunity of tracking the activities and the learning process.

Annotation – scaffold knowledge building

References to selected resources are stored in the LearnWeb2.0 repository. Different references to the same resource can be added to the repository in different learning contexts. Resources in LearnWeb2.0 can be bookmarked, tagged, rated and discussed by other users who are allowed to access them (Figure 7). The categorisation of information by naming things is seen as an important activity of learning. Using tags to label the resources help students to make an effort of categorise the resources in a certain domain, thus engaging them in higher-level cognitive processes. Hence, the LearnWeb2.0 community can collaboratively identify the best learning resources for specific learning domains. Furthermore, the system automatically tags objects with the query terms used by learners when retrieving these objects. Comments on particular learning resources can further be used by authors to improve their resources.

Figure 7: Resource annotation window (v.1)

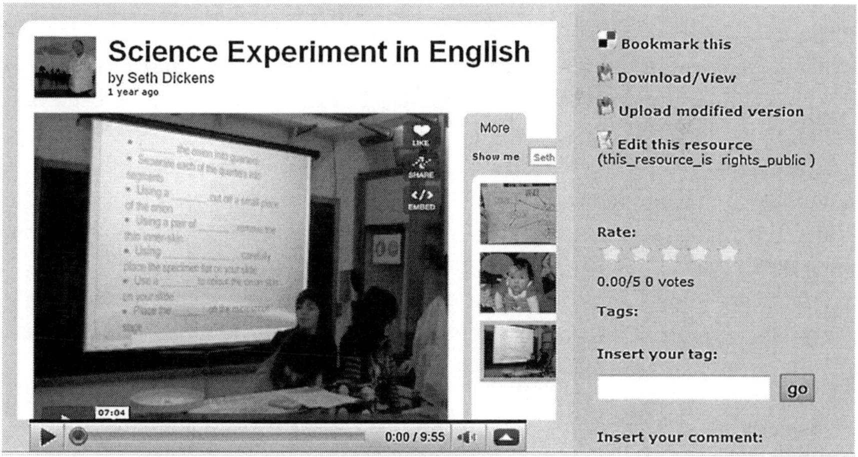

3.2.3 Comparison with existing solutions

In this section several interesting related systems are presented and compared with the LearnWeb2.0 system (v.1).

The *Graaasp*[14] system is "a Web 2.0 application that can serve simultaneously as an aggregation, contextualization, discussion, and networking platform, a shared asset repository, or an activity management system[15]" (Li et al., 2010, p. 163; Bogdanov et al., 2010).

Whilst in Graaasp the main focus lies in project management and activity organisation, LearnWeb2.0 was designed as a collaborative tool for searching and sharing resources found in social networks, and working with them in a critical way.

MIT OpenCourseWare[16] (OCW) is a large-scale repository of learning materials for undergraduate and graduate level courses started in 1999–2002 and is supported by a number of universities around the world. OCW materials are stored in the form of textual or multimedial documents including lecture notes, exams and interactive demonstrations. Whilst OCW sources can be integrated into LearnWeb2.0 as modules, the latter additionally provides means for the collaborative creation of course supporting materials rather than for their storage only.

ITunesU[17] is a podcasting platform which integrates the OCW repositories and other sources. The lecture podcasts can be viewed on mobile devices of the student to perform self-directed learning without spatial and temporal restrictions. LearnWeb2.0 allows for organisation of resources of different types including podcasts.

Edshare[18] is a content learning and teaching repository created by the University of Southampton. Users create and manage educational content in a Web 2.0-like way. LearnWeb2.0 additionally helps students to find relevant material on the Web.

The *OpenScout*[19] European project aims at building an online portal with materials for management education. Going beyond these projects, LearnWeb2.0 is a search and exploration system that allows for organisation of resources from all over the Web.

Metamorphosis+[20] is a semantic social platform for sharing educational resources across the Web. It is based on Linked Data and Service-oriented

---

14 http://graasp.epfl.ch

15 http://www.role-widgetstore.eu/content/graasp

16 http://ocw.mit.edu/index.htm

17 http://www.apple.com/education/itunes-u/

18 http://www.edshare.soton.ac.uk/

19 http://www.openscout.net/

20 http://metamorphosis.med.duth.gr/

principles. Smart search and enrichment mechanisms allow users not only to search for educational resources across the Web, but also to enrich existing metadata with original structured annotations. LearnWeb2.0 provides a similar functionality and extends it with the possibility to store search results in meaningful groups, rate and discuss them.

Web 2.0 tools such as Microblogs (Borau et al., 2009), Wikies and Forums can support learners' communication, collaborative project work and cultural competence training. Typically such tools provide specific functionalities in a closed environment. LearnWeb2.0 goes one step further and supports appropriate media types in an integrated way, providing an open environment where users can find different types of resources and share them with their colleagues and friends in their social networks.

Among the available open source e-learning platforms which declare themselves to be "collaborative", there is a basic lack of functionalities which support collaborative learning and in particular specific processes of reflection and metacognition. *Synergeia*[21] was designed putting particular attention on facilitating knowledge building. The description of the system reported in the following paragraph is taken from the official Website (http://bscl.fit.fraunhofer.de/).

> "Synergeia is a software system developed within the ITCOLE research project funded by the European Union in 2001–2003. It is designed to support collaborative knowledge building in school classrooms. It provides a shared, structured, web-based work space in which collaborative learning can take place, documents and ideas can be shared, discussions can be stored and knowledge artifacts can be developed and presented. In Synergeia teachers can structure, seed and guide work to facilitate knowledge building in their classrooms using the Knowledge Forum[22] and the Thinking Types. It is important for students to reflect upon the role that a note they are entering will play in the knowledge building process. Discussion within the knowledge building areas is scaffold with a set of thinking type categories for the notes. Before users can enter a note, they have to decide what category of note they want to add to the existing discussion. For instance, do they want to state the problem that is to be pursued, propose a working theory, deepen the knowledge that is already there, or make a meta-comment about the knowledge building process that is taking place (Rubens et al., 2005)? In Synergeia it is possible to have different sets of thinking types for different approaches to knowledge building".

LearnWeb2.0 does not provide such a functionality yet, but the researcher intends to investigate it further and to include it into the system. Preliminary

21 http://bscl.fit.fraunhofer.de/
22 http://www.knowledgeforum.com/

studies have already been done by the researcher in the field of functional linguistics and presented in 2010 towards an integrated descriptive visual/verbal tagging/annotational system based on a hierarchy of icons and guided menu choices (Section 9.2.2).

4 Design-based research and evaluation methodology

> "A third 'mixed methods research' approach, involves the combined use of qualitative and quantitative methods with the hope of offering the best of both worlds."
>
> (Dörnyei, 2007, p. 20)

After the design of the system for specific user requirements the next step in the research was the evaluation of the LearnWeb2.0 platform in specific CLIL and ESP (*English for Specific Purposes*) setting scenarios adopting an *Iterative evaluation-driven design-based* research approach (Darn, 2003).

In the following section the notion of *Iterative evaluation-driven design-based* research is defined. Further details about the empirical research can be found in Section 4.2. The description of the first evaluation cycle according to the users' feedback is presented in Chapter 5.

4.1 Iterative evaluation-driven design-based research

The notion of *design-based research* was introduced by Brown (1992) and Collins (1992), who described *design experiments* as a way to advance design, research and practice concurrently in a principled way. According to Wang and Hannafin design-based research is

> "a systematic but flexible methodology aimed to improve educational practices through iterative analysis, design, development, and implementation, based on collaboration among researchers and practitioners in real-world settings, and leading to contextually-sensitive design principles and theories."
>
> (Wang & Hannafin, 2005, p. 6)

The methodology is pragmatic (refines both theory and practice), grounded (design is conducted in real-world settings), interactive (designers are involved in the design processes and work together with participants), iterative (processes are iterative cycles of analysis, design, implementation, and redesign), flexible (designers can make deliberate changes when necessary), integrative (mixed research methods are used and methods vary during different phases) and contextual (research results are connected with the design process and the setting).

The purpose of *interactive* and *iterative evaluation* is to improve a system "through continuous learning" (Mirijamdotter et al., 2006, p. 84). In contrast with traditional evaluation methodologies the study is not conducted "objectively" (i.e. independently of the context) and its goal is not only to give an accurate representation of the actual situation, but the intention is to involve actual users in an interactive and qualitative process of *formative evaluation*. Developers, evaluators and stakeholders (users of the system involved in the evaluation) have to work together to test the system, collect the feedback and implement the improvements in the new version.

On the basis of this, an *Iterative evaluation-driven design-based* research methodology has been adopted in the present doctoral work with the intention of investigating and improving relationships between educational theory, designed artifact, and practice. The initial idea was to design and implement a new educational environment based on the integration of the latest web-services and technologies, namely LearnWeb2.0, as described in Section 3.2. To reach this ambitious goal, an iterative evaluation was planned to improve the usability and the effectiveness of the system in supporting the design of materials for CLIL courses (Section 5.1). To carry out a complete iterative evaluation-driven research it was necessary to involve experts from different disciplines (e.g. computer scientists, educators) as well as different stakeholders (e.g. teachers and students). The contribution of their expertise was very important for team work. In particular, at the L3S Research Center in Hannover, different steps were carried out, namely:

(1) Design and implementation of a first version of the LearnWeb2.0 environment, incorporating initial ideas on architecture, functionalities and interface. Specification of the basic functionalities for the collaborative search and sharing system. Definition of a conceptual design and a basic structure for the system (Section 3.2);
(2) Analysis and evaluation of the design and usability of the LearnWeb2.0 system in various scenarios: identification and collection of the users' requirements in different settings;
(3) Preliminary matching of the requirements with the existing LearnWeb2.0 functionalities;
(4) Evaluation of the system in two university courses (in Hannover, Germany, and in Pavia, Italy), to get feedback from the teachers and the students about what worked well and what had to be improved (Chapter 5);
(5) Identification and definition of the priorities for the new functionalities to be adopted and implemented (Section 5.3).

The specific role of the researcher within the research team-work was that of *educational technologist* (Section 2.6). In particular, by referring to several pedagogical approaches and educational theories, it was important to analyse the various scenarios to be supported by a technological environment, and also to be a reference point for the other parties involved (i.e. developers of the environment and users participating in the evaluation, including teachers and students). As an educational designer in general, the role of the researcher was not only to elicit data, but also to facilitate the communication between the different project stakeholders: developers and users (i.e. teachers, students and researchers) and to design and provide a suitable environment to support different scenarios (e.g. educational and for research). "As Lightbown summarises, it is essential for researchers to enter into dialogue with classroom teachers – not only so that teachers can know what researchers are saying, but also so that researchers can hear what teachers are saying" (Dörnyei, 2007, p. 193).

Dörnyei explains that "collaboration in educational scenarios can take several forms, from the researcher owning the project and co-opting a participating teacher, to real collaboration where researchers and teachers participate equally in the research agenda" (Dörnyei, 2007, p. 191). For the present research work, the involvement was of the second type, where the teacher was leading the pedagogical approach and the researcher was taking care of supporting the sharing and collaborative activities through technology. The effort was to guide and to iterate the development and the evaluation through the various phases (e.g. design, development, evaluation, analysis…) involving the stakeholders in the improvement of the system. In the educational settings, the specific effort was to support the teaching and learning process as a tutor and facilitator. While in research-project settings, the role of the researcher was to support the content and activities organisation, and to facilitate communication and collaboration between the participants.

In the following sections, details about the empirical research are provided. The various steps of the iterative designed-based evaluation are visualised in the GANTT chart below (Figure 8) and described in more detail in Chapters 5 and 6.

4.2 Evaluation and data collection

4.2.1 Course setup

The educational technology background gave the researcher a solid base to start analysing different learning scenarios, to detect possible problems, to better understand learning conditions and thus facilitating the learners' collaborative processes.

Two preliminary case studies were carried out with the intention of collecting users' requirements and feedback to improve the support of various learning

Figure 8: Iterative evaluation GANTT chart

Task	Start	End	Dur
LearnWeb2.0 evolution	1/1/08	31/12/13	1513
2008- 2009 (TENCompetence platform)	1/1/08	31/12/09	504
2010 LearnWeb2.0 v1	1/1/10	31/12/10	253
2010 evaluation scenario - (CLIL Seminar, Hannover)	7/4/10	14/7/10	70
2010 evaluation scenario - (Dentists, Pavia)	4/5/10	1/6/10	20
2011 LearnWeb2.0 v2	1/1/11	31/12/11	252
2011 evaluation scenario (Leinbizschule, Hannover)	26/9/11	14/10/11	14
2012 evaluation scenario (YELL project, Udine)	24/1/12	25/7/13	381
2012 LearnWeb2.0 v3	1/1/12	31/12/13	504
2013 LearnWeb v4	1/5/13	31/12/13	168

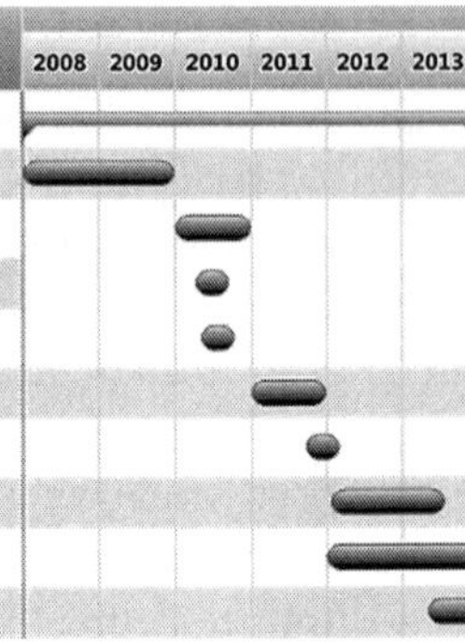

scenarios. In particular the LearnWeb2.0 system was used and evaluated in two university courses in the summer semester 2010, one at the Leibniz University of Hannover in Germany, the second at the University of Pavia in Italy. Preliminary evaluation of the Hannover course is described in Marenzi et al. (2010) and in Marenzi and Zerr (2012).

In 2011 and 2012 two different case studies were considered, one at the Leibnizschule high school in Hannover (described in Section 6.1), the other at the University of Udine, Italy (described in Section 6.2). The evaluation was carried out in real learning scenarios to get useful feedback according to the actual requirements of the various users. Working in a real teaching and learning situation implied having a few constrains on the design of the evaluation studies, since real learning scenarios cannot be handled in the way laboratory experiments can. However working under these constrains provided "invaluable asset of an audience for effective customisation of computer-based teaching" (Scanlon et al., 1998, p. 10). The case studies did not have the ambition of addressing a larger population but simply to collect insights into the learning requirements and goals of the specific users, so as to better define and design suitable educational support for them.

In order to design the evaluation it is necessary to identify the purpose of introducing the technology into the teaching and learning situation, and to consider the purpose of students' use of the system (e.g. find authentic materials for CLIL in Hannover, share teaching experiences in Udine). Many variables within the four settings were different, for example: the national context (Germany and Italy), the field of study (e.g. language teaching, intercultural communication studies, medicine), the learning approach and the learning goals (e.g. trainee teachers, dentists, high school students), the course design and the learning tasks (e.g. more open in the CLIL seminar, more guided at the Leibnizschule). Some variables were similar, such as the collaborative group project work methodology, the different types of assignments, and the need to collect various kinds of resources (e.g. written text and multimedia).

All scenarios were designed as *blended learning*, where students could meet in person as well as online. The organisation of the learning environment is very important because the context can influence the ways in which learners collaborate: learners and teachers may have different perceptions, understandings and expectations of the learning situations. All these features may affect the ways in which learners behave during collaborative interactions. Intending to take into account several educational aspects and perspectives, the adopted research approach was to consider and collect information from a variety of sources both qualitative and quantitative, also to "avoid possible fallacies one method may have when used solely" (Rummel et al., 2011, p. 368). Each technique provided useful information about the value and effectiveness of a specific part of the learning process supported by a computer. Of course, in a multi-layered learning experience where a variety of additional teaching resources are used (including face-to-face activities and offline interaction with the teacher), it is difficult to establish what is the actual contribution of the online system on the learning process. Particularly in these cases, to evaluate the effectiveness and the perception of the system by the students, qualitative methods such as observations and interviews are necessary.

In the following sections the "mixed method research" approach is described as well as the adopted data management and analysis methodology.

4.2.2 Data elicitation

The two main research methods adopted in the past, based either on quantitative or on qualitative data elicitation do not provide enough exploratory capacity if applied separately. The researcher agrees with Dörnyei (2007, p. 163) when he argues that "a more constructive approach is to view qualitative and quantitative research as a matter of degrees or a continuum rather than a clear-cut dichotomy". As Dörnyei remarks, after the "paradigm war" in the 1970s and 1980s, which emphasised the ideological differences between qualitative and quantitative research, researchers of the two alignments started to accept each other and began to integrate the two approaches. Furthermore, considering that today's research scene is becoming increasingly interdisciplinary and complex, researchers increasingly feel the need to complement one method with the other (Johnson et al., 2007). The present doctoral work follows Dörnyei's suggestion of adopting a third "mixed method research approach, involving the combined use of qualitative and quantitative methods with the hope of offering the best of both worlds" (Dörnyei, 2007, p. 20). According to him, "mixed method research involves different combinations of qualitative and qualitative research either at the data collection (typical examples are consecutive and interrelated questionnaires and interview studies) or at analysis levels" (Dörnyei, 2007, p. 45).

The goal of the researcher is to take advantage of the complementary aspects of the two different approaches to analyse the research purpose (i.e. providing new learning opportunities and course designs) looking at it not only from different angles, but also in its continuous evolution. But, *how can different research paradigms be efficiently integrated?* To combine the different methods and to integrate the results and findings of the inquiries in a disciplined and consistent way, an *Iterative evaluation-driven design-based* research was carried out where qualitative phases were dominant, and the data collection as well as the analysis process had an iterative and recursive nature.

The researcher collected data of various types including the LearnWeb2.0 activity logs as well as online pre- and post-questionnaires and interviews at the end of the courses, to get feedback from the teachers and from the students who used the system to carry out their project work. She also took into consideration the e-mail messages that students sent to ask for technical support, and the Skype calls with teachers to define the course design. The goal was to test what functionalities worked well and what was missing in the first PHP-based release so as to improve the system according to the users' requirements. The dimensions included in the analysis, as suggested by the CIAO evaluation framework[23] (Scanlon et al., 1998), were *context* (learning scenario and rationale of use of the software), *interaction* and collaboration (methods of interaction of students with the system and communication with each other), *attitude* and *outcomes* (user satisfaction and perception of using the system, as well as changes in the use of the various functionalities). The methods of data collection adopted were aimed at describing the learners' satisfaction in using the LearnWeb2.0 platform to support their collaborative activities (e.g. system design and usability) as well as at describing the interactions among the learners.

Quantitative data – System logs

The quantitative evaluation was based on the log files of the LearnWeb2.0 platform (Section 5.1.4 and 5.2.4) to collect data on the processes by which students

---

23 http://citeseerx.ist.psu.edu/viewdoc/download?doi=10.1.1.104.4527&rep=rep1&type=pdf

interacted with the computer and with the online learning materials. The system keeps track automatically of the activities carried out by the students such as number of searches, number of uploaded resources, number of resources viewed or edited by the user, number of annotations (comments, tags, ratings). User actions and navigation through the application pages can be aggregated for each user and session from the log files. "Logged user actions include resource selection, rating, commenting or tagging, as well as search and group membership" (Marenzi et al., 2010, p. 209).

Mixed data – Questionnaires

Observations of users were made by the researcher during the activities to identify possible technical or methodological issues. Questionnaires and interviews were used to explore furthers those issues and to better understand the students' personal perception of the learning experience (Scanlon et al., 1998).

In the first three scenarios (CLIL, ESP and at the Leibnizschule) "The mixed evaluation included two questionnaires delivered on-line through Google Document forms; questions asked about the use of Web 2.0 tools and of specific LearnWeb2.0 functionalities meant to support collaboration" (Marenzi et al., 2010, p. 207). Multiple-choice questions and checkboxes, were followed by a text-field to collect additional more extensive comments. The first questionnaire checked the students' previous experiences and their expectations about the starting course, while the second questionnaire evaluated the use of LearnWeb2.0 at the end, to check whether and how its specific functionalities supported the learning process, and whether students perceived it as a useful tool for their future studies and work. The goal was to verify whether the use of Web 2.0 tools such as LearnWeb2.0 supports the students' learning process, and how. More details can be found in Marenzi et al. (2010).

Questionnaire design - While designing the questionnaire the researcher referred to Dörnyei's book *Questionnaires in Second Language Research: Construction, Administration and Processing* (2003). GoogleDocs questionnaires were created and delivered online to obtain an automatic record and automatic visualisation of the data.

Piloting the questionnaire. The researcher discussed the questions together with the teachers and with two students who worked as tutors in the CLIL seminar to check whether the questions were understandable and plausible to them (as target users).

Question types. Closed-ended questions (e.g. multiple choices, checkboxes, grid, and Likert scales) were included together with open-ended questions (e.g. *behavioural* questions and *attitudinal* questions) that require a qualitative analysis.

The pre-course questionnaires collected students' previous experiences and expectations and included *behavioural questions* about previous learning experiences and the use of Web 2.0 tools, and *attitudinal questions* to find out students' expectations about the starting course. An overview of the GoogleDocs results is given in Appendix 2(a, c) for the CLIL seminar, and in Appendix 3(a, c) for the case study at the Leibnizschule. The post-course questionnaires collected students' feedback about their recent learning experience using LearnWeb2.0. The researcher's interest was in how they accessed the digital information, how they perceived the way they worked on the assignments, and to what extent they felt they were supported by LearnWeb2.0 during their learning. An overview of the GoogleDocs results is given in Appendix 2(b, d) and Appendix 3(b, d).

In the YELL scenario (*Young English Language Learners*, described in Section 6.2), the focus was more on the creation of an online community for trainee teachers rather than on sharing learning contents within the classroom (even though knowledge sharing had a strong role). In this case, the teacher in Udine, in agreement with the educational technologist and considering the different nature of the case study, decided to adopt a different kind of questionnaire divided into two sections: Section 1 was about the use of the YELL portal (yell.uniud.it), Section 2 asked about the use of the YELL social platform (LearnWeb2.0) both for studying and for professional purposes. The questionnaire used for the YELL pilot study is reported in Appendix 4.

The goal of the Appendices is to provide the documents used for the data elicitation, to give evidence of the various modalities of collecting, organising and analysing data in different settings.

Qualitative data – Follow-up interviews

The interviews investigated more in-depth questions about the students' experiences and opinions. Guided interviews in a group format were used at the end of the seminar in Hannover and in Pavia to ask the respondents to explain or illustrate the results obtained through the study, as well as their general opinion about the use of LearnWeb2.0 to support their collaborative work. The interviews were semi-structured, including a list of pre-defined questions but leaving room for variation and flexibility to let the students add their personal comments and suggestions. Four students volunteered at the end of the course in 2010 in Hannover. It was one-shot group interview on a voluntary basis. The interviews were recorded by the researcher after the end of the seminar using a laptop and a microphone. The author transcribed the recordings herself afterwards. The *Interview Guide for the use of LearnWeb2.0*, used as basis for the guided interviews in Hannover, is provided in Appendix 1.

In Pavia the teachers interviewed the students during the oral exam. Individual interviews were carried out and sent via e-mail to the researcher who translated them from Italian into English afterwards.

Other collected data

E-mails and Skype calls were used outside the classroom by the researcher to communicate and to interact with students and teachers.

E-mails. The official support e-mail address (learnweb-support@l3s.de) provided by the technicians at the L3S Research Center was not used much. Students in Hannover preferred to wait till the next lesson to report problems which occurred or to ask the researcher questions directly. Students in Pavia mainly used their personal e-mail addresses to ask for technical assistance (mainly for password or access problems). E-mails were a good opportunity for communication in the YELL scenario where interactions between participants, teachers and the researcher took place mostly online.

Skype calls were organised mainly with the teachers in Pavia and in Udine to agree on the activities design, on the required LearnWeb2.0 functionalities and customisation, and on the evaluation methods.

Iterative evaluation timeline

The following chart (Figure 9) visualises the evaluation timeline of the various releases of the system driven by the two main design-based research cycles carried out to investigate the system usability (in 2010) and the users' requirements (in 2011 and 2012). In the last row the evaluation instruments used in the various case studies are reported.

4.2.3 Data management and analysis

When interactions among participants are totally or partially mediated by computers, it is easy to collect big amounts of data on the online activities, but it is more complex to find suitable indicators to analyse those data. A combination of various methodologies (qualitative, quantitative and social network analysis techniques) is often required to monitor, analyse and evaluate the learning process using data coming from different sources. Martinez-Mones, Harrer and Dimitriadis (2011) give an overview on many difficulties that both researchers and practitioners can encounter when dealing with interaction analysis tools in Computer Supported Collaborative Learning settings.

The researcher collected and considered various types of data for the analysis, both shared with colleagues or derived by users. In the first case, the researcher kept the minutes of the periodic meetings (feedback from the users:

Figure 9: Iterative evaluation timeline

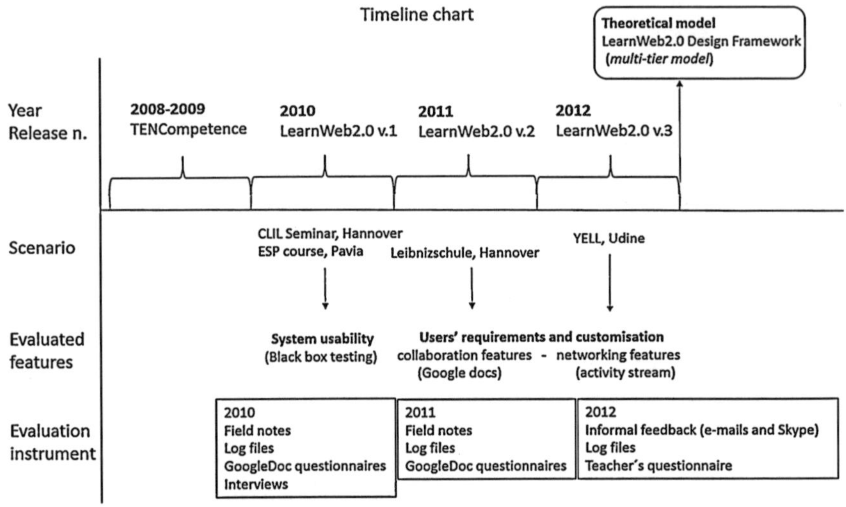

teachers and students) and the record of the Skydev Logbook, which was used as "research log" system to keep track of the software changes (both requested and implemented). Data deriving from the users' evaluation were collected in Excel files and used to record the results and to visualise them in graphs and charts.

Informed consent – Anonymity and guarantees of confidentiality

At the beginning of the course students were asked to sign a *Research consent form* as written consent to participate in the research study and evaluation. Anonymity of the participants was guaranteed: the Log files (ID) and data were stored encrypted on the server (e-mail address is not mandatory while creating the LearnWeb2.0 account), the online questionnaires were anonymous (the respondents were not asked to give personal details), the interviews were organised on voluntary bases.

The mixed methods research also helped in the analysis of the data. The following section gives a short synthesis of the procedure adopted for the data analysis during the first evaluation cycle in 2010. A more detailed analysis of the results is reported in Section 5.1 for the CLIL seminar, in Section 5.2 for the ESP course, in Section 6.1 for the Leibnizschule and in Section 6.2 for the YELL pilot study respectively.

Data analysis

The case studies did not carry out a large-scale questionnaire survey, therefore they did not provide a representative sample of users for the various settings. In 2010 the two classes included 19 students in Hannover and 19 students in Pavia. The data about the use of the system were collected through online GoogleDocs questionnaires. Numbers and statistics were analysed to compare the different classes in Hannover and in Pavia and to analyse how they used the system to carry out their group work. The numerical data were visualised through the GoogleDocs facility and analysed manually. The open questions were exported into Excel tables and analysed manually by the researcher. Written analysis extracts from word-based narrative accounts of the respondents are reported in the published papers to give evidence of the representativeness of the actual results, so as to validate the researcher's inferences. During the second cycle, a larger number of users were involved: 52 students at the Leibnizschule in Hannover and 26 postgraduate trainees in Udine as a starting point for a growing community.

The researcher took into account the different learning requirements and the design of the courses (e.g. interests and motivation of the teachers and of the students in the different settings), as well as the different cultural and social circumstances of the various scenarios (two in Germany and two in Italy) to further interpret and better understand the reactions and acceptance of the e-learning environment by the users. For example, the relevance of the various types of data was designed and interpreted differently from the teachers and the students in Hannover (CLIL) and in Pavia (ESP). In Hannover the activity on the platform was on a voluntary basis, as well as the task of answering the questionnaires. In Pavia the teachers explicitly indicated LearnWeb2.0 as the main system to create a corpus or collect and store resources, and the writing functionalities, such as comments and questionnaires, were considered part of the written exam to assess the English as well as the students' skills in organising their group-work. This facilitated the greater acceptance of and participation in the online activities of the Pavia students.

Interviews were recorded on a voluntary basis paying special attention to the individual experiences of the participants, to find out their opinion on the learning process, and to collect feedback to improve the learning environment. The researcher recorded the interviews using the Audacity software on her laptop. She made the transcriptions and considered each verbal protocol in relation with the activities carried out by the participants while using the LearnWeb2.0 system, searching for resources or working with peers. While reporting the users' quotations the researcher edited minor linguistic inaccuracies to facilitate reading. Analysing these data the researcher was able to check what functionalities worked well and what was missing. Discussion with the teachers focused on how to improve the system according to the actual users' requirements. The primary goal was to support students in specific scenarios and to use their feedback for the iterative evaluation and improvement of the e-learning environment, before being able to generalise the findings for the CLIL methodology in general.

On the other hand, as mentioned earlier, *Design-based research* goes beyond perfecting a particular artefact or program. The intention is rather to inquire more broadly into the nature of learning in a complex scenario and to refine learning theories and methodologies, also generating general and innovative models. According to this, in Chapter 8 the LearnWeb2.0 framework is presented to integrate and embed the technical environment into an appropriate pedagogical theory, that is *multiliteracies*.

5 First evaluation cycle: system design and usability

> "What we need is project-based learning, with students having the opportunity to engage in learner-centered collaborative projects, working together with their classmates and with others around the world, using a variety of technological means."
>
> (Warschauer, AILA Review 14, 2001, p. 57)

During the summer semester 2010 a proper iteration phase of the evaluation-driven design-based research started using LearnWeb2.0 to support active learning through collaborative search in a CLIL seminar at the Leibniz University of Hannover in Germany, and in an ESP course at the University of Pavia, in Italy. The following sections (5.1 and 5.2) discuss in detail the two CLIL and ESP courses respectively. A preliminary discussion of the CLIL study was presented in Marenzi et al. (2010).

The preliminary evaluation cycle discussed below focused on the LearnWeb2.0 system design and usability to collect feedback from the users and improve the functionalities of the tool. The experience in the CLIL context was very interesting and produced a lot of valuable research results and improvements both for the LearnWeb2.0 system design and for the theoretical research. Online questionnaires and interviews were used to collect feedback from the students about their previous experiences in using e-learning platforms and social networks, as well as their satisfaction in using LearnWeb2.0 as a support for their learning process.

The questions addressed in the first phase of the research (Marenzi et al., 2010) and presented in this chapter are:

- *How can a platform for collaborative work and collaborative searching be appropriately used and adapted in different university contexts so that it helps in the process of learning how to teach English in a CLIL context and in the process of learning how to improve English as a foreign language?*
- *What pedagogical and project design should be used to support teaching and learning CLIL concepts at university level and to foster student reflection on methods and materials appropriate for CLIL?*

To answer these broad exploratory research questions, a flexible and comprehensive research method is fundamental. In answer to the first research question the following sections describe the pedagogical design of the two courses and discuss how it enhanced students' learning processes. In answer to the second research question the evaluation designs, as well as promising preliminary evaluation results are described in Section 5.3.

5.1 First case study: CLIL (Content and Language Integrated Learning)

CLIL is one of the most promising approaches to foreign language teaching and learning to emerge in the last 20 years that attempts to take into consideration the needs of students in the changing society. According to Marsh (2002, p. 2) "CLIL refers to any dual-focused educational context in which an additional language, thus not usually the first language of the learners involved, is used as a medium in the teaching and learning of non-language content", that is the subject.

In a globalised world, interaction with others requires a shared language for communication, and language learning and teaching are increasingly important. Knowing a language today is not only important for personal knowledge, but is crucial to live in the modern society (Warschauer, 2001, p. 55). The interplay between "cultural and linguistic diversity is one of the key facts of our time" (NLG, Cazden et al., 1996, p. 64) that has changed the very nature of language learning. Dealing with linguistic and cultural differences is a central part of our working, social, and private lives. Effective citizenship and productive work require us to interact effectively using multiple languages and communication patterns that overcome cultural and national diversities.

Internet and new technologies have changed contemporary society's interaction and meaning-making practices a lot. "New online media help transforming literacy with important consequences for language teaching" (Warschauer, 2001, p. 49). Online communication and other forms of transnational media such as broadcasting, digital TV and channels, are providing non-native speakers of English with greater communicative opportunities. New challenges for traditional school-based teaching, pedagogies and curricula are emerging. According to Marsh (2002), to be effective in a society where developing communication skills and building intercultural knowledge is important, language teaching needs to diversify classroom methodology and provide opportunities to study content through different perspectives.

For all these reasons, CLIL has been chosen as a suitable learning and teaching context for the evaluation of LearnWeb2.0 as a collaborative searching and sharing environment, aiming at renovating how informal (user-generated contents) but authentic materials can be re-used in education. This section gives an overview on the new definition of literacy and the new literacy skills required in current modern society (Section 5.1.1), it discusses how CLIL approaches these educational needs (Section 5.1.2) and presents the first case study carried out at the University of Hannover (Sections 5.1.3 and 5.1.4). This phase of the work also lead to the design of a LearnWeb2.0 model as an integrative approach for CLIL (Marenzi et al., 2012; Marenzi, 2014) which is presented in Section 5.1.5.

5.1.1 Literacy and new literacies

At the beginning of the 1960s, at the roots of computer-based self-access study, individualised learning was concerned with basic literacy: "students were deemed to be literate if they could read and understand written texts, apply grammar and spelling rules or solve simple arithmetical problems" (Rizzo, 2009, p. 19). Still in 2003 Daley reported that

> "to most people, literacy means the ability to read and write, to understand information, and to express ideas both concretely and abstractly. The unstated assumption is that 'to read and write' means to read and write text."
>
> (Daley, EDUCAUSE Review 2003, p. 33)

The development of technology, however, has recently contributed to expand the definition of literacy, based on the assumption that broader means of information and expression are now available and are crucial for education (Meyer & Rose, CAST[24], chap 5). For today's students having basic literacy skills is no longer enough, they also need to acquire technology skills for exploring, communicating, and accessing information, for investigating, thinking critically and evaluating data, for communicating and actively collaborating with their peers. The definition of *literacy* in a digitised society is rapidly changing as new technologies for information and communication repeatedly appear and users continuously envision new ways for exploiting these technologies.

An array of definitions is emerging such as for example:

Information Literacy: The ability to identify what information is needed and to locate, access, evaluate the content and use information;

Digital Literacy: "The ability to use digital technologies, communication tools and networks to locate, analyse, interpret, consume and create information" (ICT Journal[25]);

Media Literacy: "The ability to communicate competently in all media forms — print and electronic — as well as to access, understand, analyse and evaluate the images, words, and sounds that comprise contemporary mass media culture" (KQED education network[26]);

---

24 http://www.cast.org/library/books/ltr/chapter5.html

25 http://esjournals.org/journaloftechnology/archive/vol2no8/vol2no8_5.pdf

26 http://uw.kqed.org/edresources/plans/Media%20Literacy.pdf

Critical Literacy: The ability to discern, challenge and evaluate the meaning and purpose of a text (written texts, visual applications, spoken words, or virtual environments) to question the values, attitudes and beliefs behind them.

In the modern technological society independence and functions have changed and extended to "include multiple literacies such as visual, media and information literacy with a stronger focus on an individual's capacity to use and make critical judgements about the information they encounter on a daily basis" (National Adult Literacy Database[27], *Literacy the Foundation of Learning*, p. 1). According to the UNESCO:

> "Literacy is the ability to identify, understand, interpret, create, communicate, compute and use printed and written materials associated with varying contexts. Literacy involves a continuum of learning to enable an individual to achieve his or her goals, to develop his or her knowledge and potential, and to participate fully in the wider society."
>
> (UNESCO[28])

Digital literacy and information navigation

Technology influence the way information is searched, found, and used by people. Today, educators largely agree that printed media is no longer the dominant source of communication and must be seen in relation to other reference systems. One of the difficulties to be faced in online environments is to cope with the various types of 'writing' or 'reading' that take place: more information is available than in books and sometimes online written text is less accurate and precise. Additional concerns arise from the risk of *information overload* and *knowledge fragmentation*[29]. In a networked world the new literacy skill, beyond connecting text and image, is one of information *navigation* and *exploration* which entails the ability to know how to navigate through confusing, complex information spaces. The idea of 'information navigation' does not involve just reading, rather also interacting with contents and feel comfortable doing so. Dealing with hypertextual environments such as one finds on CD-ROMs or websites involves clicking to move from one field to another so as to capture, save, and download materials relevant to one's own projects. Thus, in addition to the linear cognitive skills needed for the traditional reading of print material, *digital literacy* responds to the need to read hypertexts that are often

27 http://www.nald.ca/library/research/nwwlp/literacy/lfl.pdf

28 http://www.unesco.org

29 http://www.next-tell.eu/project/introduction/

multidimensional requiring the linking of images, graphics, texts, and increasingly audio-video materials (Baldry & Thibault, 2006b).

Furthermore, with large amounts of information available on the Web, the ability to synthesise and recognise connections and patterns is very important (Siemens, 2005). The new kind of learning is *discovery* based, involving browsing through the constantly emergent sets of digital resources, and developing meta-skills for reasoning about contents and evaluate what is actually found in digital media. In this sense, reasoning is not only intended in a deductive and abstract way, rather it involves observation and critical evaluation of concrete experiences. In his article *Growing Up Digital* Seely Brown refers to the concept of *Bricolage* previously suggested by Claude Levi-Strauss. Becoming an effective *digital bricoleur* means having the ability "to find something - an object, tool, document, a piece of code" choosing from a finite set of materials which apparently bear no relation to the current project, "and use it to build something you deem important" (Seely Brown, 2000, p. 14).

In a global information environment, *digital literacy* involves switching from websites and interacting with people from different countries and cultures, thus requiring contextual understanding and literacy skills that focus more on the ability to communicate, interact and share rather than on reading information as an individual. Digital technologies, including the rise of social networks and online gaming, help people to easily connect to their friends and to other peers who share the same interests, even if geographically distant. Besides using a wide variety of technologies and of digital devices in their daily life (e.g. watching TV and movies, listening to music online and offline) young people are increasingly engaged in actively playing computer games and in creating social network pages using MySpace or Facebook. For this reason young people need to learn how to negotiate and participate in these multiple, distributed online networks becoming active rather than passive in interpersonal contexts. In general digital literacy skills are becoming increasingly important to facilitate interaction and participation in the modern society. Starting from these foundations, experts suggested the urgency of "developing *media literacy* as part of standard educational training" (Kellner, 1998, p. 107).

Critical literacy

Critical literacy includes the critical analysis of the huge amount of resources and media materials that currently immerse us, and the ability to recognise the reliability of such sources. The materials and the messages made available in the digital society are so polymorphous and multivalent, that a special sensitivity is required to understand complex meanings and different interpretations

(Kellner, 1998). To make effective use of information found online, it is necessary to interpret it critically and select the most reliable and suitable to the information need. In this regard, "it is more important that learners acquire skills of analysis rather than factual information" (Byram et al., 2002, p. 19). Critical literacy also includes a critical understanding of media and how they convey meaning, for example being aware "how media can affect their audiences" (Kellner, 1998, p. 109).

Still, critical media pedagogy is in its infancy and it is just beginning to produce experimental results. It is important to use authentic materials in the classroom, but also to ensure that learners understand their original context and intention. Different sources and materials should be used (Mehisto, 2012) to enable learners to compare and to analyse the resources available from different perspectives, in this way promoting multicultural education and sensitivity to cultural differences. Furthermore, students must attain a critical-reflective media literacy in order to be able to resist being manipulated by the media and instead use them to articulate their own interests. Van Heertum and Share advocate a *critical multiple literacy* education which they describe as follows:

> "Following the critical pedagogy of Paulo Freire (1970, 1998) and his contemporaries, it would not be a set curriculum with prescribed teaching practices or universal curricular content. Instead, it would offer a basic theoretical foundation and critical pedagogical strategies, including the deconstruction of media texts, the creative production of media by children, and the teaching of skills in the use of various technologies required for success in contemporary society. Content would be culturally specific to the children, ensuring their interest and engagement with the material but also transcend the particularity of their experience to see the world from disparate perspectives. And open dialogue and mechanisms to allow children to participate democratically in the learning process would be integrated as key aspects of the pedagogy."
>
> (Van Heertum & Share, 2006, p. 260)

According to Lemke (2006) it is important to help teachers and learners in using existing multimedia in a critical and creative way to become independent authors of new learning materials. On one hand, students, who are often more immersed in media culture than their teachers, can contribute to the educational process by sharing their ideas, experiences, and insights. On the other hand, teachers should encourage critical discussion, debate, and analysis so that students can develop their own critical readings of media materials (Vasquez et al., 2010).

All aspects of *digital literacy*, such as collaboration and communication skills, functional skills (i.e. use of digital technologies), the ability to find and select information, cultural and social awareness and understanding, critical thinking and creativity, are closely interlinked so that developing one will often involve students making use of others. In other words, students need to be provided with the tools and learning tasks which allow them to acquire the multiple skills needed in today's society.

New literacies in education

In the modern knowledge society, where competitiveness is an increasingly important factor, education plays a strategic role towards personal achievement and social integration and equality. Schools have a very important role in preparing people to face this changing reality, and in creating the learning conditions which support them to interact in familiar, as well as in unfamiliar contexts.

Today's students are often described as *digital natives* who arrive at university as experienced *multitaskers*, accustomed to using text messaging, telephones, and e-mail while searching the Web and watching television (Roberts, 2005). On the other hand, in their handbook *Digital literacy across the curriculum,* Hague and Payton assert that "young people's confidence about their use of technology can be misleading" (Hague & Payton, 2010, p. 9). Searching for relevant information on the Web for example can be a difficult task for students who frequently struggle to select the information they need. Many students don't know how to efficaciously search terms, and many find it difficult to realise whether the information they find on websites is trustworthy. Very often users rely on the results displayed by the search engine at the top of the search results list. It is therefore not enough to assume that young people automatically have enough skills, knowledge and understanding to use technology in a correct and efficacious way. It is the teachers' role to support young people in the use of digital technology sharing their experience and critical thinking skills with them.

An additional problem is that the technology available in schools is often not relevant to support students' personal experiences and expectations. During the last decades, even when technology has been adopted in school, the tasks have not changed in a significant way and they often do not include resources provided by informal education and out-of-school experiences. As the New London Group authors suggest, "the curriculum needs to mesh more closely with students' daily life experiences and with their languages or registers, even using these as a learning resource" (NLG, Cadzen et al., 1996). With the help of new media, teachers should encourage and guide students to carry out collaborative group work activities: to search for new information from different sources, to critically analyse and select good materials, to save, change and compose, to discuss and reorganise the resources they find, to download, upload and use a range of programs. However, resource-based learning poses challenges for learners both from a technical, as well as a pedagogical perspective: often there is no teacher to structure the learning process or to prepare the learning materials. Learners are encouraged to perform the entire learning process in a self-directed manner. During the process of resource-based learning, learners have to manage a variety of tasks which should provide room for the development of *multiple literacy* skills (this is the real final goal). Amongst other challenges, learners have to choose search terms, select relevant Web pages and organise the selected results for later re-use. Learners, independently, have to assess the trustworthiness of the resources and select a variety of these resources which are relevant to their educational goals. There is a movement from task orientation to *competence* orientation. According to Kupetz (2001a, p. 9), the ultimate goal of educators "remains the empowerment of the learner to make informed choices and to use various media purposefully and peacefully." The concept of *empowerment of the learner* has a strong affinity to autonomy as it covers the goal of empowering the learner to work autonomously and be critically reflective (Kupetz, 2001b; Kupetz & Ziegenmeyer, 2006; Summer, 2010; Mehisto, 2012).

5.1.2 The Curricular Model for CLIL

CLIL is one of the teaching and learning approaches that better addresses the modern literacy requirements. The European Commission website[30], increasingly taking the lead in the sociopolitical drive to implement new Internet age curricula, recommends the benefits of CLIL in a variety of contexts: "building intercultural knowledge and understanding; developing communication skills; improving language competences; developing multilingual interests and attitudes; providing opportunities to study a specific curricular discipline or subject (the Content in the CLIL acronym) from different perspectives; diversifying classroom methodology, and increasing learner motivation and confidence in both the language and the subject being taught."

But *how are these recommendations structured within curricular frameworks or within formal models of CLIL*? Working towards a cohesive conceptual tool, in 1999 Coyle developed the 4Cs Framework (including Content, Cognition, Communication and Culture) which differs from the standards-based world languages education strategy focusing mainly on the language curriculum, as it gives much relevance to culture, bringing together language learning theories and intercultural understanding (Coyle, 1999; 2006). Zydatiß (2007) took up the 4Cs framework while defining the curricular framework for CLIL, described

30 http://ec.europa.eu/education/languages/language-teaching/doc236_en.htm (13/12/2011)

in Figure 10, according to which the role of language in the CLIL classroom differs from traditional foreign language learning in that language is a medium through which specific subject content is learned and provides a connecting link to the cognitive processes. The language needed for these curricular purposes is subject-related and everyday communicative skills are of lesser importance (Marenzi et al., 2010).

Figure 10: A curricular framework for CLIL (Zydatiß, 2007: 16)

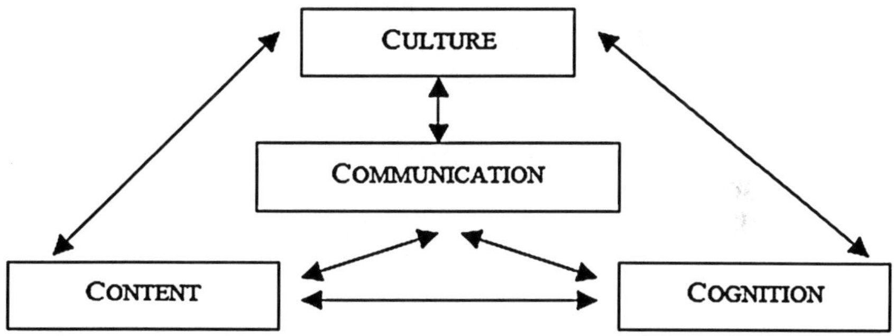

Cummins (2003) makes a distinction, relevant for CLIL, between two differing kinds of language proficiency: *Basic Interpersonal Communication Skills* (BICS) are the basic skills of listening and speaking students can easily acquire interacting with native speakers, while *Cognitive Academic Language Proficiency* (CALP) is necessary for dealing with various subjects at academic level. One of the goals in CLIL is to "help students to verbalize their thoughts appropriate to the subject manner" so as to "boost students' cognitive academic language proficiency (CALP)" (Meyer, 2010).

Supporters of CLIL argue it is superior to conventional language teaching because of its greater authenticity and frequency of exposure. "Using a foreign language as the working language for the content subject is more authentic than traditional foreign language classroom topics" (Wolff, 2003, p. 220). "Learners become more competent in the foreign language because they are exposed to it for longer periods of time than in conventional language teaching" (Marenzi et al., 2012). It is not only interaction which becomes authentic in the CLIL classroom: subject-specific materials (maps, graphs, pictures) which are used in the classroom can be more credible content-wise than foreign language textbooks. Language is presented in real-life contexts in which the natural use of language can boost a learner's motivation towards learning languages (Marenzi et al., 2010). A CLIL classroom offers an environment for *explorative learning*, where students can explore the content and experiment with specific aspects of the subject. *Discovery learning* (as in the work of Piaget, Bruner, and Papert) and *project work* are easier to embed into a CLIL environment than in a conventional language classroom (Wolff, 2002; Baldry & Coccetta, 2012; Kupetz & Woltin, 2014). "The promise of integrating both content and language learning is thus very challenging, and to be successful, good resources, a clearly defined set of objectives, and good task design are essential" (Kupetz & Woltin, 2014; Marenzi et al., 2010). Though, it is still difficult to find good and authentic materials for CLIL because a lot of resources are localised and teachers spend a lot of time preparing suitable materials for their classrooms (Mehisto, 2012). Good search strategies and tools that support teachers and students in finding useful resources for CLIL are needed. "Most importantly, CLIL teachers cannot simply *transmit* the contents of a lesson and assume that their students will understand. Rather, CLIL requires an adjustment in methodology to ensure that students understand the subject matter (whether conceptual or procedural), and teachers find additional opportunities to give them feedback regarding the language as well as the subject being taught" (Marenzi et al., 2010, p. 202; Meyer, 2010). In the light of these new learning requirements, practitioners need to reflect critically on what education, and in our case CLIL in particular, can offer. Research increasingly suggests the need of a participative design which includes collaborative searching in social networks and communication with other people in authentic contexts.

> "Selecting an appropriate mix of knowledge processes is merely the first step in designing pedagogy; the next step is to think about students' participation in those processes. There is no point in designing activities to promote selected knowledge processes if students' participation is limited."
>
> (Dooley, 2008, p. 115)

Since the goal in CLIL is to explicitly teach a subject through a foreign or additional language and implicitly to teach the language through this subject, adding collaborative searching is part of constructing the context, and hence making language learning authentic (Marenzi & Nejdl, 2012).

CLIL in teacher training

One of the key aspects of learning and teaching a language is that they entail communication among individuals and groups: it is meaningful interaction among teachers and students in which learning takes place for students as individuals and communities, and for teachers as individuals and collaborative professionals. In particular, in a teacher training context, an additional level of complexity is added, on the one hand, due to the developing quality of language competence in learners, and, on the other hand, the language and teaching competence of teachers and teacher trainers. Thus teachers and trainers need linguistic, socio-cultural and professional competences in the language they teach and the ability to transform classroom contexts into communicative environments in which learners can learn at their own pace by interacting in the foreign language among themselves and with the teacher (Block, 2003). The challenge for the language teacher is transforming teaching-time into experiential learning environments for their students focusing on how learners can learn to interact among themselves using appropriate communication in different contexts and for different communicative and educational purposes (Kupetz & Ziegenmeyer, 2005; 2006). If teachers want to promote interactive and dialogic skills in their students, they need to enact and experience this kind of communication themselves overcoming the belief that teaching is talking about something as a simple transmission of contents. The paradigm change consists in shifting from teacher-centred talk to a dialogic act, allowing students to collaborate with peers and experts, and learn by (re)constructing meaning in context (Redmond, 2011; Bortoluzzi & Marenzi, 2013).

The research activity reported in the following sections has addressed these issues by evaluating and redesigning the LearnWeb2.0 system, to provide better collaboration and interaction support in the CLIL classroom. Section 5.1.3 describes the scenario of the CLIL seminar for trainee teachers organised in Hannover, Germany, and reported in the conference paper *Supporting Active Learning in CLIL through Collaborative Search* (Marenzi et al., 2010). Section 5.1.4 presents the results of the evaluation carried out during the winter semester 2010 in Pavia, Italy, and reported in the journal article *Multiliteracies and Active Learning in CLIL-The Development of LearnWeb2.0* (Marenzi & Zerr, 2012).

5.1.3 CLIL learning scenario

2010 Hannover – CLIL English Seminar for trainee teachers

> "if a textbook presents a single perspective, then teachers can suggest that other perspectives are also possible and legitimate. One way of doing this is to find or encourage learners to find additional authentic materials which present a different view. The Internet is a rich source for this."
>
> (Byram et al., 2002, p. 18)

In the Hannover scenario a real life and explorative learning approach was adopted where trainee teachers worked collaboratively within a project, collecting and designing CLIL materials for their future pupils at school. The course was held from April to July 2010. The target group attending the "English

Language Teaching Methodology" seminar in Hannover included 19 trainee students and future CLIL teachers (Marenzi et al., 2010). 25 students registered in the seminar, but six of them lost interest and dropped out since the experiment did not provide credit points.

"In order to stress both CLIL methodology as well as contents appropriate for CLIL teaching, and to provide an active, explorative and adequately computer-supported learning environment, the seminar was structured into two phases. The first phase provided the necessary background information on CLIL, and the second involved the students in project work simulating their future CLIL teaching at school in terms of lesson design" (Marenzi et al., 2010). In particular face-to-face sessions were devoted to lay the basis for both a better understanding of the CLIL subject and effective participation in online activity, whilst online work was mainly collaborative and asynchronous. The assignments, which were designed to foster students' active and creative learning, in particular those aspects of learning involving interaction and collaboration, included tasks for individual work, group work and classroom discussions, as depicted in Figure 11. Since there was no need to restrict the students with too prescriptive guidelines, a CSCL macro script was used (Dillenbourg & Jermann, 2007). "*Computer Supported Collaborative Learning* gives guidelines on how to support students to cooperate as they interact in groups and how to solve problems in dealing both with the technology and with the content" (Dillenbourg, 2002, p. 61). On CSCL see also Section 2.4 in this thesis.

Figure 11: Assignments script in the CLIL seminar

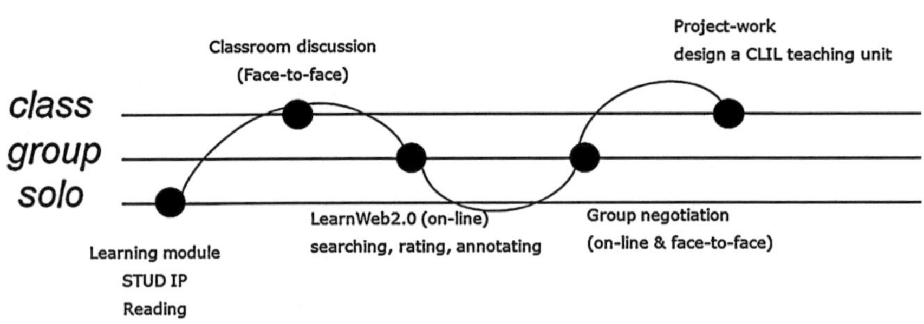

Figure 11 visualises the activities carried out in the teacher education scenario in Hannover. The overall goal of the project work was to further consolidate each trainee's expertise in applying CLIL principles and encourage the process of adjustment and further reflection and discussion.

In the initial phase of the seminar, students were required to undertake laboratory work in order to understand the basic principles of retrieving resources that are likely to support their understanding of CLIL. This phase focused in particular on the collection and integration into a lesson and/or syllabus format of appropriate CLIL materials supporting and making explicit each trainee's perception of CLIL and understanding of the constraints and affordances vis-à-vis the shaping and design of materials for CLIL ends. It was the students who determined what resources were worth collecting and including in their final teaching unit, among alternative forms of engagement from the different experiences and sources of material they brought to their learning process. The prospective CLIL teachers focused on printed media in their material design, however a new appreciation of the meaning-making affordances of modes other than the linguistic was apparent. The focus on the visual was on the organisational dimension of meaning (contents for the teaching unit in a PPT).

Phase I – Introduction and traditional face-to-face interaction. In the first part of the seminar, the procedure adopted was to move from CLIL theory to the analysis and discussion of real cases using videos. This phase included two assignments: (1) a CLIL Learning Module: reading a text on CLIL development in Germany and listening to an expert talking about CLIL and the CLIL community, (2) Reading and classroom discussion: development of observation and reflection competences by watching and discussing classroom recordings together. The organisation of the classroom discussion was flexible with less control by the teacher, allowing critical analysis on the part of the trainee teachers.

Students used Stud.IP, a self-access online learning platform for individual study. Within the seminar, Stud.IP was mainly used as a repository of text and audio-visual materials, providing a basic text by Zydatiß on CLIL from a German perspective, and expert commentaries on CLIL methodology as video interviews. Students were asked to read the relevant sections of the texts, provide an oral summary of the readings assigned and lead a group discussion on their potential application in various CLIL contexts. Video sequences of CLIL classrooms on various subjects and printed handouts of materials used in class were provided. After reading and watching the video, the most important phase was discussing what the trainees needed to read and see in order to grasp the CLIL concept from both a theoretical and practical perspective. Data from participation in Stud.IP were not included in the final evaluation since the specific goal of the research was to evaluate the efficacy of LearnWeb2.0, not the learning outcomes in general.

Phase II – Project Work. The goal of the second phase was to consolidate each student's expertise in applying CLIL principles and encourage a process of adjustment and further reflection. This phase focused on the collection and integration of appropriate CLIL materials for a lesson. In their assignments, students

(3) searched for, and discussed, authentic materials taken from the Web, and (4) designed a CLIL teaching unit in small groups (two to four students), based on a cross-curricular topic or based on their second subject (geography, history, biology). Here the students imagined and simulated their future teaching context in the classroom (Marenzi et al., 2010).

During their project work, students were invited to use the online learning platform LearnWeb2.0 to collaboratively find, retrieve and organise resources related to their subject. They wrote comments and shared them with others. They also learned how to extend their commentaries and share activities to a full range of resources found on the Web: films, pictures, podcasts, blogs, animations and other multimedia genres. This process of extension of acquisition of resources from a large dataset implies a fundamental rethinking of the constraints and affordances in the structuring of CLIL content and requires considerable reflection and practice on the part of each student. The students prepared a final presentation where they described their lesson plans for a CLIL teaching unit (Marenzi et al., 2010).

5.1.4 CLIL course: evaluation and discussion

In the following paragraphs, a detailed activity analysis is presented of how the students used the LearnWeb2.0 system based on a thorough evaluation of the online questionnaires and the LearnWeb2.0 log files. More details about the data elicitation methodology can be found in Section 4.2.

Questionnaire 1 – previous experiences and expectations [Appendix 2a]

19 students filled in the online questionnaire. From the CLIL seminar, they mainly expected to learn how to design CLIL materials and teaching units. They had already used Web 2.0 tools to search for literature and share resources, but considered social networks as a more private activity. Regarding their project preparation, students planned to use Web 2.0 tools mainly to search and share resources, and to collaborate with the other group members (Marenzi et al., 2010). In answer to the question Which prerequisites and competencies do you think are needed for collaborative self-directed learning with Web 2.0 technologies? 17 students chose searching, while only five selected collaboration. Searching and collaboration are the main features provided by LearnWeb2.0.

Questionnaire 2 – LearnWeb2.0: Perception and satisfaction with the experience [Appendix 2b]

Only five students filled in the second online questionnaire.

Search. During the two rounds of collecting resources on CLIL and subsequently on the subjects of interest, students in Hannover collected 18 videos, one PPT presentation, four pictures and three bookmarks but did not put much effort into searching multimedia resources on the Web. Among the resources they retrieved, all five students found videos particularly helpful (question 18); two students also mentioned images. However, most students mentioned that they needed additional resources to design their lesson (question 19), and mentioned books as well as conventional Web search engines as helpful sources of information. The relevance of resources depended on the subject of interest. Some of these subjects, such as for example religious instruction, are still very text-oriented and multimedia resources are not popular. Regarding CLIL methodology, it is clear that students expected to attend a course with standard lessons; they were not used to searching social platforms to discover resources (even as examples posted by people living in a specific context) that fit a particular learning goal.

Collaboration. Regarding the focus on collaborative search, sharing and commenting of resources, students in Hannover did not exploit the functionalities provided by LearnWeb2.0 (rating, tagging, commenting) because they did not work online but met in person and searched together using only one computer. The discussion and selection of the resources took place offline during those face-to-face sessions, which they found very satisfying and efficient. Consequently, they did not take much advantage of the more innovative features of LearnWeb2.0 (question 17). Personalisation for resources was selected by three of the five students and collaboration (i.e. resource sharing, commenting, and rating) only by two, as all collaboration was done outside the system. Interestingly, all students considered the use of user-generated content in formal learning positively. At question *35: Do you think that in formal learning situations, this tendency (user-generated contents) can be positive (increase creativity and motivation) or negative (difficult reliability of information sources and disorganization of the content results),* all respondent students considered user-generated content positive in formal learning situations. While at first, this seems to be a contradiction to their reluctant uptake of LearnWeb2.0, the researcher thinks this underscores the fact that the task they had to perform just did not call for the kind of resources LearnWeb2.0 is specialised in delivering exclusively.

Activity log analysis

In addition to the questionnaire-based analysis, a detailed activity analysis was carried out based on the activity logs recorded by LearnWeb2.0. These logs store each activity of a LearnWeb2.0 user together with the appropriate timestamp. 10 different activities were extracted from the logs, separated into sessions performed by users, and analysed both at an aggregate level as well as at an individual level for specific users.

Figure 12 shows the overall behaviour of the Hannover students during their course. As expected, search activities took a large part of the overall activities, about 24%, as well as upload activities with 18%, i.e. students searched for appropriate materials using LearnWeb2.0 and uploaded the selected ones into the LearnWeb2.0 repository. 42% of the activities are clearly related to search. Additionally, there was a large proportion of open_resource activities (33%) which are triggered whenever the user opens, displays or re-displays the metadata page of an already stored resource. This occurs when the user edits metadata (before and after the edit action), or when the resource is stored in a folder, or also when the user simply looks at an already stored resource to check for comments and other metadata.

Figure 12: Hannover activities logs

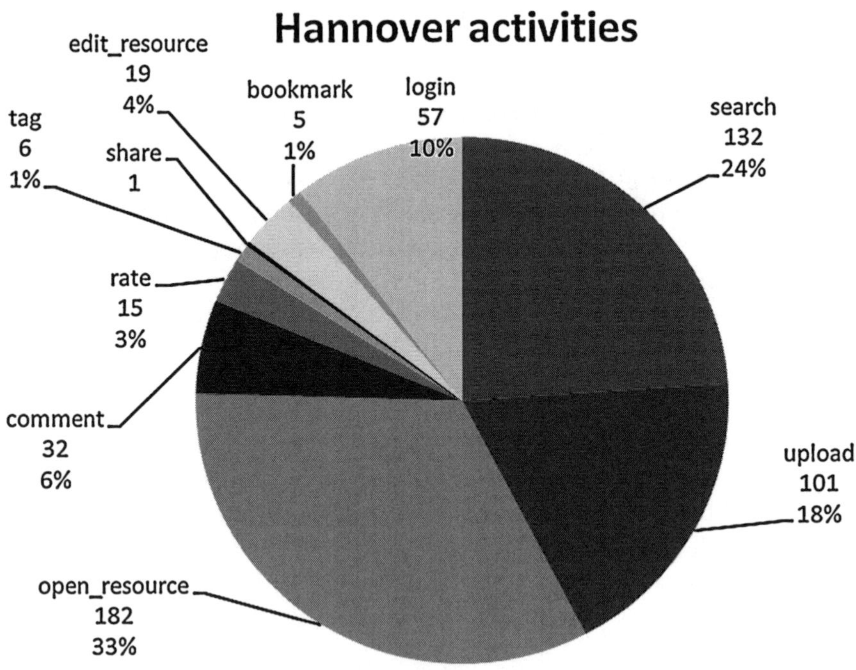

Regarding collaboration, the activity logs revealed relatively few collaborative actions. Commenting, rating and tagging only made up 10% of all activities, which is in contrast to the goal of the students voiced in Questionnaire 1, where they planned to use a Web 2.0 tool not only to search for resources but also to share them with other students and to actively collaborate with them. Possibly students did not use the sharing functionalities of LearnWeb2.0 as much as anticipated, because they collaborated and discussed sitting together at one computer, and did not collaborate online or remotely. However, some uses of the 'open resource' action may also represent a kind of sharing/collaboration behavior, where students view resources uploaded by other students in their group. More details on these aspects can be found in Marenzi and Nejdl (2012).

General issues

Technology. Students pointed out a few technical problems. Among the most significant ones, the speed of the system and the partial integration of LearnWeb2.0 with the GroupMe! component.

Transferability and Teacher Feedback. The term *transferability* describes the process of applying the research results (in the present study the LearnWeb2.0 system) of one situation to other similar situations (other contexts or scenarios). When asked during the interview whether they would use LearnWeb2.0 in other contexts [Appendix 1 - question 7] for example with their future pupils or with their future colleagues at school, students gave positive feedback:

> Stud F: When we had this discussion about the great famine in Ireland, it was very easy to find nice pictures of for example the statues in Dublin. So, yes, LearnWeb2.0 is helpful to find pictures of specific topics especially if I don't know what to search. For example in a Google search I probably need to put in "statue in Dublin" or something like that to find it, and LearnWeb2.0 got it via the text that was added by some other people as a famine related topic.

Stud N: I would think I could use it in general for school, because it does not matter what material you want to share, it doesn't matter if it's CLIL material or math or biology material, it can always be helpful.

The Hannover CLIL course teacher, made useful comments on the course focus pointing out that students showed a certain reluctance to work with the LearnWeb2.0 research prototype: "The striking phenomenon is a certain reluctance concerning research and new media. A couple of students skipped the course because their priority was CLIL and they found LearnWeb2.0 and the research involved distracting. This time the technology enhanced environment was offered as a rich learning environment because we assume that the CLIL teacher community needs social networking and students should experience it at university, but students were not forced to use it. From earlier e-learning projects we know that students sometimes have to be pushed by making the usage of technology part of their assignments. Our master students are rather focused on their credit points and do not invest time for extras."

The teacher pointed out the need for project work and task-oriented learning, but remarked that the tasks she gave her students did not really require access to a large number of resources, as they are available on the Web: "The scenarios used in the CLIL seminar supported the trainee teachers' learning about CLIL. The project work made them search for appropriate materials and the process of designing tasks for their pupils made them apply the knowledge gained about CLIL which they did creatively with all types of materials (text and digital). However, the task design was rather classical, not making the move from the personal to the worldwide Web". Further opportunities need to be designed in teacher education to enable prospective teachers to transform their beliefs so that they are able to create critical classrooms for the 21st century using new literacies and various tools of technology (Marsh, 2002).

5.1.5 LearnWeb2.0 integrative framework for CLIL

> *What is a model?*
> "Dorin, Demmin and Gabel (1990) define model as a mental picture that helps us understand something we cannot see or experience directly."
>
> (Malik & Khurshed, 2011, p. 533)

Advancing CLIL in the 21st century classroom requires both advances in pedagogy as well as in technology. The present research work provides a two-fold perspective: pedagogical – CLIL education has been placed and discussed in the context of *digital literacy*; technological - the development of LearnWeb2.0 is discussed in the Higher Education context to support collaborative learning activities in a CLIL seminar. Both aspects are brought together in this section to develop a new model which integrates and makes connections between CLIL and the wider worlds of education, meaning-making and information technology more explicit, leading to an *integrative model* for CLIL (Marenzi, 2014).

LearnWeb2.0 for CLIL

LearnWeb2.0 has been designed as a planning tool to help teachers to ensure that a particular task or project work includes different components of collaborative group-work and *digital literacy*.

As mentioned overall the thesis, collaborative group-work is different from traditional group-work where students work together to solve a joint task. Collaborative group-work requires more social interaction and enhances student discussion and reasoning on the intermediate activities to solve the task.

In a learning environment, if it is difficult to identify members' contributions and the final products is evaluated as a whole, group-work may cause some members to work less than others (Hathorn & Ingram, 2002; Johnson & Johnson, 2008). Furthermore, "organising learning in small groups does not necessarily imply that students work together and support each other in carrying out their learning tasks" (Huber & Huber, 2008, p. 113).

Table 2 summarises how LearnWeb2.0 features can support each component of *digital literacy* with a particular attention on enhancing collaboration and social interaction. For example, using the LearnWeb2.0 forum to discuss and select resources according to their reliability and relevance supports *critical thinking*, as well as collecting and organising multimedia resources in collaborative groups and folders helps students in *creatively* designing new CLIL teaching materials for different contexts. In particular collaborative search and communication are supported by LearnWeb2.0.

Collaborative search. LearnWeb2.0 provides a generic search interface for different kinds of resources (including, in the computing tradition, images, video clips, social network contacts) to match different types of subject matters. But it is not easy to find good CLIL materials for all subjects: it is still difficult to find good CLIL materials about Religion for example, as well as good multilingual resources, because most resources are localized and carry culturally loaded meaning. "For a long time only subjects such as Physics, Biology, and History were favoured for the CLIL approach" (Kupetz & Woltin, in press) because scientific experiments or historical events can be shown in videos and images.

Table 2: LearnWeb2.0 supporting digital literacy

Digital literacy components	**LearnWeb2.0 features supporting digital literacy**
Functional skills	Use of digital technologies to support the learning process
Collaborative search. Ability to search, find and select information:	Collaborative search and sharing of resources in different Web 2.0 tools and social networks such as YouTube, Flickr, Slideshare and Facebook.
Collaboration and communication	Annotation (tag, rating) and commenting of the shared resources
Critical thinking. Cultural and social awareness and understanding	Use the LearnWeb2.0 forum to discuss and organise multimedia resources according to their reliability and relevance for CLIL
Creativity	Creatively re-organise the collected resources to be reused in other contexts (e.g. to design new CLIL courses).

Using LearnWeb2.0, students as well as teachers can search in social networks and discover authentic resources (i.e. real examples posted by people living in a specific context) that fit a particular learning goal. In so doing, the LearnWeb2.0 CLIL community can collect and create a valuable repository of CLIL educational resources to be shared with other colleagues and researchers in the field.

Communication and collaboration. Accessibility to a large quantity of information on the Web though, does not always mean reliability or good quality for educational resources. Teachers have the important role of designing good tasks and activities which can help students develop critical skills and the ability to work online and collaborate in groups to analyse and select good resources. In the CLIL context, groups help users to focus on a particular learning context and accommodate all corresponding resources in one place (Marenzi et al., 2010). "Since a single resource can be useful to more than one CLIL unit, it can be added many times with different metadata (LearnWeb2.0 metadata include title, description and tags). The user can select or create a group folder within the repository where the resource will be stored. Folders are shared among the co-searchers and thus populated collaboratively. After the resource is added to the LearnWeb2.0 repository, it can be commented on, rated and tagged by all users in the same way as in other Web 2.0 platforms" (Marenzi et al., 2010, p. 207). Ratings reflect the relevance of the resource for the CLIL unit. By exchanging comments, the students and/or teacher can discuss resource quality, reliability and usability for the course and collaboratively describe the materials more precisely within the learning context. Hence, the LearnWeb2.0 community can collaboratively identify the best learning resources for specific learning domains. Comments on particular learning resources can further be used by authors to improve their resources. These discussions help to improve the work results by critically analysing materials and collections. Finally, the selected and rated resources can be used for self-directed learning and re-adapted to design new course materials.

Integrative CLIL

Given today's new communication technologies, CLIL is no longer an activity taking place in an isolated way within the confines of individual classrooms. Rather CLIL is in the process of realising its potential to transcend these confines in keeping with the changed ways, in which each and every one of us communicates in today's world. A model of CLIL that formalises these linkages to the *wider* world and its communicative practices is thus in order.

The goal in this section is to transform the *how to* model of CLIL into a more complex model which integrates and makes the connections between CLIL and the wider world of education, *literacy* pedagogy and collaboration in social networks. In particular the focus is on social interaction that is an essential part in collaborative group-work online learning. The result, depicted in Figure 13, is a new social networking model for CLIL which the researcher has called *Integrative CLIL.*

The *Integrative CLIL* model expands the 4Cs Framework (described in Section 5.1.2) as it considers the global context where the individual interacts within social networks. In this way, communication is expanded between different kinds of communities (face-to-face and online) through social networks. Content is presented with a framework of multiliteracy, and personal development (cognition and culture) is enriched by collaboration and sharing with other people. Reference to an *integrative* model can also assist in practical ways, for instance as a tool that encourages and guides dialogue with others in CLIL work providing a source of reflection on CLIL and its embracing of *digital literacy.*

Figure 13: Integrative CLIL. A social networking model

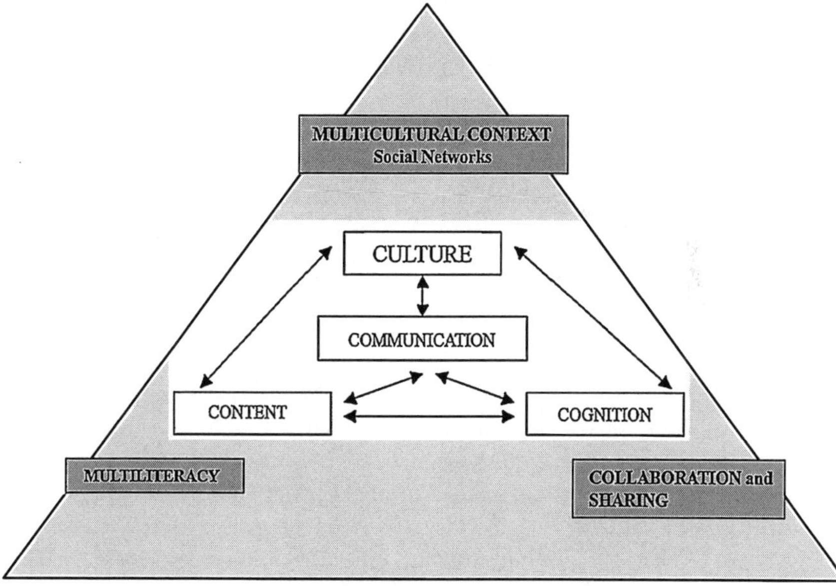

A formal model can thus help teachers to get across the tasks and activities that they wish their students to carry out with Web texts in a clear way. In this sense a model helps scaffold the learning process. Building research tools into pedagogical tools is in keeping with the starting goal of transforming the *how to* model of CLIL, into a more complex model which integrates and formalises the connections between CLIL and the wider world of education, meaning-making and information technology.

5.2 Second case study: ESP (English for Specific Purposes)

> "Learning is a gradual process of 'coming to be'. When learning takes place a person's view of the world is transformed. They take a new position to a phenomenon, a new way of talking about and describing it, and new meanings and concepts. Another way of thinking about learning is that it is the result of a process of the transformation and internalization of signs. This view of learning places modes of representation and communication at the centre."
>
> (Jewitt, 2006, p. 28)

According to Hutchinson and Waters (1987, p. 8) "ESP is an approach to language teaching in which all decisions as to content and method are based on the learner's reason for learning". It is primarily concerned with preparing learners "for chosen communicative environments" (Mohan, 1986, p. 15). The focus is on the learner's needs and on language teaching through active communication in real life situations.

Usually ESP courses are addressed to adults who already have some knowledge of English and who learn the language in order to improve their communication skills, also for professional reasons. The term "specific" in the acronym refers to the specific purpose for learning English. The ESP content can be related to very different subjects varying from computer science to business management, law or tourism. Since students learn the vocabulary and can re-use the structures that they learn at school in a meaningful context (for example at work, or if they move in a foreign country), they are more motivated to interact with other English speakers and to read texts in English. This practice reinforces the relevance and the knowledge of the subject which is taught and increases the motivation to improve their English.

At university level in particular, the work of defining terms is an essential requirement for any student: what Faculty a student is enrolled in, the capacity to discuss terms from the standpoint of their definitions, interpretations in specific contexts is paramount – "it entails knowledge of scientific English, in the widest meaning of the term" (Rizzo, 2009, p. 13). To learn English at university level, no matter how important grammar might be, the goal to be reached necessarily involves reflection on texts and an understanding of how texts and genres work in terms of making meaning in context (Lorenzo, 2013).

At the University of Pavia self-access e-learning in multimodal texts studies of English is used to guide students enrolled in the degree course in Dentistry in the online analysis of multimodal texts. In particular Halliday's socio-semiotic approach to English text studies (Halliday, 1978; Halliday & Matthiessen, 2004) is explored to this end, for example to answer the following questions: *How can e-learning techniques be applied to text-based studies of English? How can the multimodal analysis of texts contribute to understanding CMC (computer-mediated communication)?*

The following sections give a definition of the concepts of *media literacy* (Section 5.2.1) to introduce the multimodal text-based studies of English (Section 5.2.2) as a background for the ESP study carried out at the University of Pavia (Sections 5.2.3 and 5.2.4). This collaboration led to the integration of LearnWeb2.0 into the *Multimodal Web Search* (MWS) platform to support collaboration in multimodal corpus construction described in Section 5.2.5.

5.2.1 Media literacy

In general a *medium* can be considered as a specialised interface for the creation and distribution of content. In common usage, the term *multimedia* refers to a combination of *media* including video, still images, audio, written text that can be accessed interactively. Depending upon one's perspective, multimedia may be defined in multiple ways. Typical definitions collected by Doolittle in his white paper *Multimedia Learning: Empirical Results and Practical Applications* (Doolittle; 2002, p. 1) include the following:

- Multimedia is the "use of multiple forms of media in a presentation";
- Multimedia is "information in the form of graphics, audio, video, or movies. A multimedia document contains a media element other than plain text";
- Multimedia comprises a computer program that includes "text along with at least one of the following: audio or sophisticated sound, music, video, photographs, 3-D graphics, animation, or high-resolution graphics";
- Multimedia is any combination of text, graphic art, sound, animation, and video that is delivered by computer.

All these definitions consider the integration of more than one medium as a common aspect. From the technological point of view, separate technologies such as voice, data and video sharing resources and interact with each other, synergistically creating new functionalities. *Media literacy* thus concerns the general understanding of the various technologies available as well as the ability to use media tools with critical thinking skills: "it involves reading images critically, interpreting sounds, and seeing how media texts produce meaning in a multiplicity of ways" (Kellner, 1998, p. 110). According to Kellner, besides making students sensitive to social and cultural differences through multicultural education, they should also be made aware of how different media construct their materials in different ways. Students need to understand new representations of content and to negotiate information in multiple modes (e.g. textual, visual, audio and so on). As Daley remarks:

> "The very vocabulary of multimedia encourages approaches different from those used to write text. One creates and constructs media rather than writing it, and one navigates and explores media rather than reading it. [...] literacy, is no longer only about rules and their correct application. It is about finding unfamiliar kinds of text and being able to search for clues about its meaning without immediately feeling alienated and excluded from it. It is also about understanding how this text works in order to participate in its meanings (its own particular 'rules'), and about working out the particular context and purposes of the text."
>
> (Daley, 2003, p. 36)

Besides the general principles of communication, *media literacy* requires a sensitivity to the differences among the specific media, engaging students to critically analyse and dissect a wide range of media materials, including such disparate phenomena as TV news, online music events, action-adventure films, advertising, and multimedia web sites. In addition to the linear cognitive skills needed for the traditional of reading print materials, multimedia literacy requires the ability to read hypertexts that are often multidimensional, requiring the linking of images, graphics, texts, and sometimes audio-video materials. "In a global information environment, this also may involve switching from one language to another, requiring contextual understanding to read and interact with people from different cultures" (Kellner, 1998, p. 118).

Knowledge acquisition can be influenced by different types of multimedia content. Various aspects of knowledge acquisition and sharing have also been approached in relation to media literacy:

> "In the 1990s researchers investigated the influence of media and computer technology on communication and knowledge acquisition, which is to be seen in the concepts of media literacy as well as information and computer literacy. Recent work has focused on the critical use of media, especially on the Web, as reflected in the concepts of critical media literacy and critical media literacy education."
>
> (Kupetz, 2010, p. 225)

Learning theory in the past decade has expanded dramatically because of the introduction of *multimedia*. In Education, *multimedia* have been used a lot to produce *computer-based training* (CBT) courses and reference books such as encyclopedia and almanacs. A CBT lets the user go through a series of presentations, text about a particular topic and associated illustrations in various information formats. The use of *multimedia* is also becoming a major factor particularly in higher education and it is rapidly changing the curriculum in universities all over the world.

Multimodality

Going a step further, in 2000 Baldry suggested a distinction between the term *multimediality* and *multimodality*. The former refers to the integration of technologies such as the merging of personal computers and television, or phone technologies, while *multimodality* refers to the integration between semiotic resources in texts. "The term *multimodality* refers to the fact that all texts combine and integrate diverse semiotic modalities, that is to say, they use a combination of semiotic resources to produce meaning" (Baldry, 2000, p. 21).

With the establishment of new technologies and multimodal texts, communication does not happen only through spoken language, but it assumes increasingly multimodal forms which comprise the linguistic, "the visual, the audio, the gestural and the spatial modes of meaning" (Cope & Kalantzis, 2009, p. 166). In conversational interaction, the term *multimodality* refers to:

> "the coordinated deployment of non-verbal resources such as gestures, facial expression, gaze, body display, as well as verbal and para-verbal resources such as (morpho-)syntax, lexico-semantics, phonetics, and prosody".
>
> (Kupetz, 2011, p. 122–23)

Kress points out that reading itself is no longer an *interpretative* process, but more and more "a *transformative* process, where readers integrate, adjust, divide into sections, and prioritise parts of the text at will" (Kress, 2000, p. 156). For this reason, if we want to understand the various contemporary forms of representation we need to learn how to write, to read and to interpret multimodal texts which integrate the other modes with language (Jewitt & Kress, 2003).

5.2.2 Multimodal text-based studies of English

> "In language learning and teaching, text analysis that uses multimedia and hypermedia technologies can often be more effective than those which rely exclusively on printing [...] moreover, even printed texts can benefit from advances in technology by supporting [...] complex multimodal analysis that allow us to represent the entire meaning-making process to a much greater extent than was possible in the past."
>
> (Baldry, 2000, p. 22)

Text-based studies of English are, following Halliday and Matthiessen (2004), "reflections on the textual, interpersonal and ideational structure of the meaning-making processes found in genres as podcasts, forums, websites, blogs, e-mails". The suggestion is to combine various methods to study English at a university level, not only sticking to standard grammar, but also taking into account more general principles of textual organisation.

Nowadays a lot of diverse materials are available on the Web: different structures and various kinds of texts which describe the same content in various ways can be found. Written and oral language are no longer separate, but various modes such as written and oral language, visual, audio, gestural and spatial representation, are mixed in the new media (e.g. videos and websites) as well as in our everyday experience. Students can find resources and codes available to them, as well as given conventions in their contexts and cultures (or different contexts and cultures). Additionally, they can learn a language in different contexts and genres (e.g. different ways of using and learning a language in different disciplines) and not only through traditional grammar (Lorenzo, 2013). Since the digital genres found in the Web are the object of study and because the methods used when analysing and reflecting on textual properties are becoming increasingly sophisticated, reflection, comparison and analysis of text typically involves the use of computers.

The following sections relate to the scenario at the University of Pavia dealing with multimodal corpus analysis in order to develop English language skills and critical thinking (Baldry, 2000; Baldry & Thibault, 2006a). Students were encouraged to use LearnWeb2.0 to collaboratively search the Web for Public Information Films (PIFs) and create an annotated corpus of videos. The way in which generic, or genre, features are represented in individual instances of text, whether written or spoken, as well as combining language with other semiotic resources (such as colour, gaze, gesture and so on) is a major aspect of the courses in Pavia as well.

5.2.3 ESP learning scenario

2010 Pavia – ESP curse for dentistry students

The students involved in the case study in Pavia were 19 first-year undergraduate students enrolled in the degree course in Dentistry (Faculty of Medicine) taking a compulsory course in ESP (*English for Specific Purposes*). The ESP syllabus required them to apply multimodal semiotics to the analysis of English language *Public Information Films* (PIF genre), mostly dealing with medical issues. The students were encouraged to look beyond cultures where English is the mother tongue but to prefer films using English where possible in order to develop English language skills and critical thinking.

The course was held from May to June 2010. The course design included a more general part (written tasks) and a more scientific part which focused on medical aspects (oral activities and final exam). The students were divided into six groups, they used LearnWeb2.0 to search for multimedia resources relating to a specific thematic area associated with PIFs (e.g. domestic violence, road safety, and paedophilia), negotiate decisions about their choice and analyse the collected films within a peer assessment process. The course led up to a final exam presentation in which each student presented the results of the research vis-à-vis the group's conclusions and their own personal conclusions. The course was designed to improve the students' capacity to integrate skills acquired through a combination of classroom learning, e-learning and self-study (progress towards integrated skills), stress the individual and peer learning aspects and promote self-assessment. In collaboration with the researcher, the teacher structured the seminar into three phases, where the first phase provided the necessary background information on the topic and on the required activities, the second phase involved the students in project work, and the third phase required them to present the results of their project in a final presentation to the classroom. The assignments during the course included tasks for individual work, group work and classroom discussions, as described in the CSCL (*Computer Supported Collaborative Learning*) macro script in Figure 14.

Figure 14: Assignments script in the ESP course

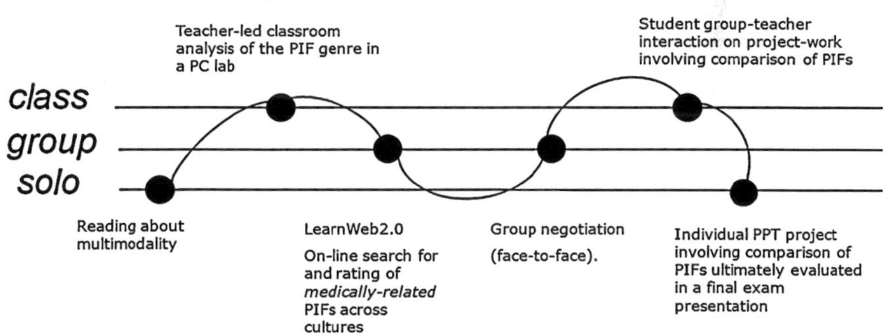

There were three phases in the activity, each with a different focus.

Phase I – Introduction and traditional face-to-face interaction. In this phase students learned about multimodal theory and how to carry out multimodal text analysis that is, studying websites, printed and digital texts in English and the ways in which these texts are used in different medical contexts (*solo* task: Reading about multimodality). The course-book (Baldry & Thibault, 2006b) is not simply an English grammar, but it provides a toolkit for the analysis of complex texts and genres. In class the teacher provided the necessary background information on multimodality and film analysis. Specifically the course dealt with the following themes: "*causality; colors in semiotic systems; context; diagrams, framing, information management, integration of semiotic resources, inter-textuality in scientific texts; meta-functional analysis, negotiation and interpersonal relations, organization of the scientific printed and web page; phonetic and prosodic elements, primary and secondary discourse genres; projection, trajectories and transitivity in medical texts*" (quotation from the course website[31]). During a teacher-led class, students carried out an analysis of the PIF genre: they analysed the characteristics of the genre and discussed their usefulness and efficacy, then they compared them with PIFs of other countries and cultures. A few preliminary activities were carried out in a computerised classroom to introduce LearnWeb2.0, search for new resources to learn to organise the resources in GroupMe! folders and collaborate in groups negotiating materials with other colleagues (i.e. commenting, tagging and rating resources).

Phase II – Project Work. In the second phase, students, partly in the classroom, partly working from home, concentrated on group project work: online searching for and rating of PIFs across different cultures, discussing their views within their group and with the teachers. Students were divided into groups and they used LearnWeb2.0 to search the Web for videos related to the PIF genre, discussed how to select appropriate resources (usually face-to-face) for their project work and created a corpus. The goal was to recommend or collect good quality resources according to the collaborative annotations of the LearnWeb2.0 community. The PIF videos had to be representative of different English speaking cultures and cover different themes for the various project-groups. After collecting the videos in LearnWeb2.0, each group of students analysed their corpus identifying the cultural characteristics and the structural schemas in the video.

"From the linguistic point of view, students were asked to acquire a specialised knowledge of English that demonstrates their understanding of how body events and processes and related ideas, theories and opinions are expressed not just through linguistic resources but through a multimodal integration of resources i.e. linguistic, visual, spatial and temporal" (quotation from the course website[30]). They learnt the language and the terminology by watching videos that

31 http://nfs.unipv.it/medicinaLM41/corso/500404/Obiettivilist.asp?cmd=resetall

talk about the content. In this phase students were interested and motivated, purposive and selective; they realised possible ways of how to represent the same contents and how to design new meanings in a creative way. Furthermore students rated PIFs and discussed how to select appropriate resources for their final project work presentation according to the characteristics of textual organisation and inter-textuality, inter-culturality, and the efficacy of the conveyed message. The discussion and the critical analysis happened more face-to-face than in the LearnWeb2.0 forum.

Phase III – Final exam presentation. In the third phase, the focus was on individual exam preparation and presentation. As Johnson and Johnson (2008, p. 26) remark, "group processing with individual feedback is more effective than group processing with whole group feedback". Students were asked to select two videos from the corpus they collaboratively created during the project work, and to analyse and discuss them in class using a PowerPoint presentation. The final exam took the form of a mini-lecture lasting 15–20 minutes, in which two films from different cultures, but with the same theme, were compared by each student. In the presentation they were expected to use language at an academic level to present the contents but also to carry out a meta-textual analysis on their work.

5.2.4 ESP course: evaluation and discussion

As in Section 5.1.4 for the seminar in Hannover, the following paragraphs present a detailed activity analysis of how the students used LearnWeb2.0 based on a thorough evaluation of the questionnaires and the system log files.

Questionnaire 1 – previous experiences and expectations [Appendix 2c]

19 students filled in the first questionnaire. Compared to the students in Hannover, students in Pavia searched more privately (question 10): 13 (69%) students already used Web 2.0 tools to search for literature for private reasons, two students (11%) used them at the university and two students both at the university and in private. As in Hannover, most students (95%) claimed they would use Web 2.0 tools to prepare the final project work for searching (question 11), 18 (95%) to collaborate and share resources within the group, 10 (53%) to annotate and comment resources.

Student expectations were both related to the course topic itself as well as to the teaching approach and tools. Student 2 mentioned the opportunity of group work "… I'm sure it will be very interesting because I think we will work in groups using very different resources, such as websites, videos and so on" and

Student 6's expectations of the course were "to study the science dentist language, to practice my English with experienced teachers, to recognise the new way to study English".

Questionnaire 2 – LearnWeb2.0: Perception and satisfaction with the experience [Appendix 2d]

At the end of the course, 17 students filled in the second questionnaire (substantially more than in Hannover).

Search. Since LearnWeb2.0's main goal is to support the searching and sharing of multimedia resources, clearly the task in Pavia (i.e. analysis of public information films) was closer to the functionalities provided by the system. Following the specific task requirements, the students in Pavia searched for videos across cultures, and were satisfied with the results. In contrast to the Hannover course, 88% of the students considered the materials they found through LearnWeb2.0 sufficient to prepare the final project work (question 6). They also found other resources, such as images, helpful in refining their presentations. During the interview Student M remarked that they retrieved all 14 films through LearnWeb2.0 "which uses YouTube or Vimeo." Students appreciated the opportunity of searching with different Web 2.0 tools simultaneously without having to access different sources in sequence.

Collaboration. As expected, search and aggregation were the most important functionalities. It is interesting to compare the almost equally high value of "discussing and commenting resources" vs. the low value for "rating" and for "tagging" resources. Rating and tagging is important in typical Web 2.0 environments, where users want to share many resources and find them again later on, and thus prefer to input short tags or rate resources. In learning contexts, where the task is to describe and comment a small number of resources, providing a longer comment makes more sense. During the final interview Student M told us that he used LearnWeb2.0 both in the classroom and at home "because through LearnWeb2.0 we can share videos and comments. [...] I made comments about the characteristics of the video (participants, processes and circumstances), the meaning of the video, and the message which is given by the video" [transcript and translation of the recorded interview carried out by the researcher]. Rating resources makes sense in an asynchronous setting, where students can use them to tell their collaborators which of the resources are most helpful.

Activity log analysis

During the course, the students in Pavia collected a total of 70 videos, three pictures and one bookmark. Compared to Hannover, they put much more effort into searching and collecting multimedia resources from the Web. The number of students in both courses was similar. Both the Pavia and Hannover students carried out the same kind of activity analysis. What is clearly visible from the Pavia activities graph (Figure 15) is the much more active use of LearnWeb2.0 by the Pavia students (about twice as many actions per student in Pavia, compared to Hannover).

Figure 15: Pavia activities

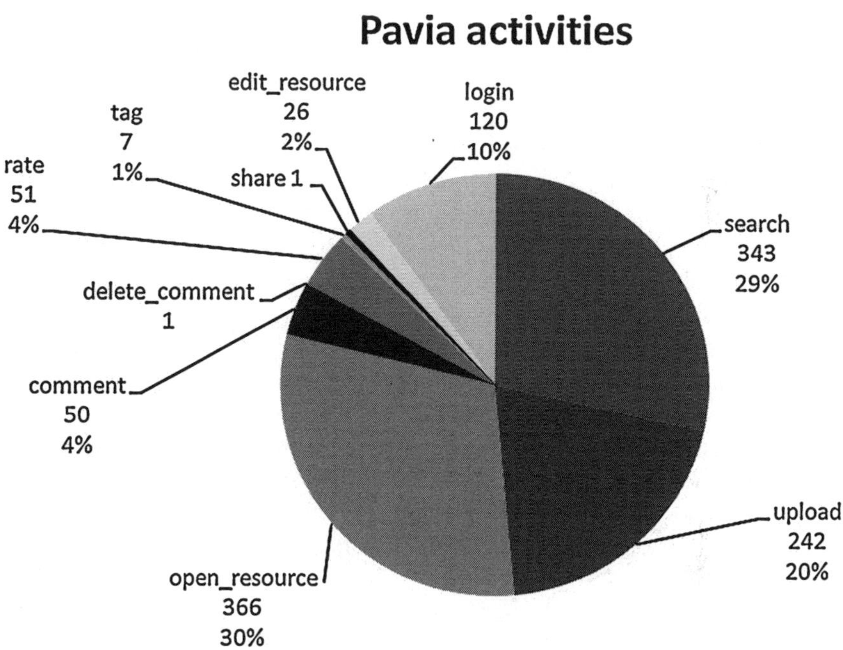

Other than that, the proportion of the actions is similar, with slightly more searching (29% vs. 24%) and uploading (20% vs. 18%) activities in Pavia. As in Hannover, relatively few collaboration actions are present: commenting, rating and tagging makes up only 9% of the activities.

General issues

Technology. Technology-related remarks made by the students in Pavia during the interviews were similar to Hannover, but more positive. The major difficulties were related to speed and technical problems: Student 1: "I found LearnWeb2.0 slow. Maybe some problems about the server which doesn't work properly." Student 9: "I had difficulties in finding the resources because the results of the searching were often too little, I needed more results. I also had problems in using the platform for many technical problems, such as the difficulty in using GroupMe!"

Transferability and Teacher Feedback. Regarding transferability, the students had interesting ideas about using LearnWeb2.0 in other contexts. Student MA told us "I think I could use it to make all kinds of research if I need some videos or pictures, for other research at the University, and I already used it for my hobby (motor bikes)."

Equally interesting are the comments made by one of the two course teachers. He pointed out the possible focus as follows: "What is the goal of LearnWeb2.0? Is it for higher education (teacher-focus) or for intelligent young adults (student-focus)? In many ways the system started out as the former but is, rightly, moving towards the latter." The teacher commented on reliability and speed of the system: "The dentistry students perceived this as the area in which much progress was made as they were testing out the system but where further progress could, should and would be made." In general, he was happy with the system: "There is no doubt in our mind that this is a system that the brightest students understand and want to integrate into their personal way of studying and existing hobbies." Regarding group work he said: "LearnWeb2.0 scored very well in this respect with us and we expect this will be the same with other teachers."

The collaboration within the course at the University of Pavia led to the integration of LearnWeb2.0 into the MWS platform to support collaboration in the multimodal corpus construction. The integrated version was used in the case study carried out at the University of Pavia in the Academic year 2011/2012.

5.2.5 Integration of LearnWeb2.0 with Multimodal Web Search (MWS)

Web pages today still contain much written text. Even so, a Web page is a visual rather than a linguistic unit, and increasingly so. A contemporary Web page is more screen-like, than page-like: 'reading' or rather 'viewing' a Web page is navigationally intricate since computer screens are designed for multiple viewing paths allowing more room for adjustment to viewer preferences. The reading path a user-reader-viewer *actually* chooses is a reflection of the efforts viewers put into their reading as their chosen pathway is just one of the many they could have chosen but did not. Visual supports help in making the written part more easily understandable. As Kress points out however, "the decreasing complexity of writing is compensated by an increasingly complex multimodality" (Kress, 2003, p. 50).

It is not easy to find educational software which supports all these ideas and allows the designing of suitable tasks. The *Multimodal Web Search* (MWS) system developed within the LivingKnowledge[32] European project at the University of Pavia, supports text exploration bringing together micro-level issues with macro-level issues: it implements a scalar model of multimodal texts described in Baldry and Thibault (2006a). LearnWeb2.0 has recently been integrated in the MWS system to provide a communication and sharing infrastructure and to support specific learning scenarios (Baldry, 2011).

MWS and Multimodal Corpus Analysis

The MWS system is a cross-website search system that enables users to specify sets of websites. The user selectively specifies the websites to be compared and the word sets such as "Multiliteracies in Education" to be detected. MWS generates a cross-site index of Internet addresses where one or more word sets are found. Individual articles can be accessed immediately from this index and further analysed in a subsequent stage in terms of their textual composition, visual and/or linguistic, within a multimodal/multisemiotic approach.

The results are also reported as a series of charts and the data retrieved can be exported in a structured format for analysis with Excel. "The main goal is to explore the Web in terms of diversity-aware dimensions in order to understand and document the differing views and opinions prevailing in differing communities over time regarding world events and trends such as climate change and immigration" (quotation from the website[33]). MWS is not intended to compete with the accuracy or completeness of a site-specific search engine, instead it explores and compares web-searches in terms of their diversity. It can be very useful for example in the classroom context where a quick-check comparative overview is required and where hunches need to be explored, illustrated discarded or refined.

MCAWeb – *Corpus construction. What is a corpus? What is a specialised corpus?*

"Corpus design includes the choice of resources, evaluation of representativeness, header content, corpus size, mark-up, which includes the choice of the system of representation chosen for the corpus, and the linguistic annotation (i.e. tagging relative to the various linguistic levels: phonetic, morphosyntactic, etc.)" (Baldry, 2000, p. 28). Multimodal corpus techniques include McaWeb (Baldry

32 http://livingknowledge.europarchive.org/

33 http://mcaweb.unipv.it/mws/

et al., 2011), a system that annotates textual hierarchies in websites (information as classification), as well as the MCA concordancing system (viewing information as relations through relational database techniques).

Concordancing – Concordancing has a well-established tradition in English linguistics, in particular in the field of language learning. Web concordancing tools such as Web Corp Live[34] look for the incidence of word patterns (e.g. collocations) with a view to looking at their typical *co-text* that is, the words that typically proceed and follow the chosen word or expression. Another type of incidence well supported by Web concordancing tools is the frequency of an expression in specific text types.

Annotation – An annotation system is a method of acting on a Web resource by adding an additional layer of information that adjusts its meaning but without modifying it. Whence this extra layer is made visible to other users, then annotation systems may be viewed as a genuine social software tool. With the advent of Web 2.0 social networking tools such as Flickr and YouTube, the possibility of sharing and analysing different kinds of materials and texts increases. There is rising awareness concerning social annotational tools (whether multimodal or language-only) available on the Internet also in educational contexts. Web annotation can be used in web-based text studies as a collaborative tool to discuss the contents of a certain resource and as rating devices for Web resources.

Since the 2010 version of MWS did not include communication and collaboration functionalities, the LearnWeb2.0 system was integrated to provide more interaction and sharing among students during the learning process (Arizzi et al., 2012). Using the two integrated systems in the next courses in the Academic year 2011/2012, students could download learning materials and form interacting groups to carry out writing activities online. They could use the communication facilities provided by LearnWeb2.0, such as comments and forums (general or by groups) to post and share their work. The discussion in the forum could contribute to the decision-making process and could be considered (directly or indirectly) for the attribution of credits. The corpus which was constructed during the course could be re-used in future courses and became the heritage of the entire LearnWeb2.0 community.

After the integration of MWS with LearnWeb2.0 the teacher in Pavia, adopted a new methodology for the oral exam presentation: instead of using PPT presentations to show the results of their analysis, students were asked to access the

34 www.webcorp.org.uk

online platform and to describe the interactions and the actual group work that they did to carry out their learning task.

Group Presentations with LearnWeb2.0

Bye bye PPT: a new solution for group presentations based on mini/micro corpora and other resources

LearnWeb2.0 as a program that allows the carrying out of searches for resources/texts, as well as uploading, sharing, commenting and rating them, provides an alternative to commercial presentation systems (such as *PowerPoint*) and avoids some of their constraints. Using LearnWeb2.0, users can describe the activities of the group they belong to (keywords they used, chosen videos, comments, rating and tag activities) and in the order they wish, to select at the time of presentation. Users can move backwards and forwards from one text/resource to another. Selected videos can be opened *inside* LearnWeb2.0 making the presentation more fluent and easier to handle at the meta-textual ('commentary') level.

It is also possible to describe the interactions between the members of a group more easily i.e. illustrate all the *behind-the-scenes* work done (forum discussions, means of communication, comments etc.), since comments and discussions will be always available in a LearnWeb2.0 community. The work of analytical comparison, so important in HE studies, is further strengthened by the fact that the *Group function* allows members to further shape their mini-corpus, and enhance its usefulness, thanks to rating, commenting and other forms of appraisal.

In the case in point, students used comments to discuss the relevance and rank the video resources in their mini-corpus. These activities give users the opportunity to build up a vast network of meta-textual ties for which a disciplined organisation (superior to that found for example in the comments sections of online news articles) is required. LearnWeb2.0 thus provides a meta-textual level capable of managing the exponential explosion of commentaries, ratings and so on, in other words, meta-texts talking about other texts.

5.2.6 Discussion

The previous sections presented two university courses which used LearnWeb2.0: one was carried out in Germany, the other one in Italy. For both courses, the tasks designed to foster students' active and creative learning have been presented, and how these tasks were supported by the LearnWeb2.0 system has been discussed. The evaluation design and the results for both courses have been presented.

Based on this, commonalities and differences in both scenarios are now discussed from the educational and cultural point of view, and how these influenced students' performance and satisfaction. It has been demonstrated that contextual dimensions such as "immediate or mediated resources or aspects of the physical, social, cultural and organisational environment influence the participants' approach to the learning activities" (Arvaja, 2011, p. 26). Additional details on these aspects for the two specific scenarios can be found in Marenzi and Zerr (2012).

Different Cultures and Expectations

Acceptance of the system – It is always a challenge to transfer the implications of research projects into the field without disturbing the natural course of the learning process but supporting and facilitating it.

CLIL in Germany has a particular historical background, which explains a focus on intercultural learning and a conventional approach towards foreign language learning (Wolff, 2002; Breidbach & Viebrock, 2012). In Hannover students expected a standard design and they worked with traditional kinds of materials (school books, references and recorded interviews provided by the teacher). The trainee teachers were free to use all kinds of materials (written/digital texts, information from the Internet, multimedia resources) to better understand CLIL and to design a CLIL teaching unit for their final project. It was more difficult for them to find relevant resources using LearnWeb2.0 because they were looking for traditional written texts, while the platform is designed to provide Web 2.0 resources (multimedia and recommendations by other people). Moreover, the role of LearnWeb2.0 was not decisive in increasing the credits so that the use of technology was considered as an additional load. When technical problems occurred, German students did not ask for technical support until the next lesson and this increased their frustration. In retrospect, the Hannover students were much more focused on their subject and on a traditional way of learning/teaching. It is clear that the students expected to attend a normal course with standard lessons.

In Italy, there is not a centralised CLIL action, and Italian schools are allowed to create flexible CLIL modules autonomously (Malvezzi-Campeggi, 2013). At the University of Pavia, students were encouraged to apply multimodal semiotics to the analysis of PIFs looking beyond cultures in order to develop English language skills and critical thinking. The LearnWeb2.0 system was central to the course, helping students to find many multimedia resources for their CLIL/ESP related tasks, the objective being to train students to think about and experiment with the principles of a specific discipline i.e. multimodality (CLIL) as well as mastering specific biomedical terminology (ESP). Students were asked to search specifically for videos regarding Public Information Films. They were encouraged by the teachers to use LearnWeb2.0 to search and organise at least 12 videos in group folders. The Pavia students were also more curious about the novelty of the system and interested in its functionalities. All students worked with the system and asked immediately when they had problems. This helped them to cope much better with some of the rough edges of the first system release as compared with the Hannover students.

Collaboration – The researcher was surprised to observe the relatively low use of collaboration functionalities in the courses. "While in Questionnaire 1 the Hannover students answered that they would expect to use Web 2.0 tools both to search and share resources, and to collaborate with other group members, during the sessions they did not use the sharing functionality in LearnWeb2.0 and did not collaborate on-line, but mainly face-to-face" (Marenzi et al., 2010). A few students explicitly mentioned that they came to the course as they wanted to learn together with other students, not remotely.

Another observation is the low use of tags both in Hannover and in Pavia. Possibly this is caused by the class work setup, where students collected a restricted number of resources, so the Title and Description were enough to describe a resource and more meaningful to use than tags.

Different Tasks – Student tasks to be performed through LearnWeb2.0 varied considerably between the two scenarios. This made the researcher aware that the tasks given by the teacher are another important factor determining student satisfaction with the e-learning platform. At the beginning of the work, during the first evaluation cycle, the researcher was not expert in CLIL, and did not know how to approach the CLIL lesson. She mainly focused on the technical support and discussed with the teacher in Hannover what possible functionalities could be suitable for the project work. The willingness of the teacher was very important to allow the evaluation even though the system was at earlier stages. The teacher accepted both the challenge and the risk to offer such an innovative perspective to her students even though no preliminary evidence of success was available.

In the second case study (ESP course in Pavia) the researcher knew the teacher, and she had gained more experience from the previous evaluation already. These two conditions led to a closer collaboration in the preparation of the tasks and during the course design. The future plan was to further investigate and experiment with different tasks and project work in future CLIL seminars in a second evaluation cycle.

LearnWeb2.0, as a system for collaborative searching and sharing of multimedia resources in a CLIL context generated so much interest while talking with colleagues in Hannover and in Pavia, that the researcher together with the colleagues at the L3S Research Center, decided to further develop and adapt the system specifically for this target audience. Given that the CLIL users' requirements were somewhat different from the users originally targeted in TENCompetence, continuing to develop the system based on iterative development and evaluation cycles as suggested by the design-based research methodology turned out to be a good idea. Developers and evaluators (researchers) as well as users of the system (university teachers and students) worked together in the first evaluation cycle to test the system, collect the feedback and implement improvements in the new release. A second improved release of the LearnWeb2.0[35] system was developed in 2010–2011 to support e-learning scenarios and CLIL courses at university level. The lessons learned during the first evaluation cycle, and the improved functionalities of the second release of the system are described in Section 5.3. The research work continued with iterative development and evaluation cycles as suggested by the *design-based research methodology* further using and evaluating LearnWeb2.0 also in other scenarios, described in Chapter 6 of this thesis.

5.3 LearnWeb2.0 (v.2): system development for CLIL

> "Internet offers a seductive deluge of information."
>
> (Salomon, 1998, p. 10)

Since LearnWeb2.0 started in 2009 as a collaborative tool for searching and sharing resources found in social networks, the most relevant functionality in the first version of the system was *search*. The feedback provided by the students during the first evaluation cycle was encouraging in many aspects, but also revealed additional improvement space at the functional as well as at the conceptual level. Using LearnWeb2.0 in the CLIL specific setting helped the researcher understand the shortcomings of the system in this context and motivated the developers to build a second substantially improved release. Activity logs, online questionnaires and interviews at the end of the courses in 2010 were used to collect feedback from the teachers and the students who used the system to carry out their project work. Analysing these data the researcher, together with the developers, was able to test what functionalities worked well and what was missing in the first PHP-based release (Section 3.2). These findings led to the re-development of the system in 2010–2011 towards the second Java-based release, improved according to the users' requirements and to the

35 http://learnweb.l3s.uni-hannover.de/lw/

insights gained by working for almost two years with the first version of the system. In particular new features and usability solutions were introduced. The attempt was to make LearnWeb2.0 more interactive and more flexible, with a particular focus on communication and collaboration.

In the following paragraphs a summary of the LearnWeb2.0 development towards the second release is given, together with a short description of the main functionalities introduced. Additional details can be found in Marenzi et al. (2010), Marenzi and Nejdl (2012), and Marenzi and Zerr (2012).

Improved functionalities

On the basis of the users' evaluation results and a deep analysis of the visual interface, new features and usability solutions were introduced in the system design after the first evaluation cycle, such as:

- Restyling of the Homepage and of the menus
- Better visualisation of the search results list
- Improved resource explorer (better consistency)
- Improved grouping functionality (better usability)

In this section the new functionalities and the major improvements are highlighted.

Efficiency – The new LearnWeb2.0 release was implemented using JAVA and JSP (Java Server Pages) technology. This led to substantial speed improvements, making searching in LearnWeb2.0 comparable to searching the Web 2.0 repositories themselves, with multi-threaded access to these services.

Single Sign On – Not all tools provide token-based authentication mechanisms. Slideshare and Delicious, for example, directly need user credentials (login and password) to access the API (*Application Program Interface*). To enable single-sign-on for those tools, encrypted credentials are saved on a server at the L3S Research Center to provide a uniform authentication interface to all tools through the LearnWeb2.0 GUI (*Graphical User Interface*) and its services.

Registration Wizard and Course Overview – To support course organisation for large numbers of students a Wizard was introduced for each specific course to allow students to create their own account directly. The Wizard also provides many necessary settings: the tutor decides whether a course should be moderated and, when this is the case, the related Overview table is attached to the course. The link to the registration Wizard for the specific course is distributed in class and each student can complete the registration form by defining a personal login name and a password. The student is automatically assigned to the new course and can start working.

Usability – User Interface and Search result view. The key component of the new LearnWeb2.0 release in 2010–2011 was the new interface which provided a better search results overview inspired by the Google and the Bing results display. The number and the size of the thumbnails in the result list were increased. A *mouse over* facility was added to allow users to preview and collect a specific resource without leaving the search context. Figure 16 shows the resource explorer with the new search filters on the left for the source and data-type selection, as well as the resource preview of the search results of the keyword "CLIL" in the middle. Supporting messages are displayed to give feedback related to the actions of the user (for example when a resource is successfully saved in a group). The major difference between LearnWeb2.0 and other search engines is that LearnWeb2.0 also indexes the resources selected by users and the corresponding metadata (tags, comments and ratings) present in the different groups. The results collected and annotated by the LearnWeb2.0 community are ranked higher than the results from other sources since they are perceived to be more relevant in the given context and also show the user what has already been stored in his/her groups by the other members.

Receiving a seamless view of all resources stored in the various Web 2.0 accounts, users are able to carry out search queries defined by their distributed Web 2.0 virtual working space in the same way as they would with their desktop search engine. "They can browse through the result list and select resources that suit their learning task best. If a user identifies a resource of interest in the result list, s/he can add it to the LearnWeb2.0 repository and share it within a user group. By clicking the "Add" button the user can automatically enrich the resource metadata with query information and add it to the repository. The selected resource is automatically tagged with the corresponding query terms. These tags can be used later for resource recommendations to friends and colleagues within the network" (Marenzi et al., 2010).

Sharing – User Groups. In social networks users can create and join various groups of interest. In 2010–2011 the LearnWeb2.0 groups were improved providing a new built-in component instead of using the external tool GroupMe! to support the collaborative learning process.

Figure 17 shows the improved view of a LearnWeb2.0 group with tabs added for the group overview, the group members and their resource folders. For each course a shared folder is available and accessible by all users enrolled in that course; in addition to this, each user can create a group and let others join. Users can create groups of learning resources (or folders) to bundle resources that belong to the same learning context in a collaborative way. They can be members of the same group so that several users can contribute resources or

Figure 16: LearnWeb2.0 Resource Explorer (v.2)

add details. Only the group owner (the creator) may edit the group details such as title and description. In the same way, only the resource owner can edit or delete the item he or she added to the group. Other users can see the items, annotate them and copy them in their own groups. "Groups help users to focus on a particular learning context and accommodate all corresponding resources in one place. In the CLIL context such groups help students focus on a particular learning task. Users can join or leave a group at any time" (Marenzi et al., 2010).

Figure 17: Resources grouped in a LearnWeb2.0 Group

The resources collected in groups are contextually visualised, in other words, a preview of the images is included and videos can be watched directly, comments and descriptions are attached in the same view. Resources can be copied from one group to another, or removed from a group.

Annotation and (formal) description – After being added to the LearnWeb2.0 repository, the resource can be commented on, rated and tagged by other users who are allowed to access them in the same way as in other Web 2.0 platforms (Figure 18). Ratings reflect the relevance of the resource. Hence, the LearnWeb2.0 community can collaboratively identify the best learning resources for specific learning domains. Comments on particular learning resources can be further used by authors to improve their resources at a meta-textual level. By exchanging comments, the students and/or teacher can discuss resource quality, reliability and usability for the course and collaboratively describe the materials more precisely within the learning context (Marenzi et al., 2010).

Negotiation and discussion – A forum module was integrated into each group to support structured communication between students. Negotiation and discussion activities are carried out in the group's dedicated forum which is moderated by the teacher. The objective of adding the forum is to allow LearnWeb2.0 users to communicate and to interact directly (users can share resources in groups and discuss and analyse them more extensively and profoundly than simply using static comments). From a pedagogical perspective, giving the opportunity of sharing ideas, explanations and interpretations in a more extensive way was meant to engage discussions and motivate collaboration between students.

Aggregation and presentation – Finally, the selected and rated resources can be used for self-directed learning and re-adapted for designing new course materials or the final exam presentation (for example using PowerPoint). As mentioned above the users collect resources in groups and hence the aggregation of resources is supported right from the search and exploration step. Users then prune the resources in a group by simply deleting the resources they feel aren't useful anymore. The resource collection in the group now represents the final aggregation of resources along with comments, tags and ratings for each resource.

Awareness – tools for processing and analysing activities

In order to improve the tutors' awareness, a log view was provided so that the course moderator can see the logs and statistics of the activities (Figure 19). The generated graphs provide usage information over time spent using LearnWeb2.0, monitoring specific user activities as well as providing insights

Figure 18: Resource annotation window (v.2)

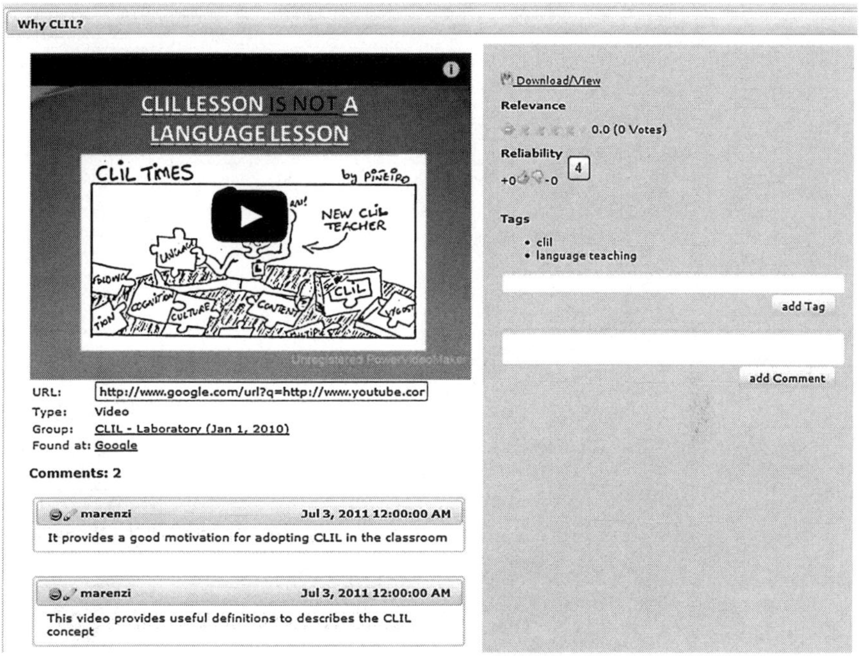

into the overall system usage and/or specific features such as searching or rating. From the left menu the moderator can also send internal notification to the classroom or to a single user. This functionality is particularly important for the courses in Pavia where the tutor has to check and to evaluate the activities of many students in several courses in parallel. It is useful for research purposes since it allows the researcher to analyse what activities/functionalities have been more frequently used by the students and improve the support to the learning process.

With the speed and interface improvements, the second release of LearnWeb2.0 is closer to a production system, and can be used without having to ignore annoying problems which were present in the first prototype. The second evaluation cycle, described in the following chapter, started in September 2011 in order to assess and evaluate the second release of LearnWeb2.0, as well as to get input for further improvements in a later cycle. A questionnaire for user interface satisfaction based on Chin et al. (1988), was prepared to collect preliminary feedback from the users during the winter semester 2011.

Figure 19: Activity logs view

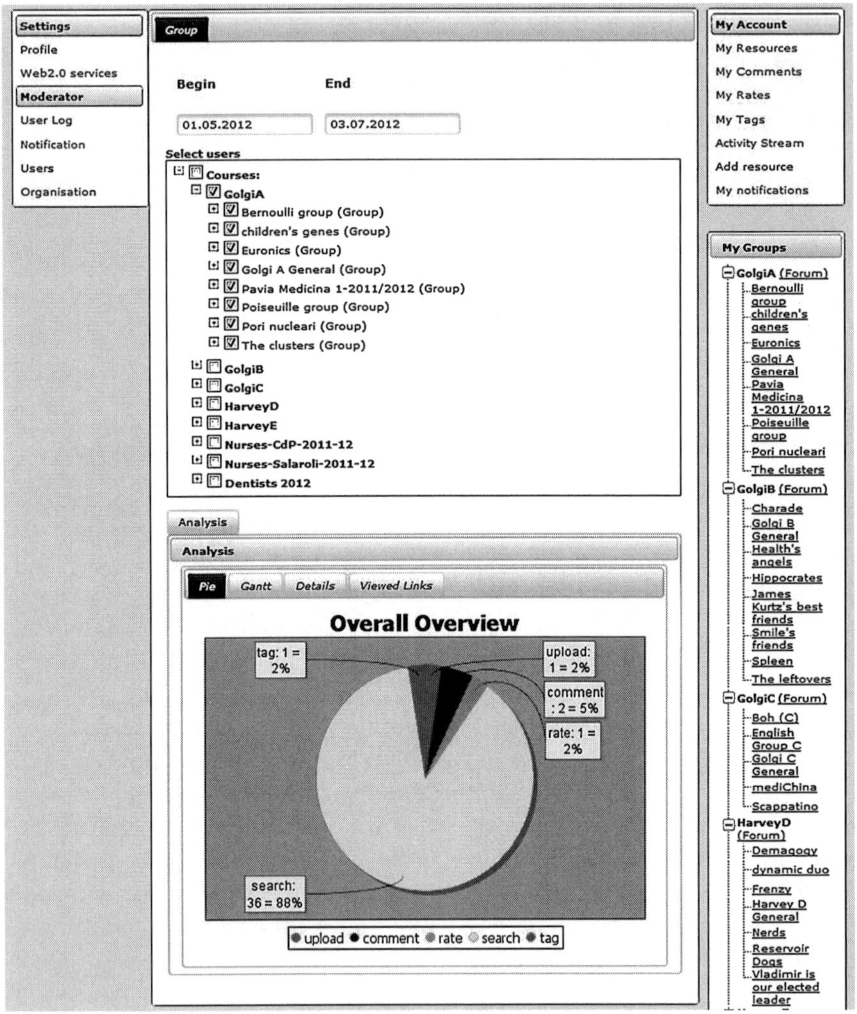

6 Second evaluation cycle: users requirements and customisation

> "...individuals differ in their general skills, attitudes, and preferences for processing information, constructing meaning from it, and applying it to new situations (Jonassen & Grabowski, 1993)". Quoted in Gouli et al. (2006, p. 179).

During the first evaluation cycle, the idea of adopting LearnWeb2.0 as a system for collaborative searching and sharing of multimedia resources in a CLIL context responded so well to the calls for support received from colleagues, in particular those concerned directly or indirectly with CLIL and/or teacher training, that the decision to redevelop and to adapt the system specifically for this target audience was made. Using LearnWeb2.0 in a specific CLIL setting helped the researcher understand the system's shortcomings and enabled the developers to build a second version which inherited most of the initial ideas and functionalities, but re-arranged them in a more integrated and user-friendly way. Constant feedback and insights from the teachers and students provided the researcher with a better understanding of how to support end-users in designing their courses.

Armed with these initial appraisals of the second release of the LearnWeb2.0 system, the researcher started a second evaluation cycle which focused less on the design and usability of the system, and more on collecting the users' requirements and customising the system to support different scenarios and learning goals. In order to define the main framework and the functionalities to be implemented to support various virtual communities, the following activities were carried out:

1) Implementation of the new functionalities in the second version to better support the CLIL scenario. Implementation of a second release of LearnWeb2.0 (in Java) to address the users' feedback and the insights gained during the first cycle, with the main changes regarding the system usability, including substantial speed and interface improvements;
2) Analysis and evaluation of other users' requirements towards a customisation of the LearnWeb2.0 system in different scenarios (Section 6.3);
3) Definition of a theoretical model and a basic structure for the system (Chapter 8).

The second evaluation cycle started in September 2011, in order to assess and evaluate the second release of LearnWeb2.0, as well as to get input for further improvements in a later cycle. A questionnaire for user interface satisfaction was prepared to collect preliminary feedback from the users during the summer semester (July 2011). Preliminary results collected in July from 21 students attending a Dentistry course at the University of Pavia showed that the users were much more satisfied with the second release of LearnWeb2.0. They appreciated the much faster speed and the clearly improved usability.

During the winter semester 2011 LearnWeb2.0 was used in a German course at the Leibnizschule high school in Hannover, in a case study involving pupils from 8th and 12th grades collecting and discussing materials from the Web relating to postwar literature (Section 6.1). During the winter semester 2012 the use of LearnWeb2.0 as a sharing platform was also evaluated by a community of teachers and researchers within the YELL project, described more extensively in Section 6.2.

6.1 First case study: learning about literature on the Web in a German school

Today, educators largely agree that printed media are not the dominant source of communication any longer and must be seen in relation to other inter-media reference systems. An integration of the didactics of literature and media is therefore desirable. Schoolbooks become partially obsolete, while Internet can help teachers in providing the latest materials for their students. However, the masses of information available on the Web are not organised and can overwhelm students. Information on the Web is increasingly accessible, but the reliability of the resources can be very questionable. Morin (1999, p. 18) notices how "our culture favors *separation* instead of *interconnection* and *analysis* instead of *synthesis*". Ranieri (2006, p. 79) writes that "an important task of Education is to teach students how to find interconnections and contextualisation of resources". Pupils must attain a critical-reflexive media literacy in order to be able to resist being manipulated by the media and instead use them to articulate their own interests (Kellner, 2004; Kress, 2003). Children must be taught how to evaluate information asking questions about its validity, comparing information with their background knowledge and with well-known sources, using new information to de-construct the external stimuli and consciously re-construct their knowledge. Often information is fragmented or de-contextualised and it is important to re-construct the relationship with the original context, or organise the resources in a structured way. Internet requires active user interaction, exploration and problematisation.

Instead of a pure acquisition of knowledge, Web 2.0 can foster inductive, integrative and synthetic learning through actively structuring collaborative and creative activities. Learning on the Web must deal with personal identification and decision processes. Open and cooperative learning arrangements are useful in task management and enable a high level of task-related activities, but good tools that can support this kind of interaction are still under development and evaluation. A few experiments have been carried out in schools in Germany to test a variety of educational software. In particular, Lower Saxony's core curriculum for high and middle-high school education in the subject German demands the expertise of "dealing with the media" including the Internet.

In Holdack-Janssen and Marenzi (2012a) a case study is presented in which students of two high school classes collaboratively searched the Web, collected and discussed materials about postwar literature, and created a final presentation. One of the main goals of the course was to teach children how to search the Web and to develop their critical competences. In the following sections, the course design is described (i.e. the teacher's methodological and didactic approach in order to develop a critical attitude to the resources), as well as the evaluation of LearnWeb2.0 in this context and the design for further improvements.

6.1.1 Learning scenario

In the case study described here, the teacher decided to introduce *media literacy* at the Leibnizschule in Hannover as part of a series of German lessons about postwar literature. 33 students from 8th grade (14 years old) and 19 students from 12th grade (18 years old) were involved in the case study, collecting and discussing materials from the Web.

The aim of the project was to teach students to search in various Web sources for new information related to the short story "An diesem Dienstag" written by Wolfgang Borchert (1947). In order to critically select suitable materials and to discuss and organise the results in final presentations, students used the second release of the LearnWeb2.0 system described in Section 5.3.

Since information available on the Web is not always reliable and suitable for use in the classroom, a further objective was to support students to carry out a critical and reflective use of online resources. Figure 20 shows the different activities carried out in the class, in the laboratory or remotely as a group from home. As uncontrolled interaction not necessarily triggers learning processes, a CSCL (*Computer-supported cooperative learning*) script was used to define some interactions to be carried out during the course.

Figure 20: CSCL classroom script – activities carried out during the project

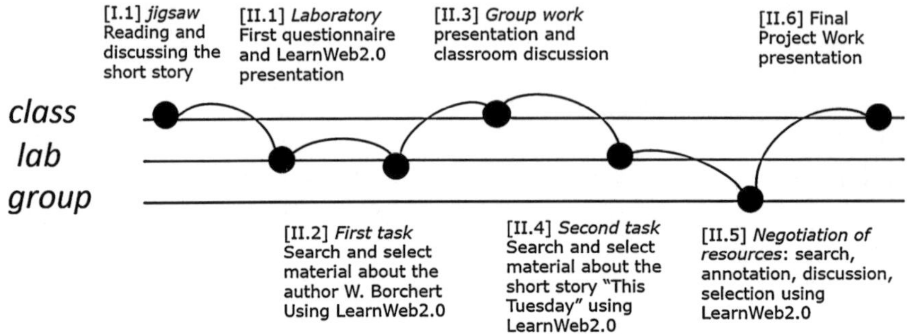

Phase I – preparation [I.1]

At the beginning of the project, the teacher presented the short story "An diesem Dienstag" in class and asked the students to develop a preliminary interpretation through a cooperative *jigsaw* process (Dillenbourg & Jermann, 2007; Dillenbourg & Hong, 2008). The organisation of a *jigsaw* activity requires a rigid coordination by the tutor, who has to identify a number of sub-topics and assign them to separate teams, as well as respect for a rigid schedule by the group participants (Pozzi et al., 2010).

Phase II – collaborative project work

Based on these preliminary self-employed working approaches, the task was to use LearnWeb2.0 to collaboratively search and analyse information found on the Web about the author Wolfgang Borchert and his short story "An diesem Dienstag" as an example of postwar literature.

Task

Create a GoogleDocs document on the topic: W. Borchert "An diesem Dienstag" as an example of postwar literature, that will be evaluated as groupwork in class.

Possible items:

- W. Borchert's biography and other works
- Short story "An diesem Dienstag"
- Postwar literature as a period, other authors, etc.
- School during National Socialism, everyday life during National Socialism
- Special features/characteristics of short stories

II.1 Laboratory – In order to collect the students' preliminary experiences regarding the use of the Web as a learning tool, they were asked to fill in an online questionnaire. Afterwards, LearnWeb2.0 was presented to the students and they were shown how to register their user accounts and to create small groups of four to six participants.

II.2 First task – The first application task was to search for suitable materials about the author Wolfgang Borchert and to select the most relevant for their project work.

II.3 Group work presentation – In the next lesson, students presented the results of their preliminary selection of resources from the wealth of multimedia resources (e.g. pictures, videos, websites...) available on the Web. Using a resource collected by the students as an example, the teacher moderated a discussion about the reliability of online resources.

II.4 and 5 Second task – The groups were assigned a second task, i.e. the creation of a presentation (using collaborative Google documents provided in LearnWeb2.0) about Wolfgang Borchert's "An diesem Dienstag" as an example of postwar literature and were then asked to present the results to the plenary. Each group worked during two sessions in class and also at home to gather resources, evaluate and comment on them, and to prepare the final presentation. Working in small groups they had the opportunity to confront themselves with their peers, reflect on their activities and prepare for discourse and presentation to the class.

II.6 Final presentation – Individual groups presented their findings.

The movement from small groups to the whole-class promoted participation in the open discussion. In Kolodner's words, "observing the discourse of others groups, students can learn from each other" (2007, p. 252). Students were also asked to fill in a final online questionnaire to give feedback about the use of LearnWeb2.0 in the project.

6.1.2 Results evaluation

This section presents some of the feedback provided by students both in the questionnaires, as well as in class. During the laboratory lessons the data were collected by the researcher in the format of field notes. More details can be found in Holdack-Janssen and Marenzi (2012a; 2012b).

Since the goal of the second evaluation phase was to collect the users' requirements and their reactions to the system, in this context the focus was in particular on the interaction with the LearnWeb2.0 system to confirm a better usability of the second release and its efficacy in supporting students in their tasks. The feedback collected in the questionnaires is presented below, as well as the results of the group work. The focus is in particular on the materials that were searched, selected and collected in the LearnWeb2.0 folders by the various groups. A discussion is also provided about the competencies and the main differences between the two classes (8th and 12th grade). Finally the students' reaction during the laboratory is reported, as well as their feedback during the course.

Questionnaire 1 – Erfahrungen der Schüler mit dem Internet [Appendix 3 (a, c)].

The first questionnaires collected the students' previous experiences in using the Web. A few examples of questions and answers are provided below. The original questionnaire was in German. The questions reported below have been translated into English by the researcher to favour the reader in the context of this thesis.

4 - Do you think that contents you find in the Internet are suitable for learning?

The majority of students considered Web contents suitable for learning (82% grade 8 and 95% grade 12). Only five students over the total of 52 did not trust the information on the Web for learning, or they preferred to read and study on paper. For one student the Web was distracting.

9 - How do you decide, whether to trust the author/source of an article/video in the Internet?

Students in grade 8 evaluated sources in a more spontaneous way, while those in grade 12 were more critical about the reliability of sources.

Grade 8	Grade 12
– According to my feeling (it has never let me down!)	– I compare several sources, and if the statements are similar, I can work with them.

10 - What do you do when you cannot judge the trustworthiness? (e.g. search for information about the author, ask a friend for his opinion…)?

Students in grade 12 seemed to be very independent and preferred to search further instead of asking other people. Younger students paid less attention or asked their parents or friends.

Questionnaire 2 – Feedback zur gemeinsamen Materialsuche über LearnWeb2.0 [Appendix 3 (b, d)].

The second questionnaire collected students' feedback on the critical use of resources from the Web and the relevance for learning. In both classes the parents of two students, concerned about privacy issues, did not sign the Research consent form, consequently only 31 students in 8th grade and 17 students in 12th grade worked with LearnWeb2.0 and filled in the second questionnaire.

14 - Have you improved your critical use of sources and materials from the Internet during the project?

In general students did not feel much improvement on this topic (only 30% in grade 8 and 18% in grade 12 answered Yes). Possibly, not enough time and emphasis was put on this issue during the project.

> Grade 12: "That one should be careful with documents on the Internet was clear to me even before. The way how to treat a source was helpful."

19 - Today the Internet is increasingly used to exchange information. Do you think this is a suitable medium to learn with in school (instead of a teacher or from books)?

In both classes students considered the Web as a possible source of information, but they would rely on the teacher's experience to better explain the learning contents and to guide them.

Grade 8	Grade 12
– Yes and no: yes, because there are more options to select from, no because the teacher can explain better.	– Only partially. The Internet is faster and offers more information about a topic, however, the trustworthiness and the quality of some sources is questionable and some information is represented poorly or not suitable for school.

Project work (Field notes)

At the beginning of each course, the researcher, together with a colleague system developer, and the teacher, organised a laboratory to describe the LearnWeb2.0 system to the students and to explain the learning goals. During the lessons in the classroom the researcher took field notes to record various aspects such as the interaction of the students amongst themselves or with the presenter, or their interaction with the LearnWeb2.0 system. A few remarks are listed below as a preliminary comparison of the two groups of learners.

Interaction in the classroom – Already during the personal presentation of the researcher and the developer, students in grade 8 showed great curiosity and willingness to interact. Most of them already knew what Web 2.0 tools are and some of them had already a Facebook or a YouTube account. In general during the course, comments were made in presence, not in the forum. Girls sat together and discussed in front of one PC, while boys worked more independently (each on one PC). In grade 12, during the introduction to the laboratory (e.g. what are Web 2.0 tools and LearnWeb2.0), students were attentive and listening, but did not interact very much, if unless asked to.

Interaction with the system – Students in 8th grade created their accounts easily by themselves using the registration Wizard and logged in, only one girl had to repeat the registration. During the initial presentation a student had already logged in and started searching for resources in LearnWeb2.0 (e.g. Bicycle MSX, Henry Main). A few children also opened the forum. 12th grade students also created their accounts easily by themselves using the Wizard and opened the forum.

Laboratory activities

Group leader and folder creation – Students in 8th grade chose a group leader and created their group folder. Since they used a few *particular* names (e.g. sexyhasen) for their group, the teacher reminded them that the administrator and the teacher can monitor the activities in the platform. Even though the children were asked to work actively in their group, they were also allowed to see what the others were doing to increase competition in the class, consequently a few children joined more than one group. A few played around for fun inventing inexistent users, deleting resources, or adding contents in their colleagues' Google documents. During the break most of the students remained in the class and started searching in LearnWeb2.0 (one group immediately searched the topic Wolfgang Borchert), or used the forum. A few checked their Facebook or YouTube accounts. After the break, students sat in different places (in different groups, so that they could discuss online) and officially started searching for resources about the author Wolfgang Borchert. Most of them easily found how to do it, only a few students asked how to open the Resource window that allows to select the Group folder. Students checked in their group folder to see all the resources collected by their colleagues in the group. The leader of group five found a group member called Lisa Lauren and she asked to delete this member from the group. Checking all groups as Administrator, the researcher found some other names which were not authorised and, in agreement with the teacher, decided to delete them from all groups.

In general students commented, rated and tagged the resources easily. Some children found some resources previously commented by the teacher and added these resources to their group as well. The goal of LearnWeb2.0 is to create a community which selects and comments good resources. So it was positive that the children reused what was already present in the community database.

Forum creation – Students in 8th grade started creating the forum for their group. The teacher warned them that she would be able to see what they write in the forum. A student asked if they could join the forum of another group and participate in their discussions. The researcher answered that the goal of the group forum is to discuss issues within the same group, to select resources to prepare the final presentation. A forum for the whole class is also available, but it is up to the teacher to use it or not. Children were a bit loud in the class, but they always used the system, they were curious and very clever in finding how to use the various functionalities.

In 12th grade the teacher asked students not to sit together in a group so that they could use comments and the forum to carry out online discussion, but they stayed where they were and talked to their colleagues in person.

Search – InterWeb limitation. When students in 8th grade searched for text, LearnWeb2.0 displayed only ten resources in the search result window, for this reason, the children started using the Google search-engine to search for additional resources. At the end of the first lesson one student asked whether he could continue to work with the platform from home.

GoogleDocs – Towards the end of the lesson in 8th grade, the presenter explained how to create a Google documents for the group and the teacher asked students to select relevant information about the collected resources and to prepare collaborative writing documents for the final class presentation. Using GoogleDocs students were able to collect written text from websites and add links and multimedia resources related to their subject of interest.

A few students already started filling in text and data in the GoogleDocs (a lot of text was found and copied from Wikipedia). A Google document was also used by the teacher to give a few introductory guidelines and to discuss the reliability of the resources. Students were asked to open their GoogleDocs and to answer the questions about reliability: search the Web for information about the resource (Author, original Website, contacts…etc.) to find additional details. Children in 8th grade needed more guidance to organise their work. One student in group GA5 pointed out that somebody else deleted the questions in the guidelines while he was answering (unfortunately GoogleDocs are public and it is difficult to prevent such episodes from happening). One girl in group GA3 noticed that their presentation about Wolfgang Borchert in GoogleDocs was empty, even though they had included some content previously: somebody deleted the content or they did not save it properly. Synchronous collaboration did not work well in the class because some students changed what the others were doing. Children complained to their colleagues when they changed their documents.

Students in 12th grade started to create Google documents in their group to collect relevant information about the collected resources and to prepare the final document for the class presentation. One student created two GoogleDocs and he asked how to delete one link. Students working in the same group collaborated in creating the GoogleDocs. They saw the changes made at the same time by their colleagues on the document and commented loudly on that. One student asked whether the GoogleDocs are public and everybody could read what they were doing. The developer explained that only people who know the URL of the document can open it, and the link is difficult to retrieve. A GoogleDocs document was also used by the teacher with a few guidelines to collect information and to discuss the reliability of the resources.

Collection Analysis

In general, the 8th grade groups collected more resources, and focused more on the author Borchert (e.g. biographies, videos, photos). The children worked in 11 groups, collecting about 10 to 12 resources each, with a minimum of one to a maximum of 18. Students in 12th grade collected fewer resources and focused more on the postwar period and its literature. In the following paragraphs, a discussion is given of a few examples of representative collections: two from grade 8 and two from grade 12.

8th grade

Group 1 collected three biographies of W. Borchert: a biography from an introductory course on German literature of the University of Tromso in Norway[36], the German Wikipedia page about Borchert, and a short biography from a project page about German history[37]. In addition, they collected a graph interpreting an essay of Borchert's[38], a YouTube video, as well as seven Flickr photos. In their presentation, students included three (!) biographies, a summary and a discussion on the short story "An diesem Dienstag", short summaries of two other essays and two pictures. They also quoted some resources that were not

36 http://www.hum.uit.no/ger/kafka/index2.htm

37 http://www.hdg.de/lemo/einfuehrung.html

38 http://home.bn-ulm.de/%7Eulschrey/home-unt.html

included in their LearnWeb2.0 group collection, for example from polunbi.de[39], which was in another group's resources as well.

Group 4 relied more on YouTube. They included three videos about the essays "Draussen vor der Tür", "Nachts schliefen die Ratten doch", and "Mein bleicher Bruder", as well as a five-part documentary about Borchert's life and work. They selected the same Tromso biography as Group 1, another short biography from a site about forbidden literature "Datenbank Schrift und Bild 1900–1960", a PDF-summary about "An diesem Dienstag"[40], and a page from the "European Students Review" journal[41] about "Die letzte Zigarette" with quotations from Borchert's short story.

They also selected a German Wikipedia article about postwar literature, a page about the history of a school "Die Schule zur NS-Zeit", and a Flickr photo. Finally, they selected a funny video of students giving a presentation on postwar literature. The collection is broad and covers a lot of different aspects; this is the most extensive collection from grade 8. The presentation starts with a biography of Borchert (from the LEMO project, selected by Group 1), it continues with a longer summary of "An diesem Dienstag" from Wikipedia, another short biography, a list of some essays, and a summary about the essay "Nachts schliefen die Ratten doch" from Wikipedia. Even though the presentation is fine, the variety of materials they selected in the LearnWeb2.0 collection is not well reflected.

12th grade

Group 1 probably gave the best presentation among the 12th grade groups. They collected two YouTube videos (i.e. "Nachts schlafen die Ratten doch", and "Das Gewitter"), as well as the YouTube documentary about Borchert in five parts. They selected the German and the English Wikipedia article on Borchert, and his biography from polunbi.de; two Wikipedia articles about "Kahlschlagliteratur" and "Nachkriegsliteratur", and one article[42] on the same topic. The resources include another page about "Schulen im Nationalsozialismus" and about "life in national socialism"[43], a website[44] including several quotations and texts from Borchert, a page about "An diesem Dienstag"[45], a very extensive website with

39 http://www.polunbi.de/
40 http://www.fundus.org/
41 http://work-out.org
42 http://www.literaturwelt.de
43 http://www.annefrankguide.com
44 http://www.gratis-gedicht.de
45 http://www.zum.de

school teaching materials, the PDF summary on Borchert[46] discussed in class, and a Flickr photo. This is a very good and a rich collection of resources. Indeed, Group 1's presentation shows the variety of resources, even though the YouTube material is not cited (probably it was not actually used, due to time constraints).

Group 3 collected fewer resources: one page about postwar literature[47], a YouTube video about the essay "Todesfuge" from Paul Celan, with no relationship to the topic, one Flickr photo, and the page about the "Inventur2008" school project from the Kantschule Falkensee, not at all related to the topic. In contrast with the small number of resources, Group 3's presentation is as good and well-structured as the one by Group 1, even though a bit shorter. Judging from the sources they cited in the final presentation, Group 3 members did not use LearnWeb2.0 much to collect their resources, but searched more often with other Web tools, including Google.

6.1.3 Comparison and conclusions

The previous section describes the project group work carried out in two German classes during the winter semester 2011. The LearnWeb2.0 system was used to explicitly include Web resources for teaching German literature at school. The experience at school was very useful for the researcher to evaluate the system in a different scenario, compared to that of the university, and to get a different point of view. In general the researchers involved in the study realised that younger children were more reactive and active during the experiment: they were curious and willing to experiment with the tool. The older students collaborated more seriously: they focused more on the collaborative tasks, but they added a smaller number of resources in their LearnWeb2.0 groups. Overall students found and selected good quality materials and they created very good presentations, also taking into account the short period of time (eight lessons).

Both classes provided useful feedback and suggestions on how to improve the LearnWeb2.0 system. In particular students asked for a larger number of search results and more diversification. They appreciated the opportunity of using a personalised environment to carry out their project work at school, as well as collaborative writing with GoogleDocs, even though there are still open issues with this. GoogleDocs should be used remotely (at home) and each student should work on different parts of the document so as not to interfere with the others. The teacher should suggest discussing the organisation of the roles

46 http://www.fundus.org

47 http://deutscheliteratur1.blogspot.com

and the structure of the GoogleDocs in the forum, to avoid conflicts while editing the presentation and to better organise the work. Since somebody deleted the original contents or they did not save their files properly, the researcher decided to save all the presentations locally on her computer, but a different solution should be found to store the final presentations without the risk of losing materials.

Additional details about the children's previous experiences and their feedback about reliability and trustworthiness of Internet resources for learning can be found in Holdack-Janssen and Marenzi (2012a). Further details about missing functionalities and the recent improvements of the system can be found in Section 6.3.

6.2 Second case study: teaching resources for Young English Language Learners (YELL)

> "Digital appliances can offer solutions, but we teachers and trainers must ask the right questions and look for the answers that suit our own educational context".
>
> (Maria Bortoluzzi, in Bortoluzzi & Marenzi, 2014)

At the beginning of 2012 a teacher and researcher working at the University of Udine, in Italy, asked to use the LearnWeb2.0 platform to support the YELL[48] (*Young English Language Learners*) project. The collaboration with the YELL group of pre-service or in-service teachers is an interesting opportunity to test LearnWeb2.0 in a new scenario since participants do not work in a class, but they form a real online community to share resources and experiences related to their work. The collaboration with the YELL group is still ongoing at the time of writing, but the experience has already been useful for the developers and for the researcher in terms of improving the system and providing the customisation of several features according to the YELL community requirements. The continuous feedback and the interest in using the system during the last period gave the researcher a lot of good ideas and motivation for further reflections. The remarks already received from the YELL community and the resulting new functionalities implemented in the third release of LearnWeb2.0 are described in Section 6.3. The following paragraphs give an account of the motivation for the YELL project (section 6.2.1), a description of the YELL pilot study (Section 6.2.2) and a short overview of the preliminary feedback resulting from the first pilot study within the community (Section 6.2.3). More details about the Udine

48 http://yell.uniud.it/

experience can be found in Bortoluzzi and Marenzi "*YELLing for Partnership: A social platform for sharing practice and reflection in teacher training for language learning*" (in press). Finally Section 6.4 provides a discussion and directions for further developments.

6.2.1 YELL scenario

2012 Udine (IT) YELL: Teaching resources for *Young English Language Learners*

Pre-service and in-service teacher training for primary and nursery school teachers in Italy has become in recent years a relevant issue for trainers and university courses especially in the field of English as foreign or second language. In spite of the multilingual and intercultural context in which teachers work in today's nursery and primary schools, the recent reform[49] of pre-service teacher training for school teachers in Italy has made English the only dominant foreign language and virtually the only foreign/second language taught in primary and nursery schools. In this context, experienced school teachers are often recruited to teach ESL (*English as a Second Language*) to children even if their own proficiency in the language is low, and they are not trained in second language teaching.

Within this context, a group of trainers, trainees and school teachers have decided to transform a problem into an opportunity and offer to a wider community of teachers a peer-learning peer-teaching platform in which trainee teachers, school teachers and teacher trainers can share, discuss, find materials, reflect on their practice and improve on it.

In collaboration with the L3S Research Center, the YELL community started using the LearnWeb2.0 social platform that has been adapted to their needs for improving language skills, reflecting on learning and teaching planning and practices, gaining confidence as teachers through sharing, developing and sharing quality and innovative materials and Web resources. In the YELL scenario, the LearnWeb2.0 platform is intended as a virtual environment to meet the teaching community (i.e. trainees, teachers and trainers), to share and negotiate ideas and collaborate creatively (through the community forum); it is also used as a search engine (to search for and explore resources on the Web), and as a multimodal and multimedia repository for teaching and learning materials (to develop and share innovative coursework materials with peers and re-contextualise it transforming it into peer-teaching and peer-learning materials). It is intended to

49 D.M. 249, 10 September, 2010.

offer a shared virtual space but also an individually customised space for learning from, sharing and discussing with colleagues, future colleagues and trainees. The evaluation of the training activities are carried out through observation, logs and surveys about its different uses. Feedback from participants about the education assets and the perceived drawbacks of this virtual community and environment will feed into its future developments. According to the teacher: "LearnWeb2.0 for YELL has the potential of becoming an innovative use of social platform for teaching and learning. It is open to multilingual uses and it can represent a precious means of sharing resources for community and minority languages in which teacher training materials tend to be less widely accessible to trainees".

6.2.2 The pilot study

During the winter semester 2012 the teacher in Udine used the LearnWeb2.0 platform with her students attending the course of English as a foreign language for young and very young learners ("Corso di studi di Formazione primaria e dell'Infanzia") at the University of Udine, in Italy. Students participating in the case-study attended the third year of a four years undergraduate course which allows them to teach in primary and secondary schools. The group consisted of 26 postgraduate trainees (25 female and 1 male), all Italian native speakers and foreign users of English. They had all chosen to follow the non-obligatory English course and they all had (at the very least) a B1.2 linguistic competence[50] in English, while some had already a B2 competence. The majority of the group was between 22 and 26 years of age (19 trainees, the age range of the other 7 is between 30 and 44).

The sample is rather small but representative of the pre-service teacher-training programme at the University of Udine (the overwhelming majority of female students, their age range and ICT literacy level for learning and teaching). The English course in presence with two teachers lasted 50 hours in total.

The LearnWeb2.0 system was included in the YELL Web portal so that it is accessible as a tool among other opportunities and initiatives and more integrated in the activities of the community. The relevance of the YELL platform as a means of creating a professional community that could last beyond their English course was mentioned at the start of the course: it was explained that, by using the YELL platform, the trainees had the opportunity to become part of a collaborative virtual community that could accompany them beyond the end of

50 Common European Framework of Reference. http://www.coe.int/t/dg4/education/elp/elp-reg/cefr_EN.asp

the English course and during their future professional life as teachers of English to children. All members of the community created a personal account using the same registration Wizard and accessed the shared space where every YELL user could contribute and participate in the discussions. To better integrate the system within the activities of the group and to introduce it smoothly to the participants, the teacher, in collaboration with the researcher, designed and suggested a few preliminary tasks to be carried out, so that participants could start using the platform and get used to the searching and collaboration functionalities. This strategy resulted very successful since it involved the participants more actively in the activities, they learned in advance how to use the system, and they were more enthusiastic in using the functionalities available during the actual project work. The list of tasks, previously discussed and agreed with the researcher, is reported in the following frame.

Preliminary tasks to get used to the system functionalities

The YELL website and platform will be used throughout the course to post materials online and to share resources. Let's explore it and become serious YELLERS!

1. Explore the main YELL website (http://yell.uniud.it/).
    1. What are the most important sections for you?
    2. What would you add which is not present?
    3. What would you expand on?
    4. What is less relevant for you as a future teacher of English?
2. Search the resources of the different groups (Materials and Projects) on YELL platform (http://learnweb.l3s.uni-hannover.de/lw/)
    5. Click on all the groups and decide what are going to be the most relevant for you after you have explored them.
    6. Tag the resources and comment on them. Why do you think this activity can be relevant for you as a teacher?
    7. Learning goal: relevance of tags and comments.
3. Learning how to search using the YELL platform.
    8. Think of a keyword you find relevant for you as a teacher, go on a web search using the facilities of the platform: refine your search, expand or restrict it according to what you need.
    9. Share and upload one important link you find in this way.
4. Focus on some sections which you find particularly relevant for you in the link:

10. Add to the YELL platform five websites that are not yet present among the platform resources. Of course you have to check that they have not been uploaded first.
11. Please, keep track of what you have added and be ready to explain why you think those sites are relevant for teachers.

5. Add to the YELL LearnWeb2.0 platform one or more websites you know of and are relevant for you and are not yet present in the platform. Keep track of what you added.
6. Using the forum, ask your classmates to comment on and tag the websites you added.
7. How do you think this platform can be useful to you as a language teacher?
8. Please talk to a classmate/tutor in school who does not follow the English course and present the YELL LearnWeb2.0 platform to her/him. Can you record her/his reaction?

After these preliminary training activities to use the platform, during the winter semester 2012 the YELL platform was used to: searching and exploration of resources for teaching and learning; annotation and discussion among trainees and experts of resources for teaching and learning (tagging, commenting, annotating resources collaboratively); upload and aggregation of resources in a multimedia repository for teaching and learning materials (share with peers and use their materials, comment on them and contribute to them). The course teachers emphasised the relevance of collaboration offline and online. Participants carried out the activities mostly online; the platform was used also at times in class where, however, there was only one computer connected to the Web. The final project, which contributed to the coursework assessment, was finally posted on the platform to be shared with fellow trainees and future colleagues.

From the early stages of the pilot study, the researcher started collecting direct feedback for the teacher and from the YELL users via e-mail, or through Skype meetings. This close collaboration while using the system was very useful for collecting specific requirements and for addressing those requirements on time by providing new ad hoc LearnWeb2.0 functionalities. In addition, a formal evaluation was prepared to collect feedback and comments from the students through a final questionnaire at the end of the course in February 2013. The questionnaire is provided in Appendix 4. The analysis of the results, in particular as regards the evaluation of LearnWeb2.0 as YELL platform, is reported in the following section (6.2.3). Additional details about the evaluation results of this case study are reported in the journal article Bortoluzzi and Marenzi

"*YELLing for collaborative learning in teacher education: Users' voices about the social platform LearnWeb2.0*" (2014).

6.2.3 Feedback and evaluation

Filling in the YELL questionnaire was not obligatory, but strongly advised (while having no influence on the final mark). 26 out of 32 students, that is all the students regularly attending classes, filled in the final questionnaire. The questionnaire included research questions divided into two sections: Section 1 was about the use of the YELL portal (yell.uniud.it), Section 2 asked about the use of the YELL social platform (LearnWeb2.0) both for studying and for professional purposes. The following paragraphs focus on the feedback collected in the second part of the questionnaire and, more specifically, on the LearnWeb2.0 functionalities. The questions required the respondents to rate the platform's functionalities on a scale from 1 to 10. The results showed the general appreciation of the users for the platform, but some of the results were contradictory. As regards sharing, users appreciated sharing resources within the groups and among the groups (rated mainly as useful and as rather easy to do) but in the open-ended answers 14 out of 26 students remarked that the platform could be more user friendly. The qualitative analysis of the open-ended answers was done manually by the teacher in Udine. More details about the students' perception of the platform in terms of usability and professional relevance can be found in Bortoluzzi and Marenzi (2014).

A contradictory aspect that was revealed in the quantitative section of the questionnaire was the use of tags: users found tags rather useful (Figure 21) and easy (Figure 22), but then when they were asked how much they used this functionality, the answer was surprisingly low (Figure 23).

One of the respondent even noticed that she only tagged her own resources, not what other colleagues posted. These results are in keeping with the study "*Evaluating the benefits of social annotation for collaborative search*" (Abel et al., 2009a) where social annotations are only considered as secondary relevance indicators for search results: title and description are viewed as more important. It has been shown that, when sharing resources in a relatively small corpus, users prefer writing comments rather than using light-weight mechanisms such as tagging. Organising resources in meaningful groups is enough for categorising, sharing and re-finding materials. Nevertheless, in an open-ended answer one trainee mentioned the use of comments in a very positive way saying:

MDMB 368 'The aspect I like best in the YELL social platform is the possibility to comment the different projects and also to express ideas/opinions.'

Figure 21: Tags and comments (how helpful)

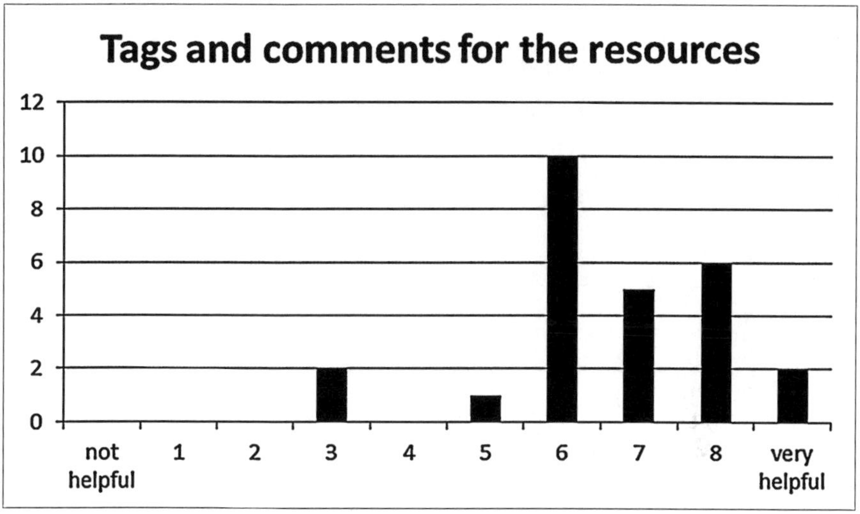

Figure 22: Creating tags and comments (how easy)

Some answers in the feedback can be grouped into two categories related to *problems* the users encountered while using the platform (such as: lack of user-friendliness and intuitiveness of use, need for a clear user-guide, need for more

Figure 23: Creating tags and comments (how often)

time in class to learn how to use the platform) and *suggestions* to solve the problems they noticed (allowing more time for the learning process of using a new tool, more widespread use of platform needed to share experience with more teachers/lecturers, etc., request to introduce a chat system). In fact during the case study the second release of LearnWeb2.0 was used. Thanks to the feedback collected through the questionnaire, the problems related with the user-friendliness, accessibility and usability of the platform have been already improved at the time of writing, as described in the following Section 6.3.

6.3 LearnWeb2.0 (v.3): new customised features

The following sections summarise the new functionalities introduced in the third release of the LearnWeb2.0 system (http://learnweb.l3s.uni-hannover.de/lw/, online at the time of writing) according to the users' requirements. The experience at the Leibnizschule in Hannover and with the YELL initiative in Udine was very useful to test the efficacy of the support provided by LearnWeb2.0 in addressing different requirements and learning goals. At the Leibnizschule the focus was more on pedagogical issues related to formal education. The YELL project gave a more open point of view of a community of adults oriented to their future work as teachers in school. Both groups provided useful feedback and suggestions on how to improve the LearnWeb2.0 system: students at school provided very pragmatic feedback and requests; the YELL teachers also requested structural modifications (e.g. welcome page) and raised ethical issues (e.g. thumb down) as described below.

In the following paragraphs the feedback collected in both case studies is listed, together with the resulting update and newest functionalities implemented in the third release of the LearnWeb2.0 system. The features are listed according to the order in which they occurred while using the platform (from registration and login to the actual use of the services). The group of users, students or trainee teachers, who requested the corresponding feature, are displayed in brackets. Additional details can be found in Marenzi et al. (2010), Marenzi and Nejdl (2012), and Marenzi and Zerr (2012).

6.3.1 General access

Registration Wizard (8th grade) – Using the same Wizard to register the accounts for the class every participant can see the list of the groups in the Group Overview table and join or leave a group at will.

Welcome message (YELL) – The teacher would like to send a welcome message (e-mail at the registration) that new users will find in their mailbox when the user creates her/his account (after they have signed in). A button will be provided in the YELL profile so that the administrator can switch on and off the feature at need. This has not yet been implemented.

Home page and login (8th and 12th grade) – After the logout there was no login possibility: to login again the user had to start from the Home page once more. The login has been provided in all pages in the new release. Users can now go back to their personal home page using the LearnWeb2.0 logo on the top left corner of each page.

E-mail address (8th and 12th grade) – One student asked to delete the e-mail address she had already typed in into her profile. It was not possible to delete the e-mail address if the user typed it in during registration. It was mandatory to type in the e-mail address at registration, it was possible to type in even a fake e-mail address, but it was not yet possible to leave the field empty at the time of the course. This has been fixed in the new release. Now the e-mail address field is no longer mandatory. If the user provides an e-mail address at registration, s/he can edit and change it afterwards in the user's profile.

Welcome page (YELL) – For the YELL community it was important to identify the group and to welcome new users. The moderator asked to put the logo on the front page and requested editing rights for the welcome message in order to add new information if needed. She also requested a User Guide summarising the main features of LearnWeb2.0 [The User Guide is provided in Appendix 5].

User's profile (YELL) – Users can easily update their profile and change their password. In addition, for YELL users it would be really nice to add images and text in the profile (apart from the picture/photo) and to customise one's space as a teacher or trainee maybe with links to one's own blog, or website, or Facebook account. Currently this is not a high priority for the general users, but the developers will keep this suggestion in mind.

Change/retrieve password (8th and 12th grade) – From the LearnWeb2.0 home page users can now retrieve lost passwords.

6.3.2 Search functionalities

Search results (8th and 12th grade) – In particular children asked for a larger number of search results and more diversification. Infinite scrolling was missing in LearnWeb2.0: when students searched for text, LearnWeb2.0 displayed only ten resources in the search result window. A larger number of search results and more diversification have been provided in the new release (Figure 24) first through *paging* and then through infinite scrolling.

When many resources related to a specific query are already stored in LearnWeb2.0 the first search results page is full of LearnWeb2.0 resources and fewer are displayed from the Web. Sometimes there are also pointers to old resources which have been deleted (for example when a video is no longer available in YouTube). In this case, the pointers to resources that are no longer available on the original source are not displayed in LearnWeb2.0.

Figure 24: LearnWeb2.0 search results window (v.3) – multimedia results

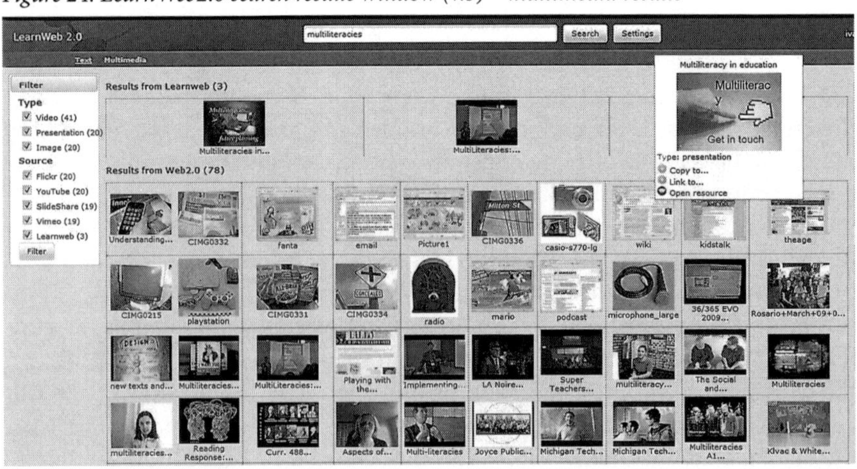

Visualisation of search results

Ranking (YELL) – For the YELL users it was important to be able to improve the order of resources, especially with a large number of data. The visualisation of the search results has been improved so that the results already stored in LearnWeb2.0 are displayed earlier in the top part of the page: the newest resources are visualised first, in the top left corner of the search results page. Furthermore, using the Filter on the left, it is possible to add or to exclude from the search results resources which are already stored in the LearnWeb2.0 database (Figure 24).

Customisation has been also requested, so that the order of the resources can be personalised by the user according to the relevance (stars) or alphabetically. Ideally it should be possible to choose customisation for each single group. In the future the possibility for the user to rank the resources according to the title (in alphabetical order), the date of retrieval, the type and the relevance (stars) will be introduced. This will be an option that users can choose in their profile and that will be valid for all the groups users are involved in.

Textual results (8th and 12th grade) – Students were asked to find textual information for their project work besides multimedia resources. *Bing* text search results have been added (Figure 25) to return *Wikipedia* entries as well as any other page on the Web.

Text vs Multimedia resources (YELL) – The difference between *text* and *multimedia* resources for users can be misleading. Web pages are displayed as a list in the text view (Figure 25). For the community of YELL teachers, Web

Figure 25: LearnWeb2.0 search results window (v.3) – text results

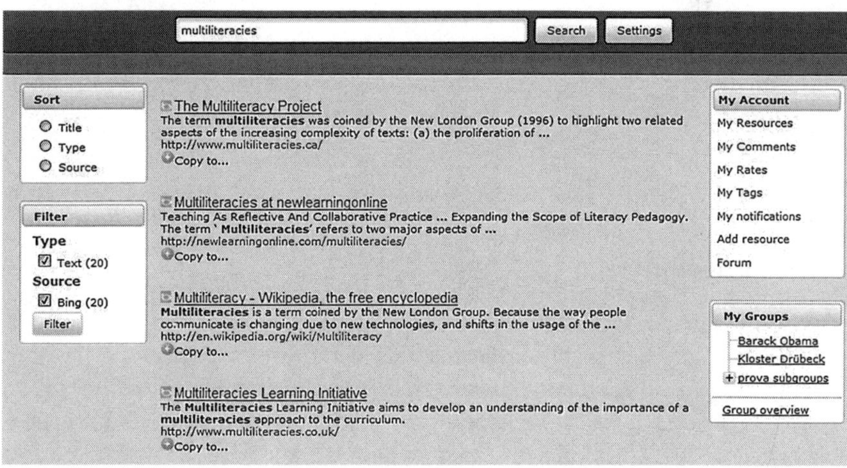

pages are intuitively multimodal since they include various types of resources (e.g. written text, pictures, videos, banners …). In the third release the search results are distinguished in Web, images and videos.

Thumbnails (YELL) have been provided for PDFs so that the first page of the document is displayed as a preview. PDFs files stored in LearnWeb2.0 are handled as text in the results list view.

Advanced search (YELL) – dealing with various topics and various groups, the resources were spread among various folders and were difficult to retrieve. Users can now search more precisely inside LearnWeb2.0 by selecting specific groups from a drop-down menu (Figure 26).

Figure 26: Group selection option

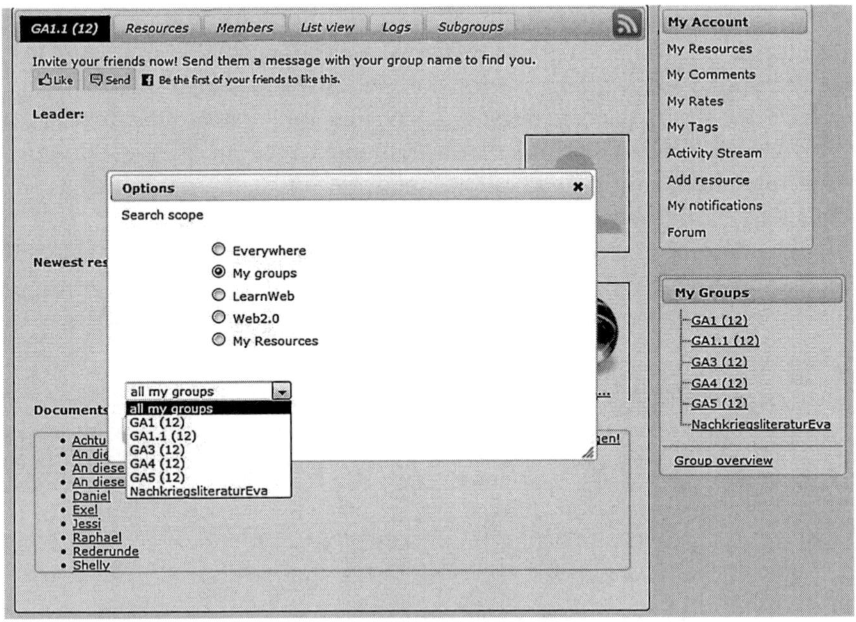

6.3.3 Collaboration functionalities

Edit resources (YELL) – Previously it was not possible to edit resources (e.g. edit the title, or change comments and tags). This feature was particularly important in both scenarios to correct typos or to refine the description of the resources. The edit function has been extended now to title and comments, and it is possible to delete tags. Additional information has been added to the single resource such as the author, the group where the resource has been stored, and the source (i.e. where the resource was originally found).

Thumb down (YELL) – The moderator raised the ethic issue of the *thumb up* and *thumb down* rating system, which can be read as a form of judgment, or even worse as a verdict. For this reason this control has been hidden in the YELL environment. Only stars-rating is available to vote the relevance of resources.

Delete resources (YELL) – The YELL administrator can add, delete and check anything s/he deems useful for the group. This means that if somebody posts materials that are irrelevant, offensive or outside copyright, the administrator can delete them. Single users can only delete what they post, not even the links established by others (that is the links of resources across groups).

Open resources (YELL) – When opening a resource, both in the search result window and in the groups, the content appeared in the same window (replacing LearnWeb2.0) and not in a new window. For this reason users would close the window and exit the platform. To go back to the previous LearnWeb2.0 page instead, they should have used the "back" button in their Browser. This problem has been solved and now resources are opened in a new independent window.

Groups – A new layout has been designed to present the collection of resources in a more social network and community-oriented style. The visualisation has been improved so that the description of the resources is clearer and more complete (Figure 27).

Additional metadata have been provided for each resource to determine the group where the resource is stored, as well as the author (i.e. who stored the resource in LearnWeb2.0 first). In the group overview, the latest resource shown was the oldest instead of the newest. This has been changed according to the students' request. Furthermore, it is now possible to copy or to move resources between groups using the "Copy to…" or the "Link to…" button. "Copy to" is used to create a new instance of a resource, which can have different meanings or interpretations in different contexts (for example the picture of an eagle as an animal in biology or as a metaphor in poetry). "Link to" allows to create in the new group a pointer to the original resource, maintaining the same annotations and descriptions. In this way the same resource appears in two different groups with the same metadata.

Terminology (YELL) – The teacher of the YELL group also raised the issue concerning the term 'leader' which is displayed to identify the author and moderator of a group. From the technical point of view, it is necessary to identify the member who creates the group, in order to give her/him administrative rights for that. In the teacher's view however, since LearnWeb2.0 is a collaborative platform, the terminology should highlight this equality and

Figure 27: New group resources view

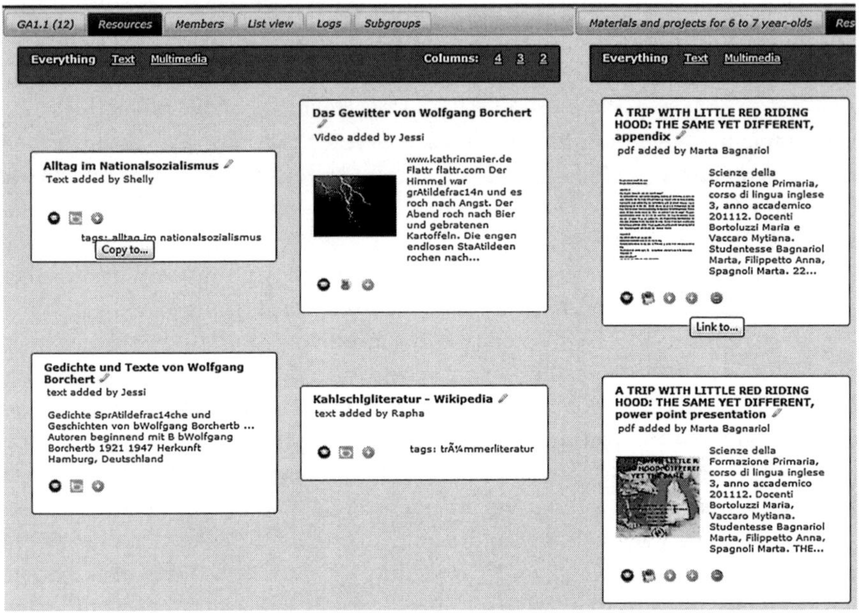

collaboration instead of defining 'leaders'; for this reason another term should be adopted in the future.

Subgroups (YELL) – Groups may also include subgroups to better organise the resources in several folders and provide a list of activities carried out by the group members. Subgroups have been visualised as *daughter* groups not as *sister* groups (that is to say indented in a lower level) to distinguish them in a tree-like menu.

GoogleDocs (8th and 12th grade) – Google documents have been integrated to provide collaborative writing facilities and allow creative production of learning artifacts by students. Teachers can also use Google documents to create activities or questionnaires, or to coordinate project work (for example a Google document could be used to create a timetable to set up objectives and shared goals, to schedule the activities, and to keep track of the progresses).

The evaluation showed that collaborative writing using Google documents is still tricky due to issues such as anonymity: documents are external to LearnWeb2.0 and public, causing privacy issues and making it possible for students to play around for fun. Since users appear anonymously, it is difficult to control their activities. The problem of anonymity and public documents should be solved using personal accounts (i.e. each student should create a Google account so as to be recognisable as a user).

In 12th grade the request was to delete GoogleDocs links if accidentally created. This functionality has been provided in the new release of the system.

Presentation editor – The presentation of work is the crucial final step of any learning process. A collaborative presentation editor has been added recently to allow the group to present the results as a slideshow. It is a shared space for collaborative presentation of the content of the group such as pictures, videos, documents, and comments. Specific tools should support and encourage users not only to share resources but also to elaborate and creatively develop shared results. The new presentation editor allows users to create presentations on the fly using the resources from their groups without the need of switching platforms or using different tools. The group members may work together to select the resources from the group and organise them to be presented in various contexts.

To keep the user informed about what happens in the platform, two notification features have been provided, namely the RSS feeds and the activity logs.

RSS feeds – "As Web 2.0 is a very dynamic information environment, new learning materials can arrive at any moment. To support ongoing learning activities LearnWeb2.0 can keep its users updated on new resources relating to queries, even if these resources were published after the search query was issued. This functionality enables users to monitor new resources corresponding to a particular learning task. For each searching activity LearnWeb2.0 provides an RSS feed which can be used as a standing query in an RSS aggregator. This feed can be shared with co-searchers to inform them about mutual search activities and support exchanges of search results. In the top right corner of each group view there is an orange RSS feed button which allows subscribing to the feed and receiving a notification as soon as a new resource is added to the group" (Marenzi et al., 2010, p.206). Recently the possibility of inviting friends to join the LearnWeb2.0 groups through Facebook has been introduced (Figure 28).

Figure 28: RSS Feed and Facebook invitation

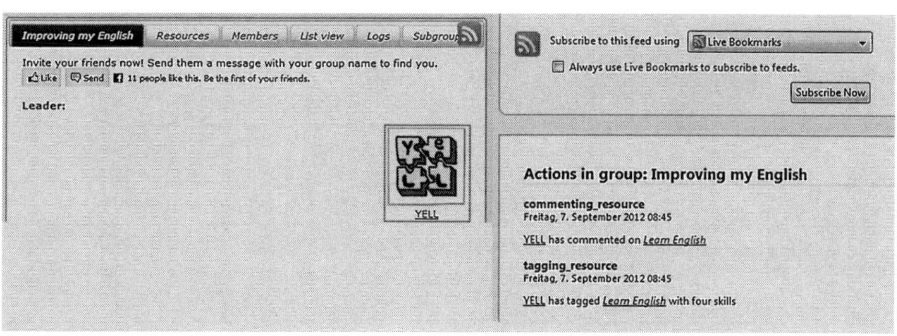

Activity logs – providing support for community building

LearnWeb2.0 provides three types of logs:

1. In the user's profile the history of the users' activities gives a visualisation of the activities carried out by a single user (Figure 29). The activities carried out

Figure 29: User's activity logs

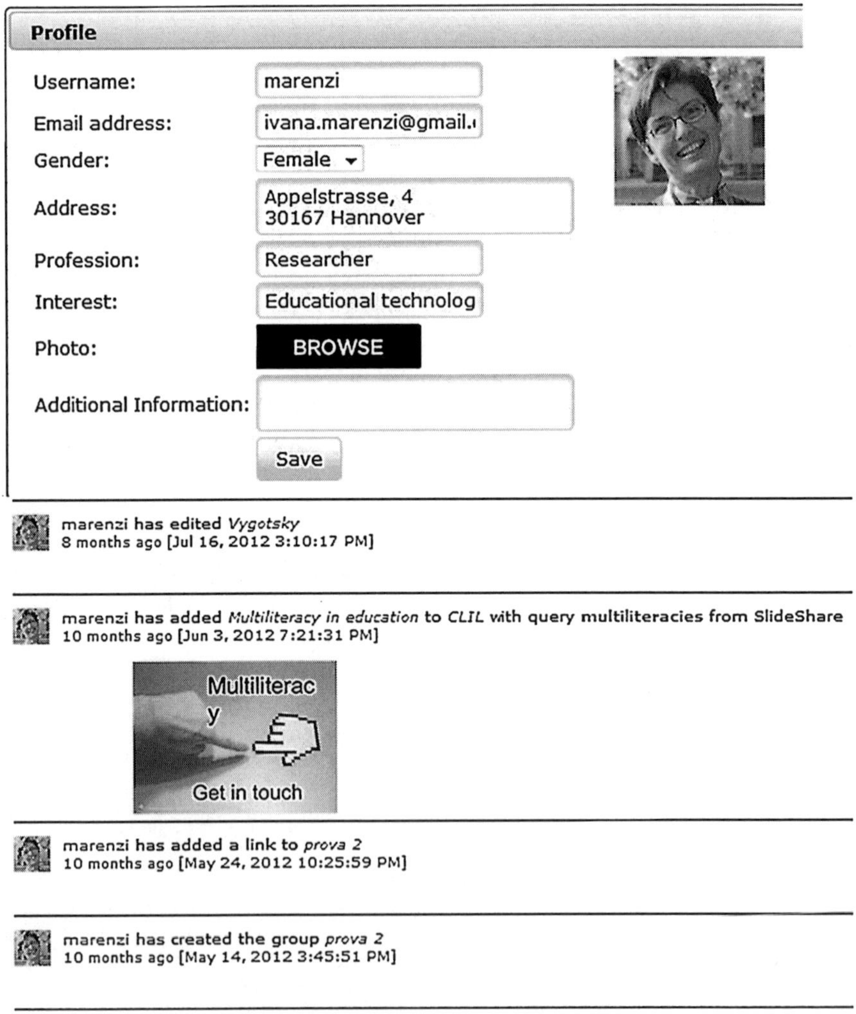

by the members of a specific group are listed in chronological order in the group view (Figure 30).

2. Visualisation of the *logs as networks (Facebook/social)*: activity of the members of the single group. The log list provides information about the user who saved the resource, the group where the resource is stored, the time when the resource was stored and possible tags assigned to the resource. A click on the thumbnail allows the opening of the resource view directly from the log list.

Figure 30: CLIL – Laboratory Group activity log

3. In the "My account" menu the user finds the groups activity stream which provides a list of all activities carried out in all groups belonging to the same environment.

These activity views have been introduced with the goal of developing a sense of community and belonging so that participants can be updated about what is happening in the virtual community and find their relation with the others. The social networking layer helps create a sense of awareness and responsibility needed in order to sustain a community, and the group represents the collection of the users' knowledge.

The YELL administrator asked to collapse the logs overview-list in the welcome page. This customisation has been introduced.

6.4 Conclusions and directions for further developments

The previous sections presented two case studies carried out during the second evaluation cycle of the LearnWeb2.0 system in order to collect and refine users' requirements and improve the pedagogical efficacy of the system accordingly. At the end of the second cycle, a summary and comparison between all the various scenarios involved in the research study can be made.

Short comparison of the four scenarios

CLIL and ESP

In the two scenarios carried out during the first evaluation cycle in 2010, the learning activities focused mainly on learning the contents and producing a final project work, rather than augmenting the social interaction between participants. In the CLIL Seminar, the reflexive part on the "practice of teaching" and "learning to teach" was guided through materials suggested by the teacher (in the Reader or in STUD-IP), or collected by the trainees from books or online (in LearnWeb2.0). In Hannover, as well as in the ESP course in Pavia, the final goal of the project work was the creation of educational materials for future CLIL classes (in Hannover), or the creation of a corpus of PIF videos about medical topics (in Pavia). The project work was *product-oriented*, focusing on learning activities and on producing learning content. The role of the researcher was mainly to provide technical support for task-specific activities such as searching and sharing resources, and less on enhancing or moderating social interaction or online collaboration between the participants. The task for trainee teachers for example was not to design specifically an *online* teaching unit for their future students, but was rather more open. They chose a traditional format to design their final teaching unit. For this reason, during the seminar trainee teachers were not specifically instructed in online interaction and dynamics, and also did not interact much online to carry out their tasks. Sharing knowledge and results was done mainly in the classroom with face-to-face reports and discussions.

Leibnizschule

During the second evaluation cycle, the experience with the 8th and 12th grade classrooms at the Leibnizschule high school was more *process centred.* Since students were younger and needed more guidance to carry out their tasks, the teacher paid attention to the fine-grade structure of the learning activities. The first activity was a *jigsaw*, where a more complex task was explicitly broken down into parts which could be mastered individually or in smaller groups. In the end, the partial solutions were exchanged and summarised as a final solution. Even though the *jigsaw* activity was carried out in the classroom, this approach contributed to generating 'positive interdependence' between learners (Swain, 1993; Szewkis et al., 2011) who were required to acquire specific expertise to exchange their knowledge with each other to build a final common understanding. This interaction was also present during the rest of the course (both in the classroom and online). Students were more active online and willing to interact socially with colleagues of other groups, for example in the Forum, even though sometimes they played around for fun inventing for example inexistent users.

YELL

The YELL experience was much more focused on the *potential of the community* (interaction and sharing with other teachers) and enhancing social competencies (strategy of community of teachers sharing their experiences). YELL is a community of teachers where interactions and networking are considered important aspects to foster professional development. One of the main goals (shared between teachers, trainees, researchers and developers) is to contribute and maintain a peer-learning and peer-teaching environment in which participants can find and share materials and ideas, reflect on their professional practice, and learn from other colleagues, also from different levels of schooling. The activities go beyond the specific course, but they are meant as an opportunity to create a network of experts to serve as a reference during the future professional life of the participants. For this reason, participants were more eager to interact online and to consider the YELL platform as the main learning and sharing environment. This perspective led the learning activities and facilitated the feedback response that addressed both the acceptance of the LearnWeb2.0/YELL platform and the needs of the community. In this respect the answers users gave on their perception of their identity within the community are interesting. For example, many respondents wrote that "being part of the community promotes teachers' creativity offering new stimuli and peer collaboration", and also that "belonging to this community will be even more relevant when they are full-time teachers in school". All respondents considered the platform to be a useful professional tool. However the questionnaire showed that more guidance in the professional use of the system is required. Interestingly, there seems to be a correlation between problems using the platform and the fact that users had never used a social platform before for professional purposes. The difficulties some of them experienced in using YELL for learning and for their professional life may have been influenced by some aspects of the system release they used, but were certainly increased by their inexperience with social ICT tools for professional use. 19 out of 26 trainee teachers responded they had never used a professional platform before; one did not answer. The six users who gave examples of platforms they use, listed websites, blogs or portals. Only two out of 26 gave examples of social platforms. They gave two examples neither of which was specifically professional: www.anobii.com (shared bookshelves) and Facebook for learning individually with fellow trainees.

According to the teacher in Udine, "This confirms that the use of the YELL platform in teacher education is a positive step ahead in *multiliteracy* for learning and teaching". In order to support the process of learning how to use the platform efficiently for professional purposes, expert users will be identified who can welcome new users, show them around and introduce them to the community (expert YELLERS). This will also establish stronger links with school communities.

In light of the positive experience with the YELL pilot study, in 2013 the teacher in Udine decided to enlarge the community extending it to more experts users and creating the TELL (*Teen English Language Learners*) group. Since the YELL/TELL scenario is still ongoing, the researcher expects to collect further interesting feedback from the next phases of the project.

Thanks to the feedback and the insights already collected during the various evaluations from the students and from the teachers using the system in the various scenarios, the researcher is much more confident about supporting users (teachers and students) in their course designs, including tasks which can be supported by LearnWeb2.0, and she finds it easier to understand when technology is necessary and helpful (or not) in improving teaching and learning in specific situations. From the technical point of view, it was possible to identify many things that did not work and many aspects that had to be improved. The current version of the LearnWeb2.0 platform has overcome most of the problems raised by this group of users. It speaks of the quality of the initial ideas and architecture that the new release inherited most of the initial ideas and functionalities, but in addition provided them in a much more integrated and user-friendly way. In addition to the improvements to the current release, the researcher is already discussing with the developers the design and implementation of new features that can improve the system usability and collaboration between users (a short anticipation of future directions is given in Section 9.2).

In particular, the researcher realised the need for a stronger pedagogical framework as a basis for further development of LearnWeb2.0. Chapter 7 describes this new research framework and the corresponding investigations towards the adoption and enhancement of the *multiliteracies* approach.

III
New Research Framework and Conclusions

7 New research framework and refined research questions

> "[…] *literacy* education is about actively communicating in an unfamiliar context and learning from your successes and mistakes."
>
> (Kalantzis & Cope, 2008, p. 203)

At this stage of the research, after three years of evaluation and continuous change, the system had improved a lot from the usability point of view. On the other hand, the need for a stronger pedagogical base was urgent. While at the beginning, the main goal of the research was to enhance the development and the usability of LearnWeb2.0 as collaborative search and sharing system, in 2012 the researcher realised the need to re-route the basic research questions towards a new pedagogical framework.

The researcher decided to look more deeply into the *multiliteracies* approach to better embed LearnWeb2.0 in an educational context. The *multiliteracies* and the *Learning by Design* approach were chosen because they suggest a flexible approach to pedagogy which takes into account the modern social changes and stresses learner autonomy and creativity. These issues are effectively supported by LearnWeb2.0 since it allows searching for authentic resources on the Web. Often it is difficult to find good and authentic material on the Web since a lot of resources are localised and teachers spend a lot of time preparing suitable materials for their classrooms. LearnWeb2.0 provides tools for collaborative search which can help teachers and students find reliable and authentic materials for their classroom; the LearnWeb2.0 annotation functionality and the forum support discussion and *critical thinking*; the opportunity to collect and organise multimedia resources in collaborative groups and folders can help students in *creatively* designing new learning materials for different contexts.

The new research questions investigated the pedagogical setup and the project design more closely in order to better support the learning process in language courses at university level. In particular they investigate:

- *How can the LearnWeb2.0 functionalities be integrated with the pedagogical notion of the multiliteracies approach, and how can this integration be represented through an appropriate model?*
- *What course design should be used? How should LearnWeb2.0 be used in various learning scenarios?*

To answer these questions, the researcher studied the *multiliteracies* approach and the *Learning by Design* framework thoroughly to reinforce the pedagogical setup of the doctoral work research and the application of LearnWeb2.0 in various scenarios.

7.1 Multiliteracies pedagogy

The development of digitalised technologies has been influencing the social community (culture and ways of communication), as well as what constitutes *literacy*. In the past literacy was centered mainly on basic language skills (i.e. reading, writing, listening, and speaking) with the introduction and use of new technologies and visual texts, "we now encounter multiple kinds of literacies which are embedded in multimodal texts" (Cope & Kalantzis, 2000, p. 5).

The traditional literacy teaching, based on the ability to read, write, listen and speak a language is no longer enough to ensure that all students benefit from education in ways that allow them to participate fully and equally in public, community, and economic life. The *multiliteracies* pedagogy provides a framework for dealing with the changes in our digital society. In their manifesto *A pedagogy of multiliteracies: Designing social futures* the New London Group authors coined the term *multiliteracies* which addresses *textual multiplicity* as "the multiplicity of communication channels and mass media, as well as cultural and linguistic diversity" (Cope & Kalantzis, 2000, p. 9). The manifesto is influenced by the observation, that in modern society, working, public and private lives are influenced by technological development and by cultural changes, and people have to cope with a pluralism of situations and multiple social layers that are in complex relation to each other. In this context, learning to understand different ways of communication and different languages is very important in order to better understand the world around us.

The New London Group authors suggested that a new pedagogy is required to support this different learning style, as well as tools that support teachers and students in this context. In particular for language teaching and learning, grammar and vocabulary are not considered as crucial as they were in the past, instead the focus has to move to context and the various communication channels we engage with. There is the urgency of a renovation of literacy pedagogy pointing out the need for "A Pedagogy of Multiliteracies" which goes beyond the traditional curriculum focused on teaching grammar and standard forms of a language. Literacy is not a matter of correct usage, rather it is a way of communicating: we should teach how a language is used in a specific context or in a variety of discourse occurrences. The New London Group authors argued that "the mission of education is to ensure that all students benefit from learning in ways that allow them to participate fully in public, community, and economic life"

(NLG, Cadzen et al., 1996, p. 60). *Multiliteracies* pedagogy is expected to play a particularly important role in fulfilling this mission. This might involve activities such as simulating collaboration, project work, commitment, and creative involvement.

The *multiliteracies* approach shares many ideas with the constructivist concepts of scaffolding and zone of proximal development (Vygotsky, 1978) where the basic idea is that cognitive development is directly linked to social development and that the way a student learns derives from the environment in which s/he lives, from the teacher's guidance or from the collaboration with more capable peers. It adds additional important elements though. First, the notion of *Design* plays a central role in the *multiliteracies* approach. Design includes three aspects: *Available Designs* (available meaning-making resources and conventions of meaning in a particular context, which have to be gathered and understood); *Designing* (the process of shaping meaning, which involves re-presentation, transforming, re-contextualisation of the Available Designs); and *The Redesigned* (the outcome of Designing, something through which meaning-makers create new meaning-making resources and remake themselves, i.e. learn) (Cope & Kalantzis, 2000).

Second, the authors suggest a more complete range of pedagogical moves which, in addition to traditional literacy teaching and *Overt Instruction* (to transmit language rules and instil good practice from literary models) and *Situated Practice* (immersion or natural learning models), include two other pedagogical dimensions such as *Critical Framing* and *Transformed Practice.* Two important aspects are added, such as the diversity of possibly-relevant kinds of texts (any meaning-making units) that requires a critical thinking, and the agency of users who become active creators of new meanings. More details are given in Section 7.2 "The Learning by Design Framework".

In the *multiliteracies* framework, teaching and learning include a mixture of these four orientations, even though not necessarily in any particular fixed sequence. Pedagogy of *multiliteracies* must be flexible and allow alternative forms of engagement for different learners with divergent learning orientations (Kalantzis & Cope, 2004). This is well suited for supporting university courses where language learning has to go beyond sets of grammar rules and vocabulary, and instead include as an important ingredient, reflection on text as well as an understanding of how texts and genres interact towards making meaning in context.

7.2 The Learning by Design framework

"Teachers and managers are seen as designers of learning processes and environments..."
(NLG, Cazden et al., 1996, p. 73)

The main goal of the *Learning by Design Project Group* was "to examine and document the ways in which learning occurs by design to assist teachers in planning curricula for middle school classrooms in Australia" (Yelland et al., 2008, p. 198). The starting point of the *Learning by Design* project involved the re-conceptualisation of the fundamental elements of the discussion: learning, education, curriculum and pedagogy. According to the New London Group authors, "educational research should become a design science, studying how different curricular, pedagogical, and classroom designs motivate and achieve different sorts of learning" (NLG, Cazden et al., 1996, p. 73). They introduced the concept of *Design*, "in which we are both inheritors of patterns and conventions of meaning and at the same time active designers of meaning" (NLG, Cazden et al., 1996, p. 65).

The *Learning by Design* project emphasises the relationships between received modes of meaning (*Available Designs*: how people are positioned by the elements of available modes of meaning), the transformation of these modes of meaning in their hybrid and inter-textual use (*Designing*: how the authors of meanings in some important senses bear the responsibility for being consciously in control of their transformation of meanings), and their subsequent to-be-received status (*The Redesigned*: how the effects of meaning, the sedimentation of meaning, become a part of the social process) (Kalantzis & Cope, 2008). The multiplicity of texts around us (e.g. advertisements, e-mails, TV programs, video-games), provide a huge amount of messages expressed and designed in various modes involving complex relationships among visual, spatial and textual items. *Literacy* should support the learner in the recognition and comprehension of these various modalities of expression, to understand the specific meanings. But each text does not represent a single meaning: meaning can vary depending on the different contexts and the various usages (e.g. an e-mail message can be used to chat with a friend or to apply for a job). Literacy should support the learner in communicating efficaciously in diverse settings: it is not only about rules and their correct application, but it is about facing new situations and unfamiliar kinds of texts and being able to search for clues about their meaning without immediately feeling alienated and excluded (Kalantzis & Cope, 2008).

At school, teachers and students operate within a community of learners and curriculum transformation. Teachers design learning experiences in a cyclical negotiation with students, through the tasks they are assigned, learn how to apply design and use creativity to re-design teaching unit materials. They are encouraged to experiment and to creatively design new meanings in different iterations and interactions with others and with the external world "introducing agency in their learning" (Healy, 2008, p. 15). Education should support students to use creativity, innovation, and imagination to transform the resources and codes available to them, and create new representations of the world. The aim is to give students a sense of how patterns of meaning are the product of the changing contexts created by new communication technologies and the diverse and intercultural contexts in which language is used (Kalantzis & Cope, 2008). The result of the transformation is the *Resedigned*: new resources for meaning that are added to the previous available resources (the universe of *Available Designes*). According to Cope and Kalantzis (2009), the process of transformation itself, what they call "creative re-appropriation of the world", is the essence of learning. As the learner elaborates and transforms the resources available, s/he acquires new insights, new perspectives, and new ways of expression that improve his/her knowledge and his/her competence in designing new meanings. The learner transforms her/himself through learning.

In their chapter *Language education and multiliteracies* (2008) Kalantzis and Cope give a clear overview of the four pedagogical dimensions (*Overt Instruction, Situated Practice, Critical Framing* and T*ransformed Practice)* providing pragmatic examples of how to apply them in education. In the following paragraphs a short summary of their description is reported.

Overt Instruction involves systematic, analytical and conscious understanding of the elements of different modes of meaning. Students need to understand how the process of Design happens and how to describe and interpret the elements of Design. They need to develop and to use a meta-language which helps them in naming and describing the processes and the patterns of Design in meaningful ways.

Situated Practice involves immersion in experience and the utilisation of Available Designs. In a learning situation students can work with resources already available (e.g. provided by the teacher, available in the classroom or at home), or they can search for new resources and less familiar texts to be discussed, analysed and understood more closely.

Critical Framing means "interpreting the social and cultural context of particular Designs of meaning" (NLG, Cazden et al., 1996, p. 88). Students should learn how to stand back from the specific contents they are studying and analyse them critically in relation to their context. They should interpret and understand the aim of a specific Design, why that content has been designed in that way and what it means in that specific context.

Transformed practice entails the transformation of meanings so that they can be re-used in other contexts. Students may, for example, take an Available Design and apply it to a different context, or take available contents and apply a different Design to them or create a Design anew, adding something personal to the process of transformation.

To make these four dimensions more immediately recognisable as pedagogical acts, the same authors (Yelland et al., 2008) draw a parallel with the four knowledge processes of *Experiencing, Conceptualising, Analysing* and *Applying* (Figure 31).

Experiencing (Situated Practice) – Learning is situated and contextual in real world experience: it does not happen only at school, but in a variety of contexts and through different modalities such as the practical out-of-school experience, in familiar as well as in unfamiliar environments. Experiencing takes two forms: it can involve familiar forms of expression and ways of representing the world that are closer to our own

Figure 31: The Learning by Design framework (Yelland et al., 2008, p. 200)

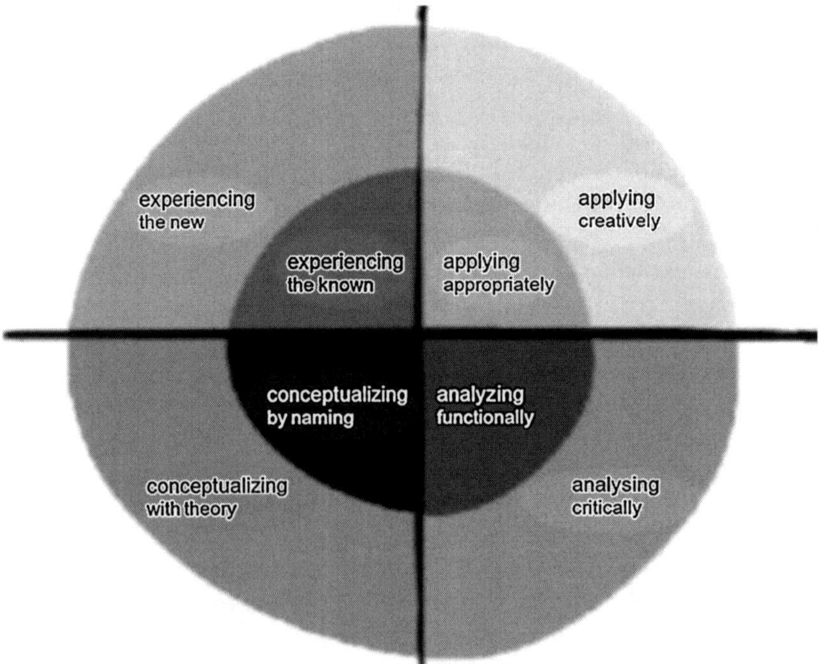

experiences, interests, and perspectives (*Experiencing the known*); in this regard, learners bring their own diverse knowledge, experiences, interests and life-texts to the learning situation. Or it can mean being immersed in new situations, reading unfamiliar texts or collecting new data (*Experiencing the new*). In this case learners are exposed to new information and texts which are close enough to their own experience to be understandable for them, so that they can connect the new information to their experience and transform it into new meanings.

Conceptualising (Overt Instruction) – Understanding concepts and theory is no longer bound to the explanation of textbooks by the teacher, but it becomes a knowledge process in which the learners are active in giving abstract names to things and in developing concepts themselves (*Conceptualising by naming*). Learners are active in making concepts explicit and in making generalisations from the particular (*Conceptualising with theory*). Learners are not taught fixed disciplinary schemas, but they put the key terms together into interpretative frameworks and they build new mental models: they become active theory-makers.

Analysing (Critical Framing) – Powerful learning also entails a certain kind of critical capacity. Analysing involves two kinds of knowledge processes: "*Analysing functionally* includes being able to draw deductive conclusions, and reasoning establishing functional relations such as between cause and effect and analysing logical and textual connections" (Cope & Kalantzis, 2009, p. 186). "*Analysing critically* involves the evaluation one's own and other people's perspectives, interests and goals. In these knowledge processes, learners interrogate the interests behind a meaning or an action, and their own processes of thinking" (Cope & Kalantzis, 2009, p. 186).

Applying (Transformed Practice) – Once the learner has got certain knowledge, s/he must be able to apply it to different contexts, understanding the complex diversity of real world situations and testing their validity (*Applying appropriately*). But learners must also be able to transfer their previous knowledge into new settings to make the world anew with innovative and creative interventions (*Applying creatively*) by bringing their personal interests, experiences and aspirations into action.

These pedagogical orientations are not to be followed in a specific and a singular sequence. Rather they are a map of the possible strategies which might be adopted by teachers to extend their pedagogical repertoires. If we want to take the learners' subjectivities into account and give them agency, we encounter a number of human differences to be addressed and the old one-size-fits-all approach is not enough to satisfy all their favoured orientations and preferences. Teachers can unpack the range of possible pedagogical moves in order to decide and adopt the most appropriate for a learner (Kalantzis & Cope, 2005). The role of technology in this respect is to support teachers in designing learning activities in different contexts and to facilitate the monitoring of the learning process.

In Section 8.1 a university course carried out in the academic year 2009/2010 with the support of the LearnWeb2.0 system is considered. The course design and the learning tasks are described based on the *multiliteracies* approach. Further details about the evaluation of the usability of the system and the pedagogical effectiveness of using LearnWeb2.0 in that scenario can be found in Marenzi et al. (2010), Marenzi and Nejdl (2012), and Marenzi and Zerr (2012) as well as in Section 5.2 of this thesis.

8 The LearnWeb2.0 design framework – a multi-tier model

> "...when the knowledge processes are made more explicit, it ensures that teachers and learners are fluent in their use and this has a profound impact not only on learning outcomes, but also on creating a positive classroom climate and becoming confident about being a lifelong learner".
>
> (Yelland et al., 2008, p. 203)

The goal of this chapter is to enhance and to integrate the *multiliteracies* approach and the *Learning by Design* framework with Web 2.0 features provided by the LearnWeb2.0 collaborative search and sharing system. According to the *multiliteracies* approach, resources are constructed and dynamically transformed by the users, through a variety of available communication channels and media, into different representations reflecting cultural and linguistic diversity. Such transformation is a result of moving through the four knowledge processes of the *multiliteracies* pedagogy (*Experiencing*: Situated Practice, *Conceptualising*: Overt Instruction, *Analysing*: Critical Framing and *Applying*: Transformed Practice). Educational setup and tools should support students in each of these processes.

The following section describes the application of the LearnWeb2.0 Design Framework in the ESP course scenario previously described in Section 5.2, revisited according to the *multiliteracies* approach. The focus here is not on introducing technology in education, but on the design of the pedagogical setup enabled by technological tools such as LearnWeb2.0, that are better suited to specific learning scenarios. A reflection on the LearnWeb2.0 contribution to *multiliteracies* education is given in Section 8.3, to explain the motivation of the researcher for connecting it with the educational context and information technology, leading to the new LearnWeb2.0 Design Framework (*multi-tier model*). This framework provides a common theoretical reference and a guide for teachers, researchers and developers when discussing how to design and to support course activities as well as to make the learning process more explicit for students.

8.1 ESP case study revisited from a multiliteracies perspective

> "One of the principles of multiliteracies education is that literacy programs must be tailored to particular contexts: no one literacy program is adequate for all."
>
> (Dooley, 2008, p. 125)

Communication and learning are dramatically changing both in social and in technological contexts, so that the development of new ways of talking about representation and communication in educational contexts becomes urgent (Cope & Kalantzis, 2009). At university level we need to find appropriate literacy pedagogy to prepare students to face the diversity of our times, e.g. different contexts and various ways of communicating and interacting with others. Language learning in particular, has to go beyond a set of grammar rules and vocabulary, but instead include the reflection on various kinds of texts as well as the understanding of how texts and genres interact towards making meaning in context (Lorenzo, 2013).

This section focuses in particular on the design of the ESP course carried out at the University of Pavia in Italy, in the Academic year 2009/2010, dealing with multimodal corpus analysis in order to develop English language skills and critical thinking. Students were enrolled in various degree courses from the Faculty of Medicine, including dentistry and nursing. They used the LearnWeb2.0 online platform to support collaborative learning activities, i.e. to search for and work with English-language *Public Information Films*, mostly dealing with medical issues (e.g. smoking and alcohol, domestic violence, road safety, paedophilia). The course was designed with an end-of-course exam in terms of group project work with a focus on multimodal text-based studies of English. Students used PowerPoint or directly LearnWeb2.0 for the final presentation of their collaborative work. A detailed description of the evidence-based evaluation of the ESP scenario can be found in Section 5.2.3 as well as in Marenzi et al. (2010), Marenzi and Nejdl (2012), and Marenzi and Zerr (2012). In the following section the course is described in relation to the four pedagogical dimensions of *multiliteracies* (i.e. *Situated Practice, Overt Instruction, Critical Framing* and *Transformed Practice*) in order to provide a specific pedagogical framework for the learning tasks. A detailed description of the scenario is given to explain the general learning goals and requirements of the course, but restructuring the learning activities using the *multiliteracies* terminology.

ESP English Language course at the University of Pavia
Faculty of Medicine (Dentistry) - FIRST YEAR (A.A. 2009–10)

The scenario of this case study has been described in detail in Section 5.2.3. In this section, the various phases of the course design and the tasks required from the students are associated to the four pedagogical dimensions of *Overt Instruction, Situated Practice, Critical Framing* and *Transformed Practice*. The goal is to explore parallels between the pedagogical moves suggested by the *multiliteracies* framework and the functionalities provided by LearnWeb2.0 which help students in the carrying out of the learning tasks.

For this purpose, the CSCL script has been adapted by introducing the four pedagogical dimensions of *multiliteracies*, as presented in Figure 32. Describing the case studies in this way provides ways for teachers to understand how to integrate the LearnWeb2.0 platform in their course design to create a sequence of effective learning activities (Marenzi, 2013; Marenzi & Kantz, 2013).

Figure 32: Course phases and multiliteracies pedagogical moves

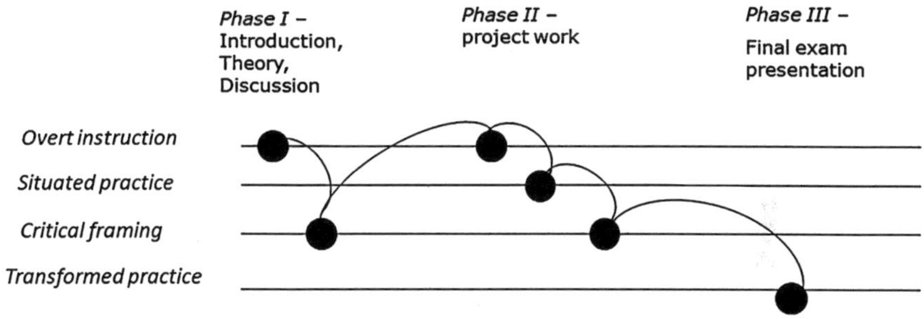

Phase I – Introduction, Theory, Discussion. Overt Instruction. In this phase the teacher provided the necessary background information on multimodality and film analysis. "Students learned about multimodal theory and how to carry out multimodal text analysis that is, studying printed, website, digital and film texts in English and the ways in which these texts are used in different medical contexts" (quotation from the course website[51]). During a teacher-led class, students carried out an analysis of the PIF genre guided by the teacher (*Critical Framing*): they analysed the characteristics of the PIF genre and discussed their usefulness and efficacy, then they compared them with PIFs of other countries and cultures.

Phase II – Project Work. Overt Instruction. In the second phase, a few preliminary activities were carried out in a lab to introduce the LearnWeb2.0 system, to search for new resources, to learn how to organise them in folders and collaborate with other colleagues negotiating materials (i.e. commenting, tagging and rating resources).

Situated Practice. Afterwards students, partly in the classroom partly working from home, concentrated on group project work: online searching for and rating of PIFs across different cultures, discussing their views within their group and with the teachers. Students were divided into groups and they searched the Web for videos relating to the PIF genre and created a corpus. The PIF videos

51 http://nfs.unipv.it/medicinaLM41/corso/500404/Obiettivilist.asp?cmd=resetall

had to be representative of different English speaking cultures and cover different themes for the various project-groups. Searching the Web is useful because a lot of diverse material is available. Written and oral language are no longer separated, but various modes such as written and oral language, visual, audio, gestural and spatial representation, are mixed in the new media (e.g. videos and websites) as well as in our everyday experience. Different structures and various kinds of texts can be found, which describe the same content in various ways (*Available Designs*). Students can find resources and codes available to them, as well as given conventions in their context and cultures (or different contexts and cultures). Additionally, they can learn a language in different contexts and genres (i.e. different ways of using and learning a language), not only through traditional grammar.

Critical Framing. After collecting the videos in LearnWeb2.0, each group of students analysed their corpus identifying the cultural characteristics and the structural schemas in the video. "From the linguistic point of view, students were asked to acquire a specialised knowledge of English that demonstrates their understanding of how body events and processes and related ideas, theories and opinions are expressed not just through linguistic resources but through a multimodal integration of resources: linguistic, visual, spatial and temporal" (quotation from the course website[52]). They learned the language and the terminology by watching videos that talk about the content. From a *multiliteracies* perspective, students also realised possible ways of how to represent the same contents and how to design new meanings by finding several examples on the Web. They rated PIFs collected in the LearnWeb2.0 groups and had online discussion on how to select appropriate resources for their final project work presentation according to the characteristics of textual organisation and inter-textuality, interculturality, and the efficacy of the message conveyed. To be successful in this phase, students needed to be purposive and selective regarding the contents (extracting only the most representative resources from a number of search results), but also interested and motivated. The opportunity of finding authentic material on the Web gave most students a good incentive to be engaged in the search and sharing activities. Students who were more used to working in a traditional way did not take advantage of the online collaborative functionalities provided by LearnWeb2.0 and carried out the critical analysis more face to face rather than in the forum.

Phase III – Final exam presentation. Transformed Practice. In the third phase of the course the focus was on individual exam preparation and the presentation

52 http://nfs.unipv.it/medicinaLM41/corso/500404/Obiettivilist.asp?cmd=resetall

of the final corpora by the various groups. Students were asked to select two videos from the corpus they collaboratively created during the project work, and to analyse and discuss them in class using a PowerPoint presentation. By comparing and analysing the videos, de-constructing the screenshots and re-constructing the content in new ways (*Redesigned*) in their PowerPoint presentations, students had the opportunity to express their autonomy and creativity, as well as their subjectivity in creating new designs by intersecting their social and cultural experiences. When they used the material (*Available Designs*) to create a new structure (*Transformed Practice*), they did not simply replicate designs they found, but they expressed their identity and their personal voice. The final exam took the form of a mini-lecture lasting 15–20 minutes, in which two films from different cultures but with the same theme were compared by each student. In the presentation students used language at an academic level to present the contents but also to carry out a meta-textual analysis on their work.

8.2 From Learning by Design to the LearnWeb2.0 Design framework

> "We find ourselves faced with a new teaching/learning process, where students manage their time and are aware of their educational goals and the path to achieving these goals."
>
> (Rizzo, 2009, p. 76)

As discussed in Section 7.2, the main goal of the *Learning by Design* project was to examine and document the ways in which learning occurs by design. In the present research work, the researcher adopted the idea of pedagogy as "knowing in action" (Yelland et al., 2008, p. 197), and she focused on learning activities that exemplify how new designs can be implemented at university level, in particular in ESP specific contexts.

The main intention when referring to the *Learning by Design* framework, represented in Figure 31, was to start from a clear base and to keep it as a common reference when discussing course design with teachers to improve each other's experiences. Referring to a model provided a source of reflection and assisted the researcher in more practical ways in her role as an educational technologist, as a tool that encourages and guides the exchange and work with other colleagues at different levels: improving understanding between teachers and researchers, giving teachers a structure to facilitate the planning of lessons, making the knowledge processes explicit also for students and giving them more agency in the learning activities.

Researchers and teachers – Referring to the same framework encourages the different participants (e.g. researchers, developers, teachers) to think more broadly about the ways in which the learning experiences (e.g. *Knowledge objectives, knowledge processes* and *knowledge outcomes*) might be structured and sequenced, as well as to find the most suitable solutions (*Designs*) to be adopted in various situations. At the beginning of the doctoral work, during the first evaluation cycle, the researcher was not expert in CLIL, and did not know how to approach the CLIL lesson. She mainly discussed with the teacher what possible technological functionalities could be suitable to support the learning activities. The willingness of the teacher was very important to allow the evaluation even though the system was at earlier stages. The teacher accepted both the challenge and the risk to offer such an innovative perspective to her students even though no preliminary evidence of success was available yet. In the second case study (ESP course in Pavia) the researcher knew the teacher, and she had gained more experience from the previous evaluation already. These two conditions led to a closer collaboration also in the design of the learning tasks.

Teachers – Collaborative learning poses to teachers new challenges as regards to classroom organisational changes and personal commitments to sustain the effort. The *Learning by Design* framework prompts teachers to consider the various pedagogical options available, "to reflect on their choices, and to document their learning programs" (Kalantzis & Cope, 2004, p. 38). It helps to scaffold the learning process where each learning element must be located in an integrated context that has relevant objectives and assessment strategies. The Framework can also help teachers in reinforcing the quality of teaching by adding more diversity while planning the tasks and activities for their students, so that they are relevant and suited to a greater range of learning styles (Kalantzis et al., 2010). In this way teachers can extend their repertoire, broaden the types of activities that their students engage in, and transform their pedagogy bringing innovation to their schools and classrooms.

Students – Students should be more directly involved in the design of their learning process, thus getting more motivated and engaged in the learning activities. If students are involved more actively in the course design, they engage with ideas in a more critical and profound way so that they are able to reflect upon what they have learned and share it with others. The importance of creating authentic tasks is a value to challenge and motivate the learners as well as to answer their need for audience and communication in innovative ways, using new technologies and various media for authentic purposes.

Empirical examples showed that original task design are often re-interpreted by the learners themselves and the actual realisations may radically differ from what might have been planned by the task designers. It is important to design "learning and teaching activities in flexible ways, both before and during the ongoing activity" (Arvaja, 2011, p. 44) for example, by offering new resources that become relevant for students' activity during the course (Dillenbourg & Tchounikine, 2007).

Building on this framework, the interesting question is how various tools, and in particular the LearnWeb2.0 system, can best be used to support students' knowledge and learning processes. Therefore the original *Learning by Design* framework has been extended in this doctoral work, by adding a third external circle which includes the activities supported by the LearnWeb2.0 features: *Search and Exploration, Annotation and Description, Negotiation and Discussion,* and *Aggregation and Presentation*. The following paragraphs describe the *LearnWeb2.0 Design* framework (*multi-tier model*) depicted in Figure 33. In particular the focus is on social interaction and collaboration.

Figure 33: Adding Web 2.0 features to the Learning by Design framework (multi-tier model) (Adapted from Yelland et al., 2008, p. 200)

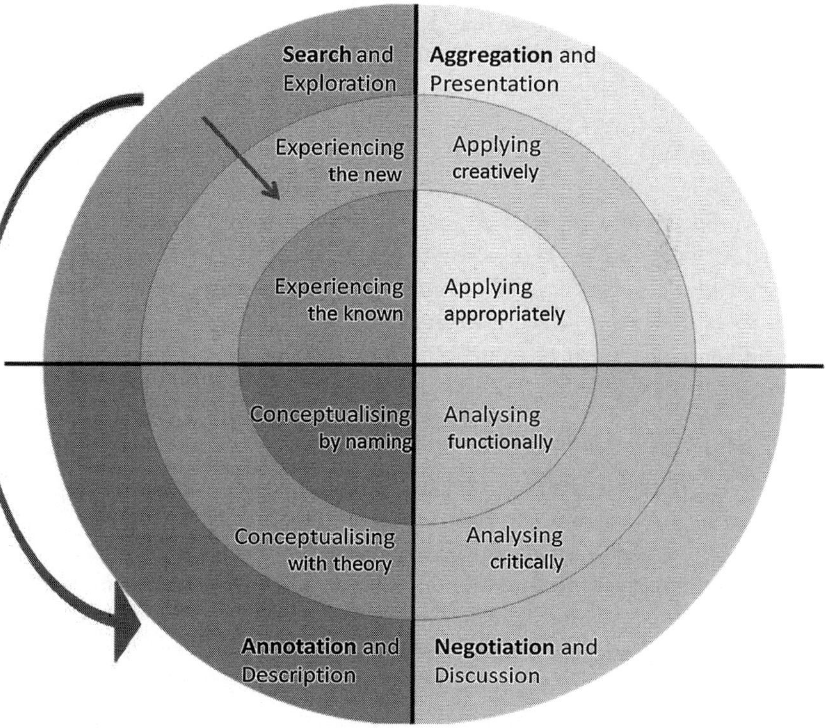

The inner arrow indicates the direction of the support: the *Search* functionality supports the knowledge process of *Experiencing*, both *Experiencing the known* as well as *Experiencing the new*. As the counter clockwise arrow shows, the activity continues with the other knowledge processes and activities. The *Annotation and Description* functionality in LearnWeb2.0 supports *Conceptualising*, the *Negotiation and Discussion* functionality supports the *Analysis* knowledge process, and the *Aggregation* functionality supports students in *Applying* what they learned in a new context. As previously mentioned though, in the *multiliteracies* framework teaching and learning include a combination of the four orientations (*Experiencing, Conceptualising, Analysing,* and *Applying*), not necessarily in any particular fixed sequence.

The following paragraphs discuss in more detail how the LearnWeb2.0 functionalities can be integrated into the pedagogical setup of the courses, to help teachers to plan appropriate learning opportunities for their students.

Experiencing through Search and Exploration

The pedagogical process of *Experiencing* is supported by the LearnWeb2.0 *Search* functionality. *Collaborative searching* of multimedia resources in social networks allows both teachers and students to find relevant resources for course material design and to experience authentic language exchange in real situations. Students have the opportunity to bring their life-worlds into the class (e.g. their resources and their personal contacts in social networks - *Experiencing the known*) and to explore new situations and immerse themselves in unfamiliar experiences (e.g. new contacts in social networks and new materials from different cultures - *Experiencing the new*). Using LearnWeb2.0 as a search engine, students can gather a big range of diverse *Available Designs* and collect various kinds of multimodal texts. For example, in Pavia students collected PIFs and websites about various topics, of different styles and designed for various purposes. Figure 34 visualises the association of the LearnWeb2.0 main functionalities within the Design/Re-design cycle.

Conceptualising through Annotation and (formal) Description

The activity of conceptualising contents (*Conceptualising by theorising*) can be supported in the classroom and carried out in face to face discussions with the teacher or with peers. In Pavia for example, during the *Overt Instruction* phase, the teacher explained the multimodal theory and set the context and the specific terminology to be used during the course. During the project work students could categorise resources (*Conceptualising by naming*) and describe them using the LearnWeb2.0 annotation functionalities such as tags and ratings. Students could use the grouping functionality to collect and categorise the resources, as

Figure 34: LearnWeb2.0 functionalities within the Design Framework

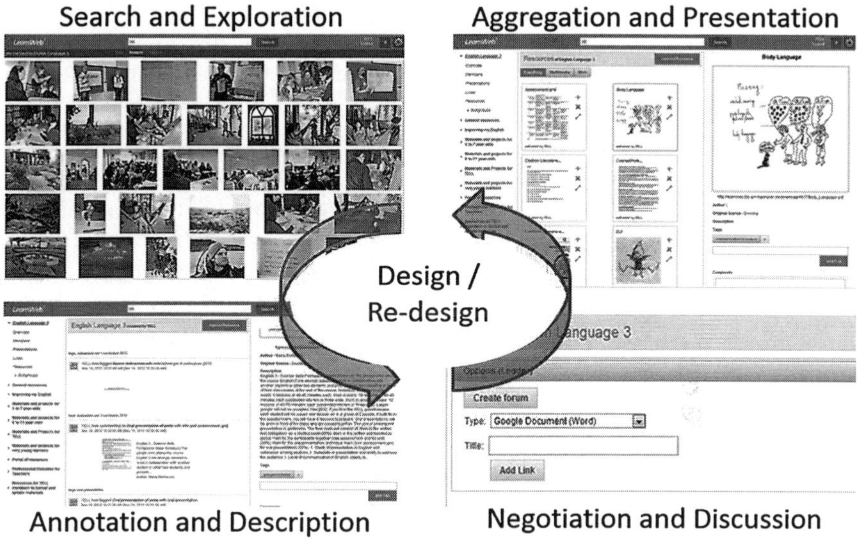

well as tags and ratings to annotate the material, characterise their ideas and build mental schemas, also to stress some issues for peer viewers.

Analysing through Negotiation and Discussion

The Forum and the commenting functionality in LearnWeb2.0 provide a powerful opportunity for peer-to-peer discussions (*Negotiation*) and critical analysis of the reliability of the source as well as the relevance of the information retrieved. Students can use comments with the group members to discuss the collected resources, make logical connections (*Analysing functionally*) and select the most relevant material for their project work (*Analysing critically*). In the Forum they are encouraged by the teacher to think critically, to learn how to reference the source of information, to compare and contrast information, and "to distinguish the relevant from the irrelevant" (Healy, 2008, p. 15). Specifically in Pavia, students were asked to analyse the various texts (PIFs) from the multimodal perspective, selecting the most relevant resources according to characteristics such as textual organisation and inter-textuality, inter-culturality, and efficacy of the message conveyed.

Applying through Aggregation and Presentation

The possibility of collecting resources in specific folders and re-organising them for the final presentation at the exam allows students to apply what they learned in the course and to use their creativity to define new meanings. At the end of the course in Pavia each group organised the previously selected material to create new meanings (*Applying creatively*), e.g. design a presentation for a different context (i.e. use PIFs in a medical context or simply to give a mini-lecture in English).

Table 3 lists the components of a learning element, defined by Yelland, Cope and Kalantzis (2008) as "A coherent bundle of learning experiences, learning tasks or activities, such as a lesson or a short string of lessons". The original table has been adapted by the researcher to include the LearnWeb2.0 functionalities so as to make the teachers aware of the available features which could be used to support the learning process. The aim is to make the connection between the knowledge processes and the technical functionalities provided by LearnWeb2.0 more explicit. The researcher suggests using this table while designing the course activities with the teachers as a preliminary guide to collect a clear list of the learning goals and to set specific strategies to scaffold the learning process. The idea is to use the table at the beginning of the design process, when the educational technologist meets the teacher to discuss the structure and the activities to be carried out during the course. Referring to a pre-defined list of items can facilitate the planning of the lessons, making the various steps explicit can improve the understanding between the teachers and the researchers collaborating in the process.

An attempt to use the table as a reference to describe the ESP dentistry course in a structured way has been made by the researcher together with the teacher in Pavia (Marenzi & Kantz, 2013). The former suggested using the *multiliteracies* framework as a common reference when consulting with teachers trying to improve each other's experiences; the teacher collaborated in the experiment to test the actual efficacy of the approach in the classroom, to analyse the course structure and to design appropriate learning activities addressing the learning goals. Table 4 (p. 162–165) summarises the results of this work. The first part of the table helps the teacher to focus on the knowledge domain and to identify the knowledge objectives; the second part of the table, including knowledge processes and outcomes, is addressed to the students and their active participation in authentic tasks. The activities are listed according to the knowledge processes to combine the project work with the technical functionalities provided by LearnWeb2.0. The teacher plans to use this structure as a basis to design the new Dentistry course during the winter semester 2013, intending to involve the students more directly in the design of the learning process and to better engage them in the learning activities.

In order to make students more aware of the course design the teacher, in agreement with the educational technologist, should discuss the CSCL script

Table 3: Overview of components of a learning element

Learning element: A coherent bundle of learning experiences, learning tasks or activities, such as a lesson or a short string of lessons (Yelland et al., 2008, p. 205)	
Learning focus	Information about where the learning element fits into the curriculum.
Knowledge domain	The subject or discipline area.
Scope of learning	The topic or theme.
Learning level	The age or year level of the learners.
Prior knowledge	What the learners already know, or are expected to know in order to be able to work on this learning element. For example, prior experience, skills, contents or tools.
Knowledge objectives	The intended learning outcomes. For example, "as a result of this learning element, a learner or a group of learners will be able to…". May include objectives in relation to experiential knowledge (learning goals to be realized in demonstrable behaviors), conceptual knowledge (learning goals to be realized in conceptual, theoretical or cognitive capacities), analytical knowledge (learning goals to be realised as an understanding of underlying dynamic and critical appraisal capacities) and applied knowledge (learning goals to be realised through problem solving, action and performance).
Knowledge processes	Different ways of knowing reflected in different types of learning activities, in which the sequence and balance may vary according to subject matter, preferred learning styles etc. The knowledge processes are filled out by content, expressing the depth and breadth of learning.
Experiencing (Situated practice)	Learning activities focused on personal experience, knowledge, skills and concrete data. *The Known:* The learning resource involves the learner's prior knowledge and life experience. Some process orientations: identify, retrieve, recall, exemplify, clarify, analyse, check, locate. *The New*: immersion in new knowledge, experience and community settings that connect with the learner to the extent that the new makes enough sense for learning to occur. Some process orientations: restate, illustrate, summarise, verify. LearnWeb2.0 functionality - *Search and Exploration*

Conceptualising (Overt Instruction)	Learning activities focused primarily on abstract concepts and theoretical synthesis. *By Naming*: defining and applying concepts. Some process orientations: define, name, give examples, classify. *With Theory*: linking concepts into a language of generalisation, or visual representation of conceptual relations. Some process orientations: generalise, synthesise, abstract, structure, organise, hypothesise, model, map, overview. LearnWeb2.0 functionality - *Annotation and (formal) Description* (comments and tags)
Analysing (Critical Framing)	Learning activities focused primarily on analysing and interpreting functions, interests and perspectives in knowledge. *Functionally*: identifying the role and function of knowledge. What does it do? Some process orientations: compare, contrast, explain. *Critically*: Interpreting personal and cultural perspectives involved in knowledge. What point of view does it represent? Some process orientations: infer, interpret, conclude, deconstruct, critique, judge, assess, appraise, argue, differentiate, discriminate, distinguish, evaluate. LearnWeb2.0 functionality - *Negotiation and Discussion* (forum)
Applying (Transformed Practice)	Learning activities focused primarily on applying knowledge, creating meanings and making a practical impact on the world. *Appropriately*: applying knowledge in an appropriate way to a specific situation or context. Some process orientations: apply, use, solve, implement, generate, plan, produce, justify, reconstruct. *Creatively*: creating new knowledge; taking knowledge from one or more settings and adapting it to a different setting. Some process orientations: transfer, translate, design, construct, invent, create, imagine. LearnWeb2.0 functionality - *Aggregation and Presentation* (Groups and Google Docs)
Knowledge outcomes	Processes for assessing the knowledge learners have acquired (experiential, conceptual, analytical and applied). Might include learner self-assessment, peer assessment, teacher professional assessment, instructional designer assessment such as an assessment task built into the learning element.

Learning pathways	Suggested follow-on activities and learning experiences, which might involve learner pathway preferences, teacher pathway recommendations, instructional designer pathway recommendations or pathway co-design as an outcome of negotiation of what to learn next.

(Figure 35) with the students at the beginning of the next course (in October 2013). As Häkkinen and Mäkitalo-Siegl (2007, p. 263) remark, "Simply offering online learning environments to students does not guarantee that they interact in a way that promotes learning". Involving the students in the co-design (or at least explain the design to them) encourages them to actively reflect on what they are expected to do and why, or what they have been doing (metacognition). The course design needs to match the curriculum, but also the perceived needs of the learners. To make the script and the learning tasks more successful and integrated into the learning experience it is useful to introduce them explicitly to the students "as a way of achieving perceived goals" (Kolodner, 2007, p. 261).

In Figure 35 the Learning by Design pedagogical processes are integrated into the CSCL script to summarise the learning activities and to make students aware of the purposes of the learning tasks. The visualisation also makes explicit the cyclic nature of the Design and Re-design process that includes action-based activities, but often requires also engaging in investigative and reflective activities to refine the group-work for the final presentation (Kolodner, 2007).

Figure 35: Explain the pedagogical intent of the course design to students (awareness)

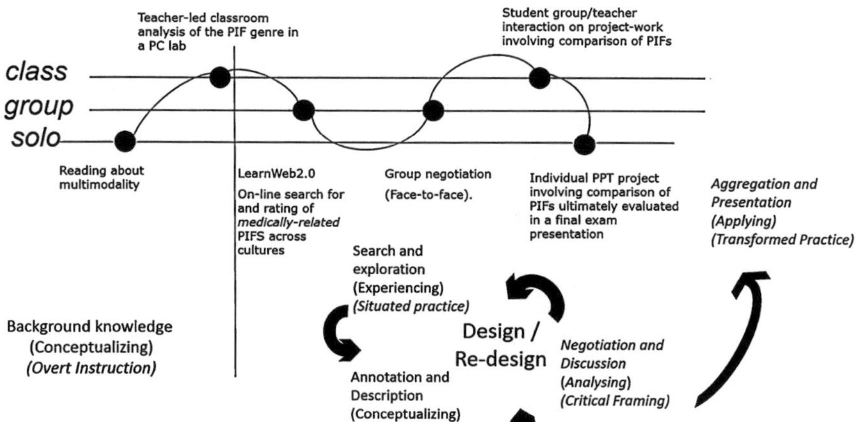

Table 4: Overview of components of a learning element (Degree Course in Dentistry)

General information First, the general course information must be described and the learning goals stated explicitly. In the following section the specific items are filled in taking into account the ESP dentistry course as an example.	
Learning focus	**L-LIN 12**
Knowledge domain	**Degree Course in Dentistry**
Scope of learning	**English Syllabus. The grammar of English multimodal texts** The aim of the course is to guide the students to reach an advanced level of autonomy in self-learning by introducing innovative methodologies and research concepts, such as the web as a *multimodal archive-cum-corpus*. Such an approach is good for ESP since it constantly connects the analysis of semiotic systems in the biomedical field focusing on discourse analysis, that is to say, on the language in use.
Learning level	First year dentistry students starting from a B2 level of the ECFL (*European Common Framework of Languages*).
Prior knowledge	To be admitted to the oral test, students must demonstrate, during the English course, that they have reached at least the C1 level (or higher) of the Common European Framework of Reference; they can do this by undertaking a written online test, printing it and taking it to one of the oral sessions.
Knowledge objectives	From the linguistic point of view, students are expected to acquire a specialised knowledge of English that demonstrates their understanding of how events, processes and related ideas, theories and opinions are expressed not just through linguistic resources but through a multimodal integration of resources: linguistic, visual, spatial and temporal (quotation from the course website[53]). They learn the language and the terminology by watching videos that talk about the content and not only, since they also expand their knowledge of vocabulary in order to express themselves better. Through the use of conceptual tools (the course book) and mediacy-support systems (LearnWeb2.0) students work on "live" multimodal texts, improving their basic literacy skills (reading-comprehension, listening-comprehension) while developing multiliteracy skills. As a result of working their way through this learning element, the students will be able to learn about multimodal theory and apply it to the analysis of multimodal texts.

53 http://nfs.unipv.it/medicinaLM41/corso/500404/Obiettivilist.asp?cmd=resetall

Course description The various phases of the course and the learning activities must be described and explicitly associated to the pedagogical dimensions and knowledge processes. In the following paragraphs the specific functionalities of LearnWeb2.0 are explicitly associated with the various phases of the learning process.	
Knowledge processes	Students will carry out a research project divided into two phases according to the knowledge acquired during the course.
Experiencing	*Situated practice.* During the first phase of the course a few preliminary activities are carried out in a lab to introduce the LearnWeb2.0 system, to search for new resources, to learn how to organise them in folders and collaborate with other colleagues negotiating materials (i.e. commenting, tagging and rating resources). Afterwards students, partly in the classroom partly working from home, concentrate on group project work, divided into groups of three people maximum. They are asked to search the Web for videos related to the PIF (*Public Information Films)* genre and to create a corpus. The PIF videos must be representative of different English speaking cultures and cover different themes for the various project-groups. Students can select a few videos from those already in LearnWeb2.0, but they have to provide a number of NEW videos in their corpus. Each group will analyse their corpus highlighting the recurrent schemes and structures and detecting cultural and identity characteristics. This work will be carried out partially in the classroom and partially at home, using various software tools such as MWS (Multimodal Web Search) and LearnWeb2.0, which will be shown during the course. LearnWeb2.0 functionality – *Search and Exploration* LearnWeb2.0 (http://learnweb.l3s.uni-hannover.de/lw/) provides a seamless web service interface to access a number of popular Web 2.0 sources and social networking systems as a storage platform with the potential to add more. Specifically for the course in Pavia, searches in YouTube and Bing are useful to find videos and additional information about the PIF genre. *Search results display window.* Resources already stored in LearnWeb2.0 are ranked and displayed first (at the top of the result window). This means that when students search for PIFs, they will find the videos stored by the students of previous courses (or other LearnWeb2.0 users) first, and then new occurrences which come from the Web (YouTube or Bing). In this way students are aware of what other students found previously and they can search for new videos, not yet stored in LearnWeb2.0. *Filter.* LearnWeb2.0 provides a filter where students can choose the tools they want to search, e.g. they can either search only in LearnWeb2.0, or exclude LearnWeb2.0 and search only in other Web 2.0 tools such as YouTube, Bing, Flickr etc…

	Suggested search keywords are: PIFs, domestic violence, Canada, or PSA (*Public Service Announcement*), drinking and driving, Australia.
Conceptualising	*Overt instruction.* During the course students will be asked, through their group-work, to present a critical analysis of medical PIF videos using subtitling techniques. The creation of subtitles in English requires students to have deep knowledge of textuality and it constitutes an important goal in the biomedical field since it allows the investigation and to discussion of the organisational principles of medical-scientific discourse in English. The textual principles taken into consideration include phasal-analysis as presented in both course-books. During the course, commercial tools will be used, as well as research tools developed at the University of Pavia which allow students to appreciate the importance of subtitles for various communities, as well as learning methods based on corpora. Lectures/laboratories will guide students step by step during the development of their projects. LearnWeb2.0 functionality – *Annotation and Description* (comments and tags) An advantage offered by LearnWeb2.0 is the opportunity of storing resources in different folders: if a video has already been found by previous classes, it can be stored again in the new group adding additional annotations and comments (also previous annotations can also be compared). After collecting the videos in LearnWeb2.0, students can use the grouping functionality to collect them in meaningful folders, categorise them (*Conceptualising by naming*). Students can describe the videos using the LearnWeb2.0 annotation functionalities such as tags and ratings to annotate the material, characterise their ideas and build mental schemas, also to stress some issues for peer viewers. Ratings reflect the relevance of the resource. By exchanging comments, the students and/or teacher can collaboratively describe the videos in more detail; discuss the quality, reliability and usability of the materials more precisely within the learning context. *Re-use of previous resources.* LearnWeb2.0 allows the community of users to profit from the previous searches and annotations. Resources already stored by other LearnWeb2.0 users are ranked according to the previous comments and ratings, so that the most reliable and relevant resources are presented first in a new search. In particular, students can see what their colleagues have already found in previous courses, learn from their experience, add new comments and improve the annotations in the resource (tags, rate the relevance of the resource for their group…). This can stimulate a bit of competition between students and motivate the new classes to add their opinions and comments to the previous ones. Of course a proper discussion can be carried out only with colleagues attending the current edition.

Analysing	*Critical framing*. During the next phase of the course, the groups will analyse their corpora and organise the final presentation for the exam. Students analyse the characteristics of the PIF genre and discuss their usefulness and efficacy, then they compare them with PIFs of other countries and cultures, gaining insight into how culture, social attitudes and different discourse genres can mould and improve their language learning. To show their ability in group collaboration, students must show they are able to use the sharing and collaborative functionalities available in LearnWeb2.0 working with other members of their group and of the classroom. LearnWeb2.0 functionality –*Negotiation and Discussion* (forum) The commenting functionality in LearnWeb2.0 provides a powerful opportunity for peer-to-peer discussions (*Negotiation*) and critical analysis of the reliability of the source as well as the relevance of the information retrieved. Students can use the comments with group members to discuss the PIF videos, make logical connections (*Analysing functionally*) and select the most relevant material for their project work (*Analysing critically*). They are encouraged by the teacher to think critically, to learn how to reference the source of information, to compare and contrast information and to distinguish what is relevant from what is irrelevant. Specifically in Pavia students are asked to analyse the various texts (PIF videos) from a multimodal perspective, selecting the most relevant resources according to characteristics such as textual organisation and inter-textuality, inter-culturality, and efficacy of the message conveyed. To avoid duplication of the same videos, students have the opportunity, provided by the available software tools (MWS and LearnWeb2.0), to carry out searches in several English speaking countries. In MWS there is also the opportunity to search for materials which are representative of different cultures where the linguistic aspect does not go beyond the necessary requirements for an English exam. In LearnWeb2.0, the search for specific countries must be specified in the query, and the results rely on the original metadata (e.g. if the person who uploaded the video in YouTube specified that it comes from Australia, or the US or GB …and so on...). The discussion and the critical analysis can be carried out both face-to-face in the classroom or in the LearnWeb2.0 online forum.
Applying	During the oral exam each student will discuss his/her written exam. Afterwards the groups will present their corpora (maximum three students per group) in a group presentation; in particular each student will have to describe his/her contribution to the whole corpus of at least 50 PIFs or 15 Health Committees videos (without subtitles).

	LearnWeb2.0 – *Aggregation and Presentation* (groups and Google Docs) Students can express their subjectivity and creativity in creating new designs by intersecting their social and cultural experiences. When they use the material (*Available Designes*) to create a new structure (*Transformed Practice*), they do not simply replicate designs they found, but they express their identity and their personal voice. In the presentation they not only use language at an academic level to present the contents, but also to carry out a meta-textual analysis on their work. The possibility of collecting resources in specific folders and re-organising them for the final presentation at the exam allows students to apply what they learned in the course and to use their creativity to define new meanings. At the end of the course in Pavia each group has to re-organise the previously selected material to create new meanings (*Applying creatively*), e.g. design a presentation for a different context (i.e. describe the selection of PIFs for the medical context or simply explain the group-work carried out for the final exam in English).
General results In this section, the expected results and knowledge outcomes must be made explicit both for the teacher to guide the course design, and for the students to better understand the pedagogical purpose of the course.	
Knowledge outcomes	The learning progress of each group will be evaluated week after week as regards the collection of videos and the subtitling process. Students must demonstrate that they have reached a good phrasing capacity in English, at least the C1 level (or higher) of the Common European Framework of Reference; students must be able to read and translate sections of the course-book as well as to answer questions about the texts chosen by the commission about the subjects discussed during the course. From a *multiliteracies* perspective, students realise possible ways of how to select appropriate resources for their final project work presentation, and how to represent the same contents in new designs according to the characteristics of textual organization and inter-textuality, inter-culturality, and the efficacy of the message conveyed.
Learning pathways	Students will be able to access LearnWeb2.0 also after the end of the course to continue using it as a personal learning environment and interact with the LearnWeb2.0 learning community.

8.3 Reflection on the LearnWeb2.0 contribution to multiliteracies education

> "[...] *literacy* education is about students in our classrooms becoming a part of the global world through mass media, the internet and the multiplicity of communication channels and through interaction with others."
>
> (Cope & Kalantzis, 2000, p. 6)

The goal of the previous sections was to integrate and make explicit the connections between the *multiliteracies* approach and information technology in the educational context. In particular the relationship between the *multiliteracies* pedagogical knowledge processes and the collaborative functionalities provided by the LearnWeb2.0 system have been shown. A *multiliteracies* approach for language learning has been described. After providing a *multiliteracies* theoretical background, a learning setup for an ESP (*English for Specific Purposes*) course carried out at the University of Pavia has been described, as well as the LearnWeb2.0 system which has been used to support the learning activities. One way of extending the *Learning by Design* framework with a technology layer has been illustrated, which draws attention to the questions on how to use technology (in particular the LearnWeb2.0 system) to support course design at university level based on a *multiliteracies* approach.

A *multiliteracies* pedagogy and the resulting theoretical framework must be flexible and allow alternative forms of engagement for different learners with different learning methods. Reflection on texts can be supported by online collaborative and sharing functionalities, but can also occur in the classroom with the teacher's support, or in small groups of peers. Although digital tools support collaborative working, a good working environment in the classroom is essential. Before digital technology can be used to support ways of working together, the classroom must be a learning place where constructive contributions are well-accepted and evaluated (Facer & Williamson, 2004). The structure and the modalities of communication and interaction of the learning elements depend on the various setups and scenarios. In general, in all aspects of *digital literacy* such as collaboration and communication skills, functional skills (i.e. use of digital technologies, the ability to find and select information, cultural and social awareness and understanding), critical thinking and creativity "are closely interlinked so that developing one will often involve students making use of others" (Hague & Payton, 2010, p. 46). Attention must be focused on the learning activities planned by the teachers and on things students *do* in order to produce knowledge. In particular, a collaborative environment such as LearnWeb2.0 is a useful system which can facilitate specific tasks (e.g. searching and organising available materials) but it is important to understand *when* and *how* to use it in an effective way.

The LearnWeb2.0 contribution to education is to support teachers and students in becoming "active designers of new meanings" (NLG, Cadzen et al., 1996, p. 65). LearnWeb2.0 can be used by teachers to design, document and publish their learning units making them available for other colleagues who can benefit from the sharing process and have access to more learning elements that they can easily adapt to their own environments. The focus is not on the specific tool per se, but on the design of the pedagogical setup that the tool contributes to, and on the activities to be carried out with the students to support and develop their learning process. The *LearnWeb2.0 Design* framework (*multi-tier model*) helps teachers who want to design activities and appropriate tasks for their students using new technologies. A model of this kind can guide teachers in the development of materials and other forms of documentation for the learning community (e.g. design materials) that can be used by the teachers with their future pupils or shared with the global community of researchers. However, it would be wrong to assume that the model and the technology presented are the same thing. They are not. Most obviously, LearnWeb2.0 could be used in non-CLIL contexts such as a community of researchers sharing their work and publications, and equally CLIL contexts could use the model while not adopting LearnWeb2.0 but different tools.

However, developing a tool that is capable of supporting and testing out a theoretical model is an asset. In this sense, the current release of LearnWeb2.0 is a redevelopment of previous versions which attempts to incorporate the theoretical model described above.

9 Conclusions and future work

"Successful models evolve through trial, use and refinement."

(Hendler et al., 2008, p. 67)

Before starting the present doctoral work about four years ago, the researcher experienced a rather different educational route, in Italy starting from a university degree in Modern Languages and Literature, through to a master in Media Science and Technology, to a position as researcher in educational technology within a research centre in Germany. Her initial goal after finishing school was to become a frescoes restorer.

In modern society which brings with it a multiplicity of changes both at a local and a global level, a fundamental challenge for everyone involved in education – administrators, teachers, parents, and students – is to teach and learn today so as to cope with an unpredictable future. Thus students are required not only to be literate, but also to be able "to self-learn and to use their knowledge and their skills in order to be successful in the environment where they live now and in the future" (Armstrong & Warlick, 2004, p. 20). The challenge for educators is to support students in emphasising skills that reflect the present increasingly digital and networked world.

Reading and understanding a written text is no longer enough to be literate. Today students are overwhelmed by a huge amount of information and digital materials published on the Web. Before studying something, they need to be able to search, identify and select reliable resources, to evaluate them in terms of their learning goals, and to organise them in meaningful ways in personal digital repositories. *Writing* and *expressing* one's own ideas and being understood by others is no longer sufficient in a multi-dimensional and multimodal world where opinions and bias make communication increasingly difficult. Students need to learn how to make their arguments and presentations more appealing by building on appropriate resources including multimedia content. Furthermore, they need to learn how to express their ideas more compellingly so as to communicate effectively in different contexts.

In a globalised world, where interaction with others requires a shared language for communication, language learning and teaching are increasingly important. Knowing a language today is not important simply for personal knowledge, but is crucial to the way we live in modern society. At times it is difficult to find relevant and authentic materials for language learning because many resources are localised and teachers spend a lot of time preparing suitable materials for their classrooms. Good search strategies and tools that support teachers and students in finding useful resources are needed. In the researcher's opinion the role of technology in this context is to enable teachers in designing learning activities that support the modern required literacy skills, and to enable students to keep improving those skills in the future. The collaborative searching and sharing system LearnWeb2.0 has been designed, developed and improved to address these issues and to support the requirements of various learning scenarios. Even though LearnWeb2.0 cannot automatically select educational resources as such, the system enables the LearnWeb2.0 community to manually select and annotate general resources as found in various Web 2.0 services, turning them into specific educational resources by rating, commenting and tagging them in contextually meaningful ways. In addition to the technological support, the researcher worked to reinforce the pedagogical setup by enhancing the *multiliteracies* approach and the *Learning by Design* framework with the Web 2.0 features provided by LearnWeb2.0. As a result, the *LearnWeb2.0 multi-tier* model has been suggested: it provides a common theoretical reference and a guide for teachers, researchers and developers when discussing how to design and support course activities as well as to make the learning process more explicit for students.

The researcher is convinced that the use of Web 2.0-based learning environments requires further studies describing and accounting for all the main deployment steps, including assessment, encouraging researchers and teachers to engage in such ventures. Much has still to be done in this direction, but the researcher is confident that facilitating interaction and collaboration among experts in the various fields involved in this paradigm change (e.g. computer scientists, pedagogues and educators) may help to find joint solutions and solve open issues illustrated in this thesis.

The following section provides a summary of the research that has been carried out for the doctoral work and the major contributions in the TEL field. Section 9.2 sketches future directions in the field of research, as well as issues that remain open for future investigations and future collaborations.

9.1 Summary of contributions

Improving education through technology needs an interdisciplinary approach, building on strong pedagogical foundations as well as on innovative technological solutions. This thesis aimed to integrate the pedagogical approach of *multiliteracies*, especially suited for language learning, with a new kind of e-learning environment, LearnWeb2.0, supporting collaborative searching, knowledge sharing, and knowledge creation.

The introductory Chapters 1 to 3 present the pedagogical and technical background, whereas Chapter 4 introduces the fundamental methodology adopted throughout the thesis, namely the *Iterative evaluation-driven design-based* research approach. The purpose of this approach is to improve a system through continuous learning involving the actual users in an interactive and qualitative process of *formative evaluation* where both developers and evaluators work together to test the system and improve the new release. With the intention of taking into account several educational aspects and perspectives (besides technology), the researcher adopted a "mixed method research" approach involving the combined use of qualitative and quantitative methods to exploit the complementary aspects of both approaches. The data collection and analysis had an iterative and recursive nature, carried out in two evaluation cycles of empirical research.

Chapters 5 and 6 describe the empirical research investigating how technology can support the four knowledge processes of *Learning by Design* (i.e. *Experiencing, Conceptualising, Analysing* and *Applying*) in various scenarios, with a focus on online interaction and collaboration from the standpoint of *Educational Technology.* Two evaluation cycles have been carried out to improve the usability of the LearnWeb2.0 system, and to check for possible opportunities for adaptation and customisation. The research questions addressed in this phase of the research (Marenzi et al., 2010) were:

- *How can a platform for collaborative work and collaborative searching be appropriately used and adapted in different university contexts so that it helps in the process of learning how to teach English in a CLIL context and in the process of learning how to improve English as a foreign language?*
- *What pedagogical and project design should be used to support CLIL teaching at university level and to foster student reflection on methods and materials appropriate for CLIL?*

The first evaluation cycle focused on two CLIL and ESP courses which were supported by LearnWeb2.0 during the summer semester 2010. Section 5.1.5 describes the *LearnWeb2.0 integrative framework*, which expands the Zydatiß curricular framework for CLIL by explicitly considering the global context where the individual interacts within social networks, and by making the importance of this global context explicit to trainee teachers. The scenarios used in the CLIL seminar supported the trainee teachers' learning about CLIL. The project work motivated them to search for appropriate materials to support a future CLIL teaching session in school. The process of designing tasks for their pupils allowed them to apply the acquired knowledge on CLIL, which they did creatively with all types of materials (text and digital) even if in a rather classical way, often not making the move from the personal to the World Wide Web. Online interaction and collaboration were not much used by trainee teachers in the specific case study, the course design did not require online collaboration since students met often in person in the classroom.

Section 5.2 describes an ESP course dealing with multimodal corpus analysis in order to develop English language skills and critical thinking. Students were encouraged to use LearnWeb2.0 to collaboratively search the Web for Public Information Films and create an annotated corpus of videos. The course was designed to improve the students' capacity to integrate skills acquired through a combination of classroom learning, e-learning and self-study making progress towards integrated skills, stress the individual and peer learning aspects and promote self-assessment. In this course, the system was central, helping students to find many multimedia resources for their project work related tasks. Students realised possible ways of how to represent the same contents and how to design new meanings in a creative way. They rated PIFs and discussed how to select appropriate resources for their final project work presentation according to the characteristics of textual organisation and inter-textuality, inter-culturality, and the efficacy of the message conveyed. The discussion and the critical analysis, though, happened more face-to-face than in the LearnWeb2.0 forum.

Section 5.3 provides a summary of the LearnWeb2.0 development towards the second release. The feedback provided during the first evaluation cycle was encouraging in many aspects, but also revealed additional improvement potential both at a functional as well as at a conceptual level. These findings led to a substantial redevelopment and extension of the system, in order for it to be more interactive and more flexible with a particular focus on facilitating the search, communication and collaboration functionalities.

The second evaluation cycle started in September 2011, so as to collect users' requirements and customise LearnWeb2.0 to support various scenarios and different learning goals. In this context, the second LearnWeb2.0 release is described and analysed in Chapter 6, as well as its integration into the setup of two courses in a German school, and within the YELL project in Udine, Italy. The experience at the Leibnizschule in Hannover was exciting. Students were enthusiastic to participate in the experiment and very engaged in using the system, but the author and the teacher realised that more guidance was needed to better organise the roles and group-work. Subsequent evaluation and discussions provided important input for further improvement of the system, especially for the presentation of final results. The second case study in this phase involved a group of graduated students working as pre-service teachers at school. Compared to students, participants in this context were more oriented at sharing educational resources and personal working experiences with colleagues online. The YELL project gave the researcher valuable input concerning the customisation of LearnWeb2.0 for a community which is not confined to a course, but which is continuing and growing over time. Compared to the first evaluation cycle, in these scenarios users were keener in taking advantage of the collaborative functionalities provided by LearnWeb2.0 and gave useful feedback to improve the efficacy of communication and sharing functionalities in the system. The evaluation results were promising, showing that the integration of Web 2.0 tools in the courses led to a much more enhanced and multi-perspective learning process than in previous editions. Section 6.3 summarises the new functionalities introduced in the third release of LearnWeb2.0 according to the users' requirements and customisation.

Building on the results of these two evaluation cycles and on the insights gained from them, in Chapters 7 and 8 the researcher focuses on a the *multiliteracies* pedagogical framework, to reinforce the LearnWeb2.0 pedagogical setup and the use of the system in various scenarios. The corresponding research questions investigated in this phase were:

- *How can the LearnWeb2.0 functionalities be integrated with the pedagogical notion of the multiliteracies approach, and how can this integration be represented through an appropriate model?*
- *What course design should be used? How should LearnWeb2.0 be used in various learning scenarios?*

Chapter 7 discusses *multiliteracies* as a conceptual framework to create a context for the implementation of a knowledge management strategy in education. In so doing, the work in this thesis enhances the *multiliteracies* approach and the *Learning by Design* framework with Web 2.0 features provided by the LearnWeb2.0 collaborative search and sharing system.

Chapter 8 discusses the LearnWeb2.0 *multi-tier model* which supports teachers in two ways: in designing their courses based on the *multiliteracies* approach, as well as in using LearnWeb2.0 to appropriately support the various pedagogical phases of the course. These final parts provide a common theoretical reference and a guide for teachers, researchers and developers, based on the results and experiences gathered through this doctoral work, when discussing how to design and to support the course activities as well as to make the learning process more explicit for students. An illustrative example of how to connect the LearnWeb2.0 functionalities to the *multiliteracies* pedagogical framework is also provided for a specific course. An important aspect of the contribution of this thesis is thus the introduction of technological support into an integrated planning and description of course design. This provides a context where teachers have to re-think the ways that they teach, and think of ways of doing things differently, using new technologies complementing the old ones. Building on these research results, the author continues to test the efficacy and flexibility of the *multi-tier model* in various communities, both in educational and in non-educational contexts (Section 9.2).

9.2 Further work: supporting collaboration in other scenarios

> "Knowledge acquired through social interaction becomes individual knowledge and individual knowledge grows and becomes more complex (Roblyer, 2000)". Quoted in Action research project (Denyer & Peacock, 2001, p. 9).

LearnWeb2.0 has been designed, developed and improved as a tool capable of supporting and testing out a *multi-tier* theoretical model. The researcher has concentrated on CLIL scenarios, in line with the focus of the *multiliteracies* pedagogy on language learning. It should be noted, though, that LearnWeb2.0 might be used in other educational contexts as well, even in non-educational contexts such as for example a community of researchers to support communication and sharing of their research results and publications. The researcher is interested in continuing to test the flexibility and extensibility of the proposed *multi-tier model*, together with the LearnWeb2.0 platform, as well as its acceptance in various kinds of communities. Therefore, this section describes a few scenarios that could be supported by LearnWeb2.0. Some of these scenarios have already started as project proposals or as case studies that are currently being observed by the researcher. Other ideas are sketched out as possible future directions.

9.2.1 CLIL through collaborative audio-visual translation (CLIL-VIDEO)

Scientific research is a driving force in human development. Nevertheless, the wider public is not fully aware of the importance of science in everyday life. It is thus a duty of science to communicate its own role to the layman and to raise youngsters' interest. This requires new communicative and teaching approaches and appealing materials. Specialised websites exist on the Web, which include collections of scientific videos specifically created for the dissemination of science, but most of these videos are in English (considered the international language of science), and only a few are in other languages (e.g. Spanish). It is an open question how translations can be provided, given that professional translations usually exceed available budgets of these projects.

LearnWeb2.0 contribution

In spring 2012 the author was contacted by an Italian researcher working at the University of Salento (Lecce) who asked to use LearnWeb2.0 with her students to carry out a pilot study on the subtitling of scientific videos. The idea for the project was based both on the CLIL approach (with the intention of developing communication skills and of building intercultural knowledge) as well as on the desire to spread scientific research results. The researcher in Lecce worked with 25 students attending the university course "Laurea magistrale in Traduzione tecnico-scientifica e intepretariato" over a period of four months, from the 1st of March to the end of June 2012. Under the teacher's supervision, the students, divided into 12 groups, were invited to watch selected scientific videos in English or in another foreign language. Then they were asked to manually transcribe the spoken text, translate it into their mother tongue, and to adapt their translation so as to create subtitles for the videos. After an introduction on subtitling theory, the students started to use LearnWeb2.0 as a common repository to collect scientific videos in English, to annotate the resources and to discuss their progresses with other colleagues or with the teacher. At the end of the course, the subtitled videos were made available publicly to the international community both through LearnWeb2.0 and YouTube[54].

The scenario and the experience gained during the pilot study have been considered as a possible starting point for a future joint project proposal involving the University of Salento and the L3S Research Center as project partners. The overall goal of the project is to create and promote a stimulating and interactive content-language learning community which fosters secondary school students' interest towards basic scientific disciplines (such as physics, chemistry, biology) as well as English and other foreign languages. The members of the community, including science specialists, linguists specialising in audiovisual translation and/or multimodal text studies, science teachers, language teachers, and students from several EU countries, will engage in collaborative activities revolving around specialised video materials selected from Web sites dedicated to the dissemination of science. The LearnWeb2.0 platform will help each teacher/researcher to organise the videos which are more suitable for his/her course or project and to share, comment and discuss them with students and international partners. The video subtitling activity will be the practical means by which students are attracted to the contents as well as the language of science, and will be a stimulus for interaction among the different

54 www.youtube.com/user/lachimicainvideo

members of the CLIL-VIDEO community. The students' work will be supported by crowd-sourcing and cooperative practices, achieved through the use of the LearnWeb2.0 platform. Furthermore, the integration of other technologies into the platform will provide community members with the possibility of engaging in innovative CLIL activities.

9.2.2 Functional searching and annotation system

Keyword-based searching on the Web (i.e. use the right keyword to find the resources we are looking for) is sometimes difficult. The current LearnWeb2.0 annotation system is unsystematic due both to the lack of an adequate choice-based annotation system, and training in how to use it. In 2010 the researcher suggested a first improvement based on choices from a limited set of fairly intuitive options drop-down menus (e.g. options, items, tags, annotations…), to be implemented for specific domains[55].

A second step would be to provide a rapid/intuitive selection based on a visual icon-based approach to help search and annotate resources. Figure 36 illustrates a possible tagging/annotation system based on a hierarchy of icons. In the example menu the selection process is simplified into one icon plus a single word (at most 2 words). It simulates how tagging of texts detected by the LearnWeb2.0 system might work with a visual focus (i.e. guided choices for immediate understanding).

Preliminary studies have already been carried out by the researcher in the field of functional linguistics and presented in 2010 towards an integrated descriptive visual/verbal tagging/annotation system based on a hierarchy of icons and guided menu choices[56]. In the context of LearnWeb2.0, such a fast and easy annotation system might also extend the current searching functionalities by a partly icon-based searching system. An icon system could be used for searching, and the search interface could be transformed into a partially automatic, partially manual annotation/tagging system. An intercultural participation model could be taken into consideration, as a possible means of going beyond language *and* text barriers using a multimodal interface which

---

55 Marenzi Ivana (2010). *Multimodal annotations.* In: Multimodal Discourse Practices – Globalization and Localisation. Seminar 65 – coordinated by Nicoletta Vasta and Eija Ventola. ESSE 2010, 24–28 August, Turin, Italy.

56 Marenzi Ivana (2010). *Textual choices and complexities: trainee teachers' reflections on the process of text and genre selections in a Web 2.0 environment.* The 22nd European Systemic Functional Linguistics Conference and Workshop. Koper, 9–12 July, 2010.

combines searching, annotating, sharing and reporting as part of a single macro function.

Figure 36: Visual icon-based annotation system

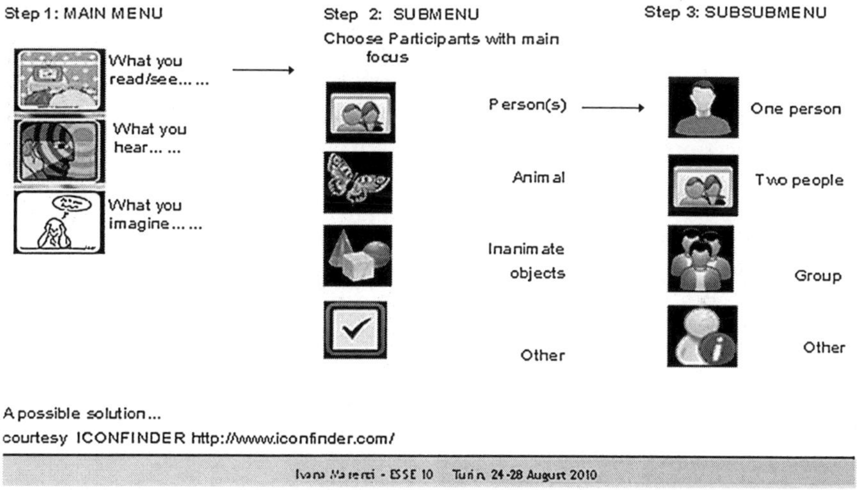

9.2.3 LearnWeb2.0 in collaborative research: the ACT project

The Italian ACT[57] (*Access Through Text*) project explores accessibility to texts by identifying potential solutions to barriers encountered by certain social groups as they attempt to access the meanings of audiovisual/multimodal texts. These include difficulties in accessing meanings made in films faced by the blind, the partially-sighted, the deaf and the partially deaf as well as difficulties, partly linguistic, partly non-linguistic, faced by young children and teenagers when attempting to access websites in English. The goal is to ensure a more precise and detailed awareness of text barriers through careful experimentation and observation of user interaction, and to suggest potential solutions or improvements that effectively remove those barriers. Three teams constitute the ACT research group: one unit of researchers in Messina (E-WARP), one unit in Udine (MACE) and one in Trieste (SABRE). From the very beginning it was necessary to have a common repository where to share materials and official documentation related to the project, as well as to record discussions and comments within the community (through the forum or by writing documents collaboratively).

57 http://mcaweb.unipv.it/ACT-ENG/

LearnWeb2.0 contribution

Starting in 2012 LearnWeb2.0 has been adopted by the research community involved in the ACT project to support the communication and sharing of their research results. Up to now, the system has been used as a search engine to search for suitable resources on the Web as well as a repository to store and to share the materials with other colleagues. The materials and the results of the research are uploaded into LearnWeb2.0 to be shared with the other members of the ACT project and then, once it has been finalised, they can be accessed by anyone who is interested. Compared to the previous LearnWeb2.0 scenarios, this is a new context of use more oriented towards the social and collaborative aspects and functionalities, and therefore an interesting line of research to be continued.

9.2.4 OER (Open Educational Resources) and educational Linked Data

UNESCO[58] (2002) defines Open Educational Resources as

> "any type of educational materials that are in the public domain or introduced with an open license. The nature of these open materials means that anyone can legally and freely copy, use, adapt and re-share them. OERs include learning objects, normally digital in nature, such as open courseware, references and readings, experiments and demonstrations, as well as syllabi, curricula and teachers' guides freely available online with minimal or no restrictions. They are principally used by educators to develop course materials, but they can also be used directly by learners." (UNESCO, 2002)

In addition to contents generated by the general public, several institutions and organisations are increasingly contributing data to the Web, making available Open Educational Resources and various datasets explicitly classified and identified as educational, or not education-specific, but anyway relevant for education (Dietze et al., 2013). Since plenty of data is published online with the aim of being reused, integrating existing educational Web resources becomes increasingly important. But, even though OERs are multiplying on the Web, it is difficult to find them since they are not uniformly classified and organised. Also, while universities, libraries, archives and other knowledge-intensive institutions contribute to increase the availability of educational resources, there are still many unsolved issues particularly with respect to Web-scale metadata interoperability and legal as well as licensing aspects. Several projects try to analyse the status of the huge amount of resources available on the Web to make them accessible not only to individual organisations, but rather to the general public as well. The

58 http://www.unesco.org/new/en/communication-and-information/access-to-knowledge/open-educational-resources/what-are-open-educational-resources-oers/

survey *Interlinking educational resources and the web of data* (Dietze et al., 2013) provides an extensive overview of current competing metadata schemas, interface mechanisms and methods to expose data on the Web. One of the statements is that "the linked data approach has emerged as the *de facto* standard for sharing data on the Web, but a number of challenges and issues as regards interoperability and interlinking of databases is still to be addressed" (Dietze et al., 2013, p. 60). The work is meant as a structured assessment and classification of existing challenges and approaches, serving as a potential guideline for researchers and practitioners in the field to find a common agreement and better interoperability. The goal of the research work is to understand what is already available and what methods can be used to connect the various datasets, to find related contents, and to make them globally accessible and exploitable.

LearnWeb2.0 contribution

At the L3S Research Center the researcher has been involved in the proposal for an internal project to enrich the current release of LearnWeb2.0 with Open Educational Resources selected and extracted from the Linked Data cloud. Besides the integration of various Web 2.0 tools and social networks providing user-generated contents, a future direction should be to integrate LearnWeb2.0 with Open Educational Resources (OER) and materials from the Linked Data cloud so as to enrich the current provision of learning materials. In this way, LearnWeb2.0 would also provide an interface to these OER materials, which often come from established institutions and organisations and are a valuable asset for courses and specific learning tasks.

Besides the standardisation, categorisation, and interlinking of the various datasets, an important issue to be considered is the maintenance and sustainability of OERs. Creating good educational resources is time and cost consuming, and after they have been created and shared, they need to be maintained and kept updated. According to Koohang and Harman (2007), communities of practice can help in improving the scalability as well as the sustainability of OERs. In this context, LearnWeb2.0 could certainly help various communities to find educational resources and create selected corpora and support categorising better access to available OERs.

9.2.5 Technological issues and further developments

> "Designing an object to be simple and clear takes at least twice as long as the usual way".
> (Nelson, 1977)

To address the needs of several scenarios the researcher, together with her colleagues at the L3S Research Center, is designing the latest release of the

LearnWeb2.0 system (namely LearnWeb$^{2(squared)}$ http://learnweb.l3s.uni-hannover.de/new/lw/index.jsf) which will be arranged around three main *perspectives*:

- A *course perspective*, managed by the teacher, where administrative tools are available to control access to the various spaces and items, for managing users, groups and participants in the specific course. Teachers are granted full control to their community of learners by means of a fine grained role-based access control panel. An internal messaging module allows the teachers to maintain direct contact with the participants and to convey further instructions during the course.
- A *group perspective,* shared within a workgroup. History reports and list of members are provided to raise awareness about the activities carried out by other group members.
- A *personal perspective* in which a student (or a generic user) can collect materials and develop his or her own ideas and projects. Photos and icons are prominently used to indicate whose workspaces or remarks are displayed, so as to provide more personal appearance.

These perspectives have special features and are regulated by access rights to make them flexible and adaptable to various scenario requirements.

Renovated user interface – Usability of a system greatly depends on the interface it provides to the user. In a collaborative system the user interface greatly influences the efficiency of the features it provides (Hearst, 2009; Shneiderman & Plaisant, 2010). Despite the latest improvements in LearnWeb2.0 a lot of information, even though rarely used, is still displayed taking away space to more relevant content.

Navigation across the system can also be improved. A new grid layout will be introduced to guide the reader through the navigation of the system. A three-column layout will be adopted to keep the user in context and engaged at all times (Figure 37). The first column displays all the groups that a user is part of. The second column includes the resources, activity stream or other content depending upon the page. The third column is used to show a preview of the selected resources. The new interface design aims at improving collaboration and search, as well as users' engagement with the system.

Query suggestions – Increasingly people search for information on the Web and use search engines to fulfil their information needs. But sometimes it is not easy for the inexperienced user to define good keywords and to formulate a query which conforms to the information intent. Often the user has to try various keywords and refine the search requirements to find good results. Keywords formulation can be made easier by providing possible suggestions as the user

Figure 37: LearnWeb² three columns layout

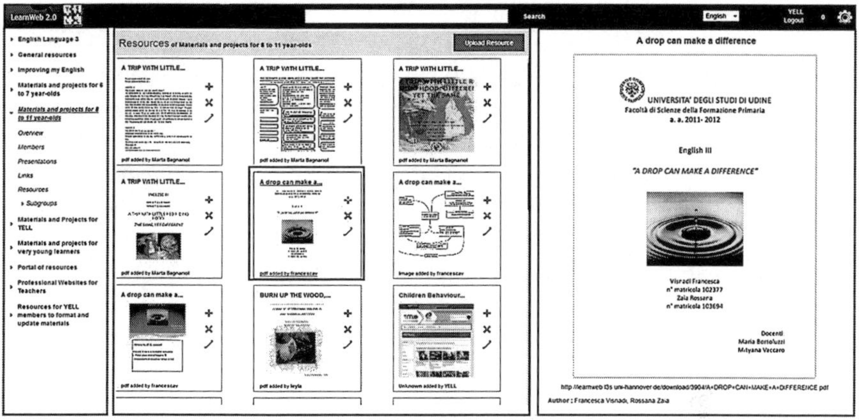

starts typing the query into the search field. Query suggestions will be provided to help users in formulating better search terms that can return relevant results.

Fact sheets – While searching for specific information, users like to see additional details about the query terms. The opportunity of presenting additional pictures and events related to a topic will be provided as a new feature in LearnWeb² (Figure 38) inspired by Google's implementation of Knowledge Graph.

Figure 38: LearnWeb² fact sheets

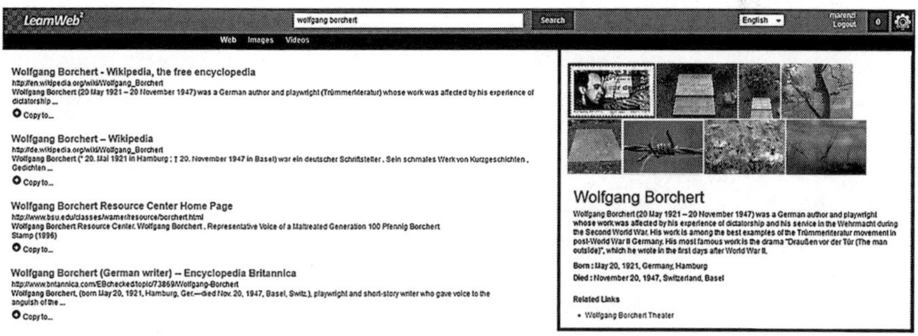

The researcher is also discussing with teachers the extension of the system in ways that more explicitly support the workflow-management and enable monitoring the whole *learning* process.

Monitoring, feedback and assessment – Web 2.0 technologies increase opportunities to access various sources of contents and to diversify the learning experience. In online learning environments, the ability to interact, collaborate and socialise, as well as peer-contribution and peer-assessment opportunities, gain more influence in the learning process. For these reasons, assessing content acquisition is not enough, rather the acquisition of competences and skills (such as online interaction and sharing, collaboration, positive interdependence, self/peer assessment) should be taken into account to reflect a more comprehensive evaluation of the literacy skills required in the 21st century society. But it is difficult to monitor and to assess these interactions in terms of knowledge acquisition and achievements. Online interaction is difficult to grasp and to assess: it is difficult to associate the involvement in online activities with actual learning on the part of the student.

In the LearnWeb2.0 system, the students' level of participation in the learning tasks, such as search for resources, upload, annotation and sharing, is currently captured by the activity logs and visualised for the teacher in the *activity logs view*, as described in Section 5.3 (Figure 19). Even though this visualisation already allows teachers to have an idea of the involvement of each student or group in the various activities, there is no clear association with the actual learning process (knowledge acquisition). The instrument is useful to gain a constant overview on the class engagement and to give feedback about students' participation, but assessment is still conducted externally using questionnaires and summative testing processes. Qualitative and formative assessment (providing developmental feedback on the acquisition of competences and skills, taking into account different sources, experts and peers) is more difficult to obtain.

To improve the current workflow-management process and to provide additional integrated formative assessment facilities into the new release of LearnWeb², the researcher is investigating current research-project findings (Harrer et al., 2013; Wesiak et al., 2013) as well as available e-assessment tools such as e-portfolio[59], and monitoring approaches such as computer-mediated discourse analysis (Herring, 2004), classroom discourse and conversation analytics (Dalton-Puffer, 2007; Kupetz 2011; Nikula et al., 2013), social network analysis (Bakharia & Dawson, 2011), learning analytics (Tull, 2012; Siemens & Gasevic, 2012), and visual analytics (Gómez Aguilar et al., 2013). Meier, Spada and Rummel (2007, p. 67) already proposed a rating scheme considering five aspects of the collaboration process to be analysed i.e. "communication, joint information processing, coordination, interpersonal relationship, and individual motivation".

As preliminary hypothesis, various types of data produced by the students during the course could be taken into account (such as text included in

59 http://www.jisc.ac.uk/whatwedo/programmes/elearning/eportfolios.aspx

comments, discussion forum, GoogleDocs, activity stream) to be analysed with natural language techniques and provide visualisation of the learning contents. In future designs, *intra-peer-assessment* (data regarding activities within the group) such as resource annotation and group discussion to select the most suitable materials for the group presentation, and *inter-peer-assessment* (constructive discussion about the work done by other groups on the final project work presented to the classroom) could be analysed and considered for the final evaluation. For this purpose, the LearnWeb² annotation system should be improved to support more detailed and comprehensive assessment criteria. Concept maps or word clouds could be used to identify major topics and understand how students conceptualised the content area (students' knowledge). Word clouds[60] could be used to summarise contents for learning as meta-cognitive tools and to scaffold sustainable learning (Meyer, 2010). In the author's view, visualisation and graphic knowledge representation techniques would provide a better overview of the learning process and allow more varied feedback and assessment designs.

Figure 39 summarises the various steps of the design-based research and the evaluation-driven evolution of the LearnWeb2.0/LearnWeb² system, including hints for possible future directions.

Figure 39: Iterative evaluation timeline – future directions

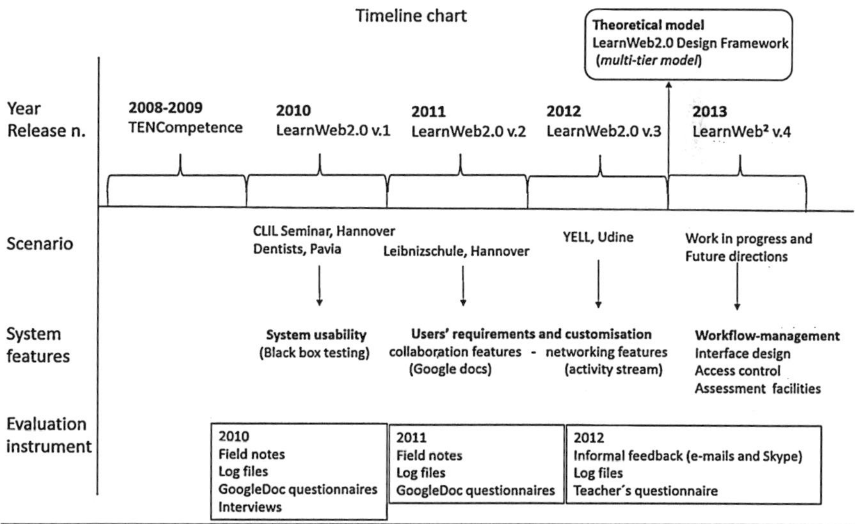

60 http://wordwanderer.org/

"Learning takes the learner into new places, and along the journey, acts as an agent of personal and cultural transformation". (Kalantzis & Cope, 2004, p. 44)

Courtesy of[61]

61 http://fc07.deviantart.net/fs71/f/2011/057/7/b/new_places_by_orioto-d3afhoo.jpg

Acronyms

API	Application Program Interface
AJAX	Asynchronous JavaScript and XML
CALL	Computer Assisted Language Learning
CBL	Computer-Based Learning
CBT	Computer-Based Training
CLIL	Content and Language Integrated Learning
CMC	Computer-Mediated Communication
CoP	Community of Practice
CoL	Community of Learning
CSCL	Computer-Supported Collaborative Learning
EDCL	European Computer Driving Licence
e-learning	electronic learning
ELMS	Education Learning Management Systems
ESAS	European School of Advanced Studies
ESP	English for Specific Purposes
GUI	Graphical User Interface
HCI	Human-Computer Interaction
HE	Higher Education
KM	Knowledge Management
IBT	Internet-Based Training
ICT	Information and Communication Technology
ICC	Intercultural Communicative Competence
ID	Instructional Design
LEaD	Learner Experiences across the Disciplines
LM	Learning Management
MOOC	(*Massive Open Online Course*)
MWS	*Multimodal Web Search*
PCM	Personal Competence Manager
PHP	Originally Personal Home Page, now it stands for PHP: Hypertext Preprocessor (recursive acronym).
RSS	RSS Rich Site Summary (originally RDF Site Summary, often dubbed Really Simple Syndication)
SRL	Self-Regulated Learning

SQL	Structured Query Language
TEL	Technology Enhanced Learning
JSP	Java Server Pages
WBT	Web-Based Training
WWW	World Wide Web
XML	Extensible Markup Language

Table of Figures

Tables

Bibliography

Abel Fabian, Frank Mischa, Henze Nicola, Krause Daniel, Plappert Daniel & Siehndel Patrick (2007): GroupMe! Where Semantic Web meets Web 2.0. In: K. Aberer, K.S. Choi, N. Noy, D. Allemang, K.I. Lee, L.J.B. Nixon, J. Golbeck, P. Mika, D. Maynard, R. Mizoguchi, G. Schreiber & P. Cudré-Mauroux (eds.): *Proceedings of ASWC 2007 and ISWC 2007*. Springer, Heidelberg. LNCS, (4825), 871–878.

Abel Fabian, Herder Eelco, Marenzi Ivana, Nejdl Wolfgang & Zerr Sergej (2009a): Evaluating the benefits of social annotation for collaborative search. In: E.Agichtein, M. Hearst and I. Soboroff (eds.): *Proceedings of the 2nd Annual Workshop on Search in Social Media (SSM 2009)*. Boston, USA.

Abel Fabian, Marenzi Ivana, Nejdl Wolfgang & Zerr Sergej (2009b): Sharing distributed resources in LearnWeb2.0. In: U. Cress, V. Dimitrova & M. Specht (eds.): *Learning in the Synergy of Multiple Disciplines*, Proceedings of the 4th European Conference on Technology Enhanced Learning (EC-TEL 2009). Springer, (5794), 154–159.

Abel Fabian, Marenzi Ivana, Nejdl Wolfgang & Zerr Sergej (2009c): LearnWeb2.0: resource sharing in social media. In: *Proceedings of Workshop on Social Information Retrieval for Technology-Enhanced Learning (SIRTEL'09)*. Aachen, Germany, (535), 1–63.

Amershi Saleema & Meredith Ringel Morris (2008): CoSearch: system for co-located collaborative Web search. In: *Proceedings of the 26th Computer Human Interaction Conference* (*CHI* 2008), 1647–56. ACM 978-1-60558-011-1/08/0.

Armstrong Sara & Warlick David (2004): The New Literacy: the 3Rs evolve into the 4Es. In: *Technology and Learning*, Research Library, 25(2), 20–8.

Arizzi Cristina, Marenzi Ivana & Jaén María Moreno (2012): Towards a sociosemiotic WebAnalytics: Higher Education TEL tools handling access and information extraction in textually complex website. In: P. Vittorini, R. Gennari, I. Marenzi, F. De La Prieta Pintado & J.M. Corchado Rodriguez (eds.): *Proceedings of the International Workshop on Evidence-based Technology Enhanced Learning* (EbTEL 12), Advances in Intelligent and Soft Computing, Springer-Verlag GmbH, (152), *67–74*. ISSN 1867-5662.

Arvaja Maarit (2011): Analyzing the contextual nature of collaborative activity. In: S. Puntambekar, G. Erkens & C. Hmelo-Silver (eds.): *Analyzing Interactions in CSCL: Methods, Approaches and Issues*. Ney York: Springer, 25–45. SBN 978-1-4419-7710-6.

Bakharia Aneesha & Dawson Shane (2011). SNAPP: a bird's-eye view of temporal participant interaction. In: *Proceedings of the 1st International Conference on Learning Analytics and Knowledge (LAK'11)*. New York: ACM, 168–173. ISBN: 978-1-4503-0944-8 DOI:10.1145/2090116.2090144.

Baldry Anthony (2000): Introduction. In: A. Baldry (ed.): *Multimodality and multimediality in the distance learning age: papers in English linguistics.* Campobasso: Palladino, 11–39. ISBN: 8884600006.

Baldry Anthony & Thibault Paul J. (2006a): Multimodal corpus linguistics. In: G. Thompson & S. Hunston (eds.): *System and Corpus Exploring Connections.* London: Equinox, (1), 164–83. ISBN: 9781904768197.

Baldry Anthony & Thibault Paul J. (2006b): *Multimodal transcription and text analysis: a multimodal toolkit and coursebook*. London: Equinox, (1), 1–288. ISBN: 9781904768074.

Baldry Anthony (2011): *Multimodal web genres. Exploring scientific English.* Como: Ibis, 1–112. ISBN: 9788871643564.

Baldry Anthony, Gaggia Alessandro & Porta Marco (2011): Multimodal Web concordancing and annotation. An overview of the MCAWEB system. In: *Identities in Transition in the English-Speaking World.* Udine: Forum Edizioni, 1, 39–60. ISBN: 9788884206930.

Baldry Anthony & Coccetta Francesca (2012): Group project work in English for Academic Purposes: background research and investigations for a blended course in tourism using Web-as-multimodal-corpus techinques. In: F. Dalziel, S. Gesuato & M.T. Musacchio (eds.): *A Lifetime of English Studies: Essays in Honour of Carol Taylor Torsello*. Padova: Il Polgrafo, 1, 311–20. ISBN: 9788871157672.

Bannon Liam J. (1989): Issues in computer supported collaborative learning. In: C. O'Malley (ed.): *Proceedings of NATO Advanced Workshop on Computer-Supported Collaborative Learning*. Maratea, Italy.

Barret Edward (1994): *Sociomedia: multimedia, hypermedia, and the social construction of knowledge*. Cambridge, Mass., MIT Press.

Block David (2003): *The social turn in Second Language Acquisition*. Edinburgh University Press, Edinburgh.

Bloom Benjamin (1984): *Taxonomy of educational objectives*. Boston: Allyn and Bacon, Boston, MA.

Bogdanov Evgeny, El Helou Sandy, Gillet Denis, Salzmann Christophe & Sire Stéphane (2010): Graaasp: a Web 2.0 research platform for contextual recommendation with aggregated data. In: *Proceedings of the 28th of the international conference extended abstracts on Human factors in computing systems*. New York, USA: ACM Press 978-1-60558-930-5/10/04. 3523–28.

Bonk J. Curt & Graham's R. Charles (2006): *The Handbook of blended learning. Global perspectives, local designs*. UK: Pfeiffer, 5(4). ISBN: 978-0-7879-7758-0.

Borau Kerstin, Ulrich Carsten, Feng Jinjin & Shen Ruimin (2009): Microblogging for language learning: using Twitter to train communicative and cultural competence. In: M. Spaniol, Q. Li, R. Klamma & R.W.H. Lau (eds.): *Advances in Web Based Learning - ICWL 2009*, Proceedings of the 8th International Conference on Web-based Learning. Berlin-Hidelberg: Springer, LNCS 5686, 78–87.

Borchert Wolfgang (1947): An diesem Dienstag. In: W. Bellmann (ed.): *Klassische deutsche Kurzgeschichten*. Stuttgart 2003, 25–29.

Bortoluzzi Maria & Marenzi Ivana (2013): YELLing for partnership: a social platform for sharing practice and reflection in teacher training for language learning. In: A.R. Natale, M.R. Dolce, S. Mercanti & C. Colomba (eds.): *The Tapestry of the Creative Word in Anglophone Literatures*. Udine: Forum editrice, 249–262.

Bortoluzzi Maria & Marenzi Ivana (2014): YELLing for collaborative learning in teacher education: users' voices in the social platform LearnWeb2.0. *International Journal of Social Media and Interactive Learning Environments (IJSMILE)*, 2(2), 182–198.

Brett Paul (1996): Using multimedia: an investigation or learners' attitudes. *Computer Assisted Language Learning Journal*. 9(2), 191–212.

Breidbach Stephan & Viebrock Britta (2012): CLIL in Germany – results from recent research in a contested field of education. *International CLIL Research Journal*, 1(4), 5–16. <http://www.icrj.eu/14/article1.html> [Accessed September 2013].

Brown Ann L. (1992): Design experiments: theoretical and methodological challenges in creating complex interventions in classroom settings. *Journal of the Learning Sciences*, 2(2), 141–178.

Brown John Seely, Collins Allan & Duguid Paul (1989): Situated cognition and the culture of learning. *Educational Researcher*, 18(1), 32–41.

Brown John Seely (2000): Growing up digital: how the Web changes work, education, and the ways people learn. *Change*, March/April 2000, 10–20. *USDLA online Journal* 16(2) ISSN 1537-5080 <http://www.usdla.org/html/journal/FEB02_Issue/article01.html> [Accessed August 2013].

Brown John Seely (2002): Learning in the digital age. In: Maureen Devlin, Richard Larson, Joel Meyerson (eds.): *The Internet & the University: Forum 2001*, 65–91.

Bruner Jerome S. (1967): *On knowing: essays for the left hand*. Cambridge, Mass: Harvard University Press.

Byram Michael, Gribkova Bella & Starkey Hugh (2002): *Developing the intercultural dimension in language teaching. A practical introduction for teachers*. Strasbourg: Council of Europe Publishing, Language Policy Division, 1–35. <http://lrc.cornell.edu/rs/roms/507sp/ExtraReadings/Section0/Section0/uploads/File1235272745204/InterculturalDimensionByram.pdf>[Accessed August 2013].

Calvani Antonio & Rotta Mario (2003): Il ruolo del tutor. *Fare formazione in Internet. Manuale di ditattica online*. Trento: Erickson, 221–250.

Calvani Antonio (2004): *Che cos'e´ la tecnologia dell'Educazione*. Roma: Carrocci, Le bussole.

Chatti Mohamed Amine, Jarke Matthias & Frosch-Wilke Dirk (2007): The future of e-learning: a shift to knowledge networking and social software. *International Journal of Knowledge and Learning*, 3(4/5), 404–420.

Chatti Mohamed Amine, Dahl Daniel, Jarke Matthias & Vossen Gottfried (2008): Towards Web 2.0 driven learning environments. In: *Proceeding of the Fourth International Conference on Web Information Systems and Technologies (WEBIST 2008)*. Funchal, Madeira, Portugal, (1)2008, 370–375.

Chin John P., Diehl Virginia A. & Norman Kent L. (1988): Development of an instrument measuring user satisfaction of the Human-Computer Interface. In: *Proceedings of the CHI'88 Conference*. ACM, 213–218.

Chomsky Noam (1965): The general properties of language. In: F. L. Darley (ed.): *Brain Mechanisms Underlying Speech and Language*, Proceedings of the Princeton Conference on Brain Mechanisms Underlying Speech and Language. New York: Grune and Stratton.

Clarke Arthur C. (1962): *Profiles of the future*. London: The Scientific Book Club.

Collins Alan (1992): Towards a design science of education. In: E. Scanlon & T. O'Shea (eds.): *New directions in educational technology*. Berlin: Springer, 15–22.

Cope Bill, Kalantzis Mary & the New London Group (2000): *Multiliteracies: literacy learning and the design of social futures*. London: Routledge.

Cope Bill & Mary Kalantzis (2007): New media, new learning. *International Journal of Learning*, 14(1), 75–79.

Cope Bill & Mary Kalantzis (2008): The social Web: changing knowledge systems in Higher Education. In: D. Epstein, R. Boden, R. Deem, F. Rizvi & S. Wright (eds.): *Geographies of Knowledge, Geometries of Power: Framing the Future of Higher Education*, World Yearbook of Education. London: Routledge, 371–384.

Cope Bill & Kalantzis Mary (2009): Multiliteracies: new literacies, new learning. *Pedagogies: An International Journal*, 4(3), 164–195. DOI: 10.1080/15544800903076044. <http://newlearningonline.com/~newlearn/wp-content/blogs.dir/35/files/2009/03/M-litsPaper13Apr08.pdf> [Accessed August 2013].

Coyle Do (1999): Supporting students in content and language integrated learning contexts: planning for effective classrooms. In: J. Masih (ed.): *Learning through a foreign language: models, methods and outcomes.* London, UK: Centre for Information on Language Teaching and Research, 46–62.

Coyle Do (2006): Content and language integrated learning: motivating learners and teachers. *Scottish Languages Review*, (13), 1–18.

Cummins James (2003): BICS and CALP: origins and rationale for the distinction. In: C.B. Paulston & G.R. Tucker (eds.): *Sociolinguistics: The essential readings.* London: Blackwell, 322–328.

Daley Elizabeth (2003): Expanding the concept of literacy. *EDUCAUSE review*, 32(2), 32–40. <http://dmp.osu.edu/dmac/readings/daley.pdf> [Accessed August 2013].

Dalton-Puffer Christiane (2007): *Discourse in Content and Language Integrated Learning (CLIL) classrooms.* Amsterdam: John Benjamins Publishing Company.

Darn Steve (2003): Design-based research: an emerging paradigm for educational inquiry. (DBRC - Design-Based Research Collective). *Educational Researcher*, 32(1), 5–8.

Demetriadis Stavros (2013): Research evidence on the impact of technology-enhanced collaboration scripts on learning. A contribution toward a script theory of guidance in CSCL. In: D. Hernandez-Leo, T. Ley, R. Klamma, & A. Harrer (eds.): *Scaling up learning for sustained impact*, Proceedings of the 8th European Conference on Technology Enhanced Learning (EC-TEL 2013). Berlin Heidelberg: Springer, LNCS 8095, XXII, 139–150. ISBN: 978-3-642-40813-7 (Print) 978-3-642-40814-4 (Online).

Demidova Elena, Kärger Philipp, Olmedilla Daniel, Ternier Stefaan, Duval Erik, Dicerto Michele, Mendez Carlos & Stefanov Krassen (2007): Services for knowledge resource sharing and management in an open source infrastructure for lifelong competence development. In: *Proceedings of the Intl. Conference on Advanced Learning Technologies (ICALT)*. Niigata, Japan, 691–693.

Denyer Laverne & Peacock Wendy (2001): Achieving balance in educational technology: using Web Quest to balance direct instruction and problem-based learning in today's classroom. *Action Research Project*. CSUS-iMET. 1–37. <http://imet.csus.edu/imet1/denyer/imet_portfolio/documents/ar_lit_review.doc>[Accessed August 2013].

Dietze Stefan, Sanchez-Alonso Salvador, Ebner Hannes, Yu Hong Qing, Giordano Daniela, Marenzi Ivana & Pereira Nunes Bernardo (2013): Interlinking educational resources and the web of data: a survey of challenges and approaches. *Emerald Program: electronic library and information systems*, 47(1), 60–91. ISSN: 0033-0337. DOI: 10.1108/00330331211296312.

Dillenbourg Pierre (1999): What do you mean by collaborative learning? In: P. Dillenbourg (ed.): *Collaborative-learning: Cognitive and Computational Approaches*. Oxford: Elsevier, 1–19.

Dillenbourg Pierre (2002): Over-scripting CSCL: the risk of blending collaborative learning with instructional design. In: P.A. Kirschner (ed.): *Three worlds of CSCL. Can we support CSCL*. Open university Nederland, Heerlen, 61–91.

Dillenbourg Pierre & Jermann Patrick (2007): Designing integrative scripts. In: F. Fischer, H. Mandl, J. Haake & I. Kollar (eds.): *Computer-Supported Collaborative Learning Series*. New York: Springer, 16, 275–301.

Dillenbourg Pierre & Tchounikine Pierre (2007): Flexibility in macro-scripts for computer-supported collaborative learning. *Journal of Computer Assisted Learning*, 23(1), 1–13.

Dillenbourg Pierre & Hong Fabrice (2008): The mechanics of CSCL macro scripts. In: *Computer Supported Collaborative Learning*. International Society of the Learning Sciences. Springer, 3, 5–23. DOI: 10.1007/s11412-007-9033-1.

Dooley Karen T. (2008): Multiliteracies and pedagogies of new learning for students of English as an additional language. In: A. Healy (ed.): *Multiliteracies and Diversity in education: new pedagogies for expanding landscapes*. Oxford University Press, South Melbourne, Vic., 102–125.

Doolittle Peter E. (2002): *Multimedia learning: empirical results and practical applications. White Paper*. <http://scr.csc.noctrl.edu/courses/edn509/resources/readings/multimediaLearningEmpericalResults.pdf>[Accessed February 2013].

Dorin Henry, Demmin Peter E. & Gabel Dorothy (1990): *Chemistry: the study of matter.* (3rd edition). Englewood Cliffs, New Jersy: Prentice Hall, Inc.

Dörnyei Zoltán (2003): *Questionnaires in second language research: construction, administration and processing.* London: LEA. ISBN 0-8058-3908-9.

Dörnyei Zoltán (2007): *Research methods in applied linguistics. Quantitative, qualitative, and mixed methodologies.* Oxford University Press. ISBN-13: 978-0-19-442258-1.

Downes Stephen (2005): E-learning2.0. *ACM eLearn Magazine.* 2005(10), 1.

Driscoll Margaret (2002): *Blended learning: let's get beyond the hype.* IBM Global Learning Services, White Paper, 2005. <http://www-07.ibm.com/services/pdf/blended_learning.pdf> [Accessed February 2013].

Evans Brynn M. & Chi Ed H. (2008): Towards a model of understanding social search. In: *Proceedings of CSCW'08,* November 8–12. San Diego, California, USA: ACM Press, 485–494.

Facer Keri & Williamson Ben (2004): *Designing technologies to support creativity and collaboration.* Bristol: Futurelab, 1–19.

Fischer Frank, Kollar Ingo, Haake Jörg M. & Mandl Heinz (2007a): *Scripting Computer-Supported Collaborative Learning: cognitive, computational and educational perspectives.* New York: Springer. ISBN 13: 978-0-387-36947-1.

Fischer Frank, Kollar Ingo, Haake Jörg M. & Mandl Heinz (2007b): Perspectives on collaboration scripts. In: F. Fischer, I. Kollar, J.M. Haake & H. Mandl (eds.): (Tran.), *Scripting Computer-Supported Collaborative Learning: cognitive, computational and educational perspectives.* New York: Springer, 6, 1–10.

Fisichella Marco, Herder Eelco, Marenzi Ivana, Nejdl Wolfgang (2010): Who are you working with? Visualizing TEL Research Communities. In: *Proceedings of ED-MEDIA 2010, World Conference on Educational Multimedia, Hypermedia & Telecommunications,* June 28-July 2, 2010. Toronto, Canada.

Gagné Robert M. (1965): *The conditions of learning and theory of instruction* (1st edition). New York, NY: Holt, Rinehart & Winston.

Gee James Paul (1996). *Social linguistics and literacies: ideology in discourses.* London: Taylor and Francis.

Gillies Robyn M. (2008): Teachers' and students' verbal behaviours during cooperative learning. In: R.M. Gillies, A.F. Ashman & J. Terwel (eds.): *The Teacher's Role in Implementing Cooperative Learning in the Classroom.* New York: Springer, 242–262.

Gillies Robyn M., Ashman Adrian & Terwel Jan (2008): The teacher's role in implementing cooperative learning in the classroom: An introduction. In: R.M. Gillies, A. Ashman & J. Terwel (eds.): The Teacher's Role in Implementing Cooperative Learning in the Classroom. New York: Springer, 1–8. DOI 10.1007/978-0-387-70892-8.

Gómez Aguilar Diego Alonso, Therón Roberto & García-Peñalvo Francisco J. (2013): Reveal the relationships among student's participation and its outcomes on eLearning environments: Case study. In: *Proceedings of the 13th IEEE International Conference on Advanced Learning Technologies (ICALT 2013)*. Conference Publishing Services, 443–447. DOI 10.1109/ICALT.2013.136.

Gouli Evangelia, Gogoulou Agoritsa, Papanikolaou Kyparisia A. & Grigoriadou Maria (2006): An adaptive feedback framework to support reflection, guiding and tutoring. In: G.D. Magoulas & S.Y. Chen (eds.): *Advances in Web-Based Education: Personalized Learning Environments*. Information Science Publishing, 178–202. <http://hermes.di.uoa.gr/lab/cvs/papers/gouli/ggpg-ple.pdf> [Accessed August 2013].

Graddol David (ed.) (2001): Applied linguistics for the 21st century. *AILA Review 14*. Catchline: AILA and the authors, 1–82. ISSN 1461–0213. <http://www.aila.info/download/publications/review/AILA14.pdf> [Accessed September 2013].

Grünewald Franka, Meinel Christoph, Michael Totschnig & Christian Willems (2013): Designing MOOCs for the support of multiple learning styles. In: D. Hernandez-Leo, T. Ley, R. Klamma & A. Harrer (eds.): *Scaling up learning for sustained impact*, Proceedings of the 8th European Conference on Technology Enhanced Learning (EC-TEL 2013). Berlin Heidelberg: Springer, LNCS 8095, XXII, 371–382. ISBN: 978-3-642-40813-7 (Print) 978-3-642-40814-4 (Online).

Halliday Michael A. K. (1978): *Language as social semiotic: the social interpretation of language and meaning*. London, Edward Arnold.

Halliday Michael & Matthiessen Christian (2004): *An introduction to functional grammar.* (3rd edition), London: Hodder education. ISBN: 978 0 340 76167 0.

Hague Cassie & Payton Sarah (2010): *Digital literacy across the curriculum.* Futurelab, 1–63. <http://www2.futurelab.org.uk/resources/documents/handbooks/digital_literacy.pdf> [Accessed August 2013].

Häkkinen Päivi & Mäkitalo-Siegl Kati (2007): Educational perspectives on scripting CSCL. In: F. Fischer, H. Mandl, J. Haake & I. Kollar (eds.): *Computer-Supported Collaborative Learning Series.* New York: Springer, 3, 262–271.

Harrer Andreas, Pfahler Kerstin, de Groot Reuma & Abdu Rotem (2013): Research on collaborative planning and reflection – methods and tools in the Metafora project. In: D. Hernandez-Leo, T. Ley, R. Klamma & A. Harrer (eds.): *Scaling up learning for sustained impact*, Proceedings of the 8th European Conference on Technology Enhanced Learning (EC-TEL 2013). Berlin Heidelberg: Springer, LNCS 8095, XXII, 139–150. ISBN: 978-3-642-40813-7 (Print) 978-3-642-40814-4 (Online).

Hathorn Lesley G. & *Ingram* Albert L. (*2002*): *Online collaboration: making it work. Educational Technology*, 42(1): 33–40.

Healy Annah (2008): Expanding student capacities: learning by design pedagogy. In: A. Healy (ed.): *Multiliteracies and Diversity in Education*. Oxford: Oxford University Press, 2–29.

Hearst Marti A. (2009): *Search user interfaces*. Cambridge: Cambridge University Press. ISBN: 9780521113793.

Held Christoph & Cress Ulrike (2009): Learning by foraging: the impact of social tags on knowledge acquisition. In: U. Cress, V. Dimitrova & M. Specht (eds.): *Proceedings of the EC-TEL 2009 Conference*. Berlin Heidelberg: Springer, 254–266. ISBN: 978-3-642-04635-3.

Hendler James, Shadbolt Nigel, Hall Wendy, Berners-Lee Tim & Weitzner Daniel (2008): *Web science: an interdisciplinary approach to understanding the web*. New York: Communications of the ACM, 51(7), 60–69. <http://www-gris.det.uvigo.es/wiki/pub/Main/PaginaRst/hendler.pdf> [Accessed August 2013].

Herring Susan C. (2004): Computer-mediated discourse analysis: an approach to researching online behaviour. In: A. Barab, R. Kling & J.H. Gray (eds.): *Designing for Virtual Communities in the Service of Learning*. New York: Cambridge University Press, 338–376.

Hesse Friedrich W. (2007): Being told to do something or just being aware of something? An alternative approach to scripting in CSCL. In: F. Fischer, H. Mandl, J. Haake & I. Kollar (eds.): *Computer-Supported Collaborative Learning Series*. New York: Springer, 3, 91–98.

Holdack-Janssen Eva & Marenzi Ivana (2012a): Learning about literature on the Web in a German school. In: P. Vittorini, R. Gennari, I. Marenzi, F. De La Prieta Pintado & J.M. Corchado Rodriguez (eds.): *Proceedings of the International Workshop on Evidence-based Technology Enhanced Learning* (EbTEL 12), Advances in Intelligent and Soft Computing. Springer-Verlag GmbH, (152), 57–65. ISSN 1867-5662.

Holdack-Janssen Eva & Marenzi Ivana (2012b): LearnWeb2.0 im Deutschunterricht. Informationssuche und -auswertung im Deutschunterricht mit LearnWeb2.0. In: P. Schlobinski & S. Torsten (eds.): *Sprache und Kommunikation im Web 2.0.* Seelze (Der Deutschunterricht 6), 64–73.

Huber Günter L. & Huber Anne A. (2008): Structuring group interaction to promote thinking and learning during small group learning in High school settings. In: R.M. Gillies, A.F. Ashman & J. Terwel (eds.): *The Teacher's Role in Implementing Cooperative Learning in the Classroom.* New York, U.S.A.: Springer, 111–132. <http://link.springer.com/chapter/10.1007%2F978-0-387-70892-8_6> [Accessed August 2013].

Hutchinson Tom & Waters Alan (1987): *English for Specific Purposes: a learner-centered approach.* Cambridge University Press. ISBN: 978-0-521-31837-2.

Ingram Albert L. (2009): Measuring collaboration in online communication. In: M. Khosrow-Pour (ed.): *Encyclopedia of Information Science and Technology, Second Edition.* Hershey, PA: Information Science Reference. 403, 2537-2541. DOI: 10.4018/978-1-60566-026-4.

Jewitt Carey (2006): *Technology, literacy and learning: a multimodal approach.* London: Routledge. ISBN: 0-415-34549-9.

Jewitt Carey & Kress Gunther (2003): Introduction. In: J. R. Lewis, C. Jewitt & *G. Kress* (eds.): *Multimodal literacy.* New York: Peter Lang, 1–18.

Jonassen David H. & Grabowski Barbara L. (1993): *Handbook of individual difference, learning, and instruction.* Hillsdale, NJ: Lawrence Erlbaum Associates, Publishers.

Jonassen David H. (1994): Thinking technology: toward a constructivist design model. *Educational Technology*, April, 34–37.

Johnson Burke R, Onwuegbuzie Anthony J. & Lisa A. Turner (2007): Toward a definition of Mixed Methods Research. *Journal of Mixed Methods Research 2007*, 112–133. DOI: 10.1177/1558689806298224.

Johnson David W. & Johnson Roger T. (2003): Student motivation in cooperative groups: social interdependence theory. In: R.M. Gillies & A.F. Ashman (eds.): *Cooperative learning: the social and the intellectual outcomes of learning in groups.* London: RoutledgeFalmer, 136–176.

Johnson David W. & Johnson Roger T. (2008): Social interdependence theory and cooperative learning: the teacher's role. In: R.M. Gillies, A.F. Ashman & J. Terwel (eds.): *The Teacher's Role in Implementing Cooperative Learning in the Classroom.* New York, U.S.A.: Springer, 9–34.

Kalantzis Mary & Cope Bill (2004): Designs for learning. *E- Learning* 1 (1), 38–93. <http://www.academia.edu/2804132/Designs_for_learning> [Accessed August 2013].

Kalantzis Mary, Cope Bill & The Learning by Design Project Group (2005): *Learning by design*. Melbourne, Australia: Victorian Schools Innovation Commission.

Kalantzis Mary & Cope Bill (2008): Language education and multiliteracies. In: Stephen May & Nancy H. Hornberger (eds.): *Encyclopedia of Language and Education* (2nd edition). Springer, Media LLC, 1, 195–211.

Kalantzis Mary, Cope Bill & Cloonan Anne (2010): A multiliteracies perspective on the New Literacies. In: Elisabeth A. Baker (ed.): *The New Literacies. Multiple Perspectives on Research and Practice*. New York: The Guildford Press, 61–87.

Kaye Anthony (1992): Learning together apart. In: Kaye A. (ed.): *Collaborative Learning Through Computer Conferences*. NATO ASI Series, Berlin: Springer-Verlag, 90, 1–24.

Kellner Douglas (1998): Multiple literacies and critical pedagogy in a multicultural society. *Educational Theory*, 48(1), 103–122. <http://pages.gseis.ucla.edu/faculty/kellner/essays/multipleliteraciescriticalpedagogy.pdf> [Accessed July 2013].

Kellner Douglas (2004): Technological transformation, multiple literacies, and the re-visioning of education. *E-Learning*, 1(1), 1–43.

Kern Richard & Warschauer Mark (2000): Theory and practice of network-based language teaching. In: M. Warschauer & R. Kern (eds.): *Network-based language teaching: Concepts and practice*. New York: Cambridge University Press, 1–19.

Kervin Lisa & Derewianka Beverly (2011): New technologies to support language learning. In: B. Tomlinson (ed.): *Materials Development in Language Teaching*. Cambridge, UK: Cambridge University Press, 328–351.

Kiernan Eamon (2001): Portfolio assessment in language education: a theoretical justification and the results of a classroom-based research project. In: R. Kupetz (ed.): *Empowerment of the learner: Changes and Challenges*. Frankfurt am Main: Peter Lang, 57–84

King Alison (2007): Scripting collaborative learning processes: a cognitive perspective. In: F. Fischer, I. Kollar, J.M. Haake & H. Mandl (eds.): *Scripting Computer-Supported Collaborative Learning: cognitive, computational and educational perspectives*. New York: Springer, 13–36. ISBN 13: 978-0-387-36947-1.

Kolodner Janet L. (2007): The roles of scripts in promoting collaborative discourse. In: F. Fischer, H. Mandl, J. Haake & I. Kollar (eds.): *Computer-Supported Collaborative Learning Series*. New York: Springer, 3, 237–262.

Koohang Alex & Harman Keith (2007): Advancing sustainability of Open Educational Resources. In: *Informing Science and Information Technology*, (4), 535–544.

Koper Rob, Krassen Stefanov & Darina Dicheva (2009): Editorial. *International Journal of Cont. Engineering Education and Life-Long Learning,* Inderscience, 19(4/5/6), 271–275.

Kress Gunther (2000): Design and transformation: new theories of meaning. In: B. Cope & M. Kalantzis (eds.): *Multiliteracies: Literacy Learning and the Design of Social Futures*. London: Routledge, 153–161.

Kress Gunther (2003): *Literacy in the new media age*. London: Routledge.

Kvavik Robert B. & Caruso Judith B. (2005): ECAR study of students and information technology. *Convenience, connection, control, and learning.* Boulder, CO: EDUCAUSE Center for Applied Research. <http://www.educause.edu/ECAR/ECARStudyofStudentsandInformat/158586> [Accessed February 2013]

Kupetz Maxi (2011): Multimodal resources in students' explanations in CLIL interaction. *Novitas-ROYAL (Research on Youth and Language)*, 5 (1), 121–142.

Kupetz Rita (ed.) (2001a): *Empowerment of the learner: changes and challenges.* Frankfurt am Main: Peter Lang. ISBN: 3-631-38751-2.

Kupetz Rita (2001b): Subjective theories of two teachers and their learners' beliefs on portfolio (self-)assessment. In: R. Kupetz (ed.): *Empowerment of the learner: Changes and Challenges*. Frankfurt am Main: Peter Lang, 27–55.

Kupetz Rita & Ziegenmeyer Birgit (2005): Blended learning in a teacher training course: integrated interactive e-learning and contact learning. *ReCALL,* 17(2), 179-196. DOI: 10.1017/S0958344005000327.

Kupetz Rita & Ziegenmeyer Birgit (2006): Flexible learning activities fostering autonomy in a teacher training course. *ReCALL,* 18(1), 63–82. DOI: 10.1017/S0958344006000516.

Kupetz Rita (2010): *Multiple Literacy*. In: Carola Suhrkamp (ed.): Stuttgart: Metzler Verlag, 225.

Kupetz Rita & Woltin Alexander (2014): Language education policy and CLIL principles. In: R. Kupetz & C. Becker (eds.): *Content and Language*

Integrated Learning (CLIL) by Interaction. Frankfurt am Main: Peter Lang, 11–27.

Lemke Jay (2006): Toward critical multimedia literacy: Technology, research and politics. In: Michael C. McKenna et al. (eds.): *International handbook of literacy and technology*. New Jersey: Lawrence Erlbaum Associates, (2), 3–14.

Li Na, Ullrich Carsten, El Helou S. & Gillet Denis (2010): Using social software for teamwork and collaborative project management in Higher Education. In: X. Luo et al. (eds.): *Advances in Web based learning - ICWL 2010*, Proceedings of the 9th International Conference on Web-based Learning. Berlin-Hidelberg: Springer, LNCS 6483, 161–170. <http://infoscience.epfl.ch/record/151683/files/ICWL2010_EPFL.pdf>[Accessed August 2013].

Lightbown Patsy M. (2000): Classroom SLA research and second language teaching. *Applied Linguistics,* 21(4), 431–462.

Long Yanjin & Aleven Vincent (2013): Active learners: redesigning and intelligent tutoring system to support self-regulated learning. In: D. Hernandez-Leo, T. Ley, R. Klamma & A. Harrer (eds.): *Scaling up learning for sustained impact*, Proceedings of the 8th European Conference on Technology Enhanced Learning (EC-TEL 2013). Berlin Heidelberg: Springer, LNCS 8095, XXII, 490–495. ISBN: 978-3-642-40813-7 (Print) 978-3-642-40814-4 (Online).

Lorenzo Francisco (2013): Genre-based curricula: multilingual academic literacy in content and language integrated learning. *International Journal of Bilingual Education and Bilingualism*, 16(3), 375-388, DOI: 10.1080/13670050.2013.777391.

Malik Sufiana K. & Khurshed Fauzia (2011): A proposed Constructive Instructional Design (CID) for teaching of social studies at elementary level. *European Journal of Social Sciences*, 23(4), 531–552.

Malvezzi-Campeggi Flaminia (2013): Content and Language Integrated Learning (CLIL): state of the art in Europe and in Italy. *Journal of Postdoctoral Research*, 1(6), 38–44. <http://www.postdocjournal.com/file_journal/589_62747169.pdf> [Accessed September 2013].

Marenzi Ivana, Demidova Elena, Nejdl Wolfgang & Olmedilla Daniel (2008a): Social software for lifelong competence development: scenario and challenges. In: H.Sligte & R. Koper (eds.): *Empowering Learners for Lifelong Competence Development: pedagogical, organisational and technological issues*, Proceedings of the 4th TENCompetence Open Workshop. April, 10–11, 2008, Madrid, Spain: SCO-Kohnstamm Instituut, Amsterdam, The Netherlands. ISBN 978-90-6813-8474.

Marenzi Ivana, Demidova Elena, Nejdl Wolfgang & Zerr Sergej (2008b): Social software for lifelong competence development: challenges and infrastructure. *International Journal of Emerging Technologies in Learning (iJET)*, 3(2008), 18–23. ISSN: 1863-0383.

Marenzi Ivana, Demidova Elena & Nejdl Wolfgang (2008c): LearnWeb2.0: integrating social software for lifelong learning. In: *Proceedings of the World Conference on Educational Multimedia, Hypermedia and Telecommunications (ED-Media 2008)*. Chesapeake, VA: AACE, 1793–1802.

Marenzi Ivana, Zerr Sergej & Nejdl Wolfgang (2008d): Providing social sharing functionalities in LearnWeb2.0. In: R. Koper, K. Stefanov & D. Dicheva (eds.): *Stimulating Personal Development and Knowledge Sharing,* Proceedings of the 5th TENCompetence Open Workshop. Sofia: Faleza Office, 9–14. ISBN 978-954-92146-5-9. <http://dspace.learningnetworks.org/bitstream/1820/1961/1/proceedings%20Sofia.pdf> [accessed August 2013].

Marenzi Ivana, Zerr Sergej, Abel Fabian & Nejdl Wolfgang (2009): Social sharing in LearnWeb2.0. *International Journal of Continuing Engineering Education and Life-Long Learning* (IJCEELL), 19(4-5-6), 276–290. DOI: 10.1504/IJCEELL.2009.028826.

Marenzi Ivana (2010): Experience as an online co-tutor in a blended English course: monitoring techniques for an online class. In: *Implementing e-Learning in English Language Teaching,* Innovative Approaches to Language Teaching Online. Roma: Artemide, 1, 155–168.

Marenzi Ivana, Kupetz Rita, Nejdl Wolfgang & Zerr Sergej (2010): Supporting active learning in CLIL through collaborative search. In: X. Luo et al. (eds.): *Advances in Web based learning - ICWL 2010,* Proceedings of the 9th International Conference on Web-based Learning. Berlin-Hidelberg: Springer, LNCS 6483, 200–209.

Marenzi Ivana (2012): Designer genres: social, interactional, technological and multimodal aspects of Web 2.0. In: M. Cambria, C. Arizzi, F. Coccetta (eds.): *Web Genres and Web Tools.* Como: Ibis, 174–214.

Marenzi Ivana & Nejdl Wolfgang (2012): I search therefore I learn. Supporting active and collaborative learning in language teaching. In: A. Okada, T. Connolly & P. Scott (eds.): *Collaborative Learning 2.0: Open Educational Resources.* IGI Global, 103–125.

Marenzi Ivana & Zerr Sergej (2012): Multiliteracies and active learning in CLIL: the development of LearnWeb2.0. *IEEE Transactions on Learning Technologies* (TLT). Los Alamitos, CA, USA, 5(4), 336–348. DOI:10.1109/TLT.2012.14.

Marenzi Ivana, Baldry Anthony & Nejdl Wolfgang (2012): Towards an integrative approach for CLIL: the LearnWeb2.0 model. In: G. Blell & C. Lütge (eds.): *Fremdsprachendidaktik und Lehrerbildung: Konzepte, Impulse, Perspektiven.* Berlin: Münster et.al: LIT, 95–112.

Marenzi Ivana & Kupetz Rita (2012): CLIL teacher training and Web 2.0. Symposium on language learning beyond the classroom. In: T. Pattison, *IATEFL 2011 Brighton Conference Selections.* Eynsham: Information Press, 126–129.

Marenzi Ivana (2013): A multiliteracies approach for supporting language learning courses at university level. In: J. Jovanovic & R. Chiong (eds.): *Technological and Social Environments for Interactive Learning.* Santa Rosa, CA: Informing Science Press, 249–276.

Marenzi Ivana (2014): Interactive and collaborative supports for CLIL: towards a formal model based on digital literacy. In: R. Kupetz & C. Becker (eds.): *Content and Language Integrated Learning (CLIL) by Interaction.* Frankfurt am Main: Peter Lang, 75–99.

Marenzi Ivana & Kantz Deirdre (2013): ESP course design – a multiliteracies approach. In: *Reshaping Learning: Transforming Education through the Fusion of Learning and Technology*, Proceedings of the 13th IEEE International Conference on Advanced Learning Technologies (ICALT 2013). Beijing, China IEEE, 221–223.

Marsh David (2002): *CLIL/EMILE – The European dimension - actions, trends and foresight potential.* Public Services Contract DG EAC: European Commission. UniCOM, University of Jyväskylä, Finland, 1–204. <http://ec.europa.eu/languages/documents/doc491_en.pdf> [accessed August 2013].

Martínez-Monés Alejandra, Harrer Andreas & Dimitriadis Yannis (2011): An interaction-aware design process for the integration of interaction analysis into mainstream CSCL practices. In: *S. Puntambekar, G. Erkens* & *C. Hmelo-Silver* (eds.): *Analyzing Interactions in CSCL.* Springer, 269–291.

Mayall Berry (2007): Children's lives outside school and their educational impact. *Primary Review Research Survey* 8/1. Cambridge: University of Cambridge Faculty of Education. ISBN978-1-906478-05-6.

Mehisto Peeter, Marsh David & Frigols Maria Jesus (2008): *Uncovering CLIL. Content and Language Integrated Learning in bilingual and multilingual education.* Oxford: Macmillan.

Mehisto Peeter (2012): Criteria for producing CLIL learning material. *Encuentro* 21, 15–33. ISSN 1989-0796.

Meier Anne, Spada Hans & Rummel Nikol (2007): A rating scheme for assessing the quality of computer-supported collaboration processes. *Computer-Supported Collaborative Learning*. Springer, 2, 63–86. DOI: 10.1007/s11412-006-9005-x.

Merrill David M. (2000): Instructional strategies and learning styles: which takes precedence? In: R. Reiser & J. Dempsey (eds.): *Trends and Issues in Instructional Technology*. Prentice Hall, 1–5. <http://id2.usu.edu/Papers/5LearningStyles.PDF> [Accessed August 2013].

Meyer Anne & Rose David H. (1998): *Learning to read in the computer age*. Harvard Education Press. <http://www.cast.org/library/books/ltr/index.html> [Accessed August 2013].

Meyer Oliver (2010): Towards quality-CLIL: successful planning and teaching strategies. *Puls* 33, 11–29. ISSN: 1577-0338. <http://dialnet.unirioja.es/servlet/articulo?codigo=3311569> [Accessed August 2013].

Mirijamdotter Anita, Somerville Mary M. & Holst Marita (2006): An interactive and iterative evaluation approach for creating collaborative learning environments. *The Electronic Journal Information Systems Evaluation*, 9(2), 83–92.

Mohan, B. A. (1986). *Language and content*. Reading, MA, Addison-Wesley

Moore Michael G. (1993): Theory of transactional distance. In: Desmond Keegan (ed.): *Theoretical principles of distance education*. London: Routledge, 22–38.

Moore Michael G. & Kearsley Greg (1996): Fundamentals of distance education. In: *Distance Education. A System View*. Belmont, CA: Wadsworth Publishing Company. ISBN 0-534-26496-4. <http://postgrado.una.edu.ve/evaluacionaprendizajes/paginas/moorecap1.pdf> [Accessed August 2013].

Morin Edgar (1999): *La testa ben fatta. Riforma dell'insegnamento e riforma del pensiero*. Milano: Rafaello Cortina.

Morris Meredith Ringel & Horvitz Eric (2007): SearchTogether: an interface for collaborative Web search. In: *Proceedings of the 20th ACM Symposium on User Interface Software and Technology* (UIST 2007). Newport, USA, 3–12.

Morris Meredith Ringel (2008): A survey of collaborative Web search practices. In: *Proceedings of the SIGCHI Conference on Human Factors in Computing Systems (CHI 2008)*. New York: ACM Press, 1657–1660. <http://research.microsoft.com/en-us/um/people/merrie/papers/collab_search_survey.pdf> [Accessed August 2013].

Nelson Ted H. (1977): *The home computer revolution*. The University of Michigan: Nelson.

[New London Group] Cazden Courtney, Cope Bill, Fairclough Norman, Gee Jim, et al. (1996): A pedagogy of multiliteracies: designing social futures. ProQuest Psychology Journals. *Harvard Educational Review*, 66(1), 60–92. <http://www.pwrfaculty.net/summer-seminar/files/2011/12/new-london-multiliteracies.pdf> [Accessed August 2013].

Newell Allen and Herbert Simon (1972). *Human problem solving*. Englewood Cliffs, N.J. Prentice-Hall.

Nikula Tarja, Dalton-Puffer Christiane & Llinares Ana (2013): CLIL classroom discourse – Research from Europe. *Journal of Immersion and Content-Based Language Education*. John Benjamins Publishing Company: 1(1), 70–100. DOI: 10.1075/jicb.1.1.04nik ISSN 2212–8433/e-ISSN 2212-844.

Norman Donald A. (1993): *Things that make us smart: defending human attributes in the age of the machine*. Cambridge, MA: Perseus Publishing.

O'Reilly Tim (2007): What is Web 2.0: design patterns and business models for the next generation of software. *International Journal of Digital Economics* (65), 17–37. <http://mpra.ub.uni-muenchen.de/4580/> [Accessed July 2013].

Pampaloni Carla (2006): e-Tutor e nuovi modelli di tutorship. *WBT E-Magazine*. June 2006. <http://www.giornalelearning.it/httpdocs/index.php?risorsa=tutorship> [Accessed February 2013].

Papert Seymour (1980): Computer-based microworlds as incubators for powerful ideas. In: R. Taylor (ed.): *The computer in the school: Tutor, tool, tutee*. New York: Teacher's College Press, 203–210.

Pavlou Andria & Kyza Eleni A. (2013): An investigation of two methods for the technological mediation of collaborative peer feedback in Higher Education. In: D. Hernandez-Leo, T. Ley, R. Klamma, & A. Harrer (eds.): *Scaling up learning for sustained impact*, Proceedings of the 8th European Conference on Technology Enhanced Learning (EC-TEL 2013). Berlin Heidelberg: Springer, LNCS 8095, XXII, 274–287. ISBN: 978-3-642-40813-7 (Print) 978-3-642-40814-4 (Online).

Petrides Lisa, Nguyen Lilly, Kargliani Anastasia & Jimes Cynthia (2008): Open Educational Resources: inquiring into author reuse behaviours. *International Journal of Technology Enhanced Learning*. Inderscience Enterprises Ltd. 1(1/2)2008, 98–117.

Pirolli Peter & Card Stuart K. (1999): Information foraging. *Psychological Review*, 106(4), 643–675. DOI: 10.1037/0033-295X.106.4.643.

Pozzi Francesca, Persico Donatella, Fischer Frank & Hoffmann Lena (2010): *Methodologies for the design of structured CSCL. Approaches to structure CSCL:*

the macro and the micro design level. Deliverable of the STELLAR European NoE, Annex 3, 48–54.

Prinsen Fleur, Terwel Jan, Volman Monique & Fakkert Marieke (2008): Feedback and reflection to promote student participation in Computer Supported Collaborative Learning: a multiple case study. In: R.M. Gillies, A.F. Ashman & J. Terwel (eds.): *The Teacher's Role in Implementing Cooperative Learning in the Classroom*. New York: Springer, 133–163.

Puntambekar Sadhana, Erkens Gijsbert & Hmelo-Silver Cindy (eds.)(2011): *Analyzing interactions in CSCL: methods, approaches and issues*. New York: Springer.

Ranieri Maria (ed.)(2006): *Formazione e ciberspazio. Divari ed opportunitä nel mondo della rete*. Scienze dell'educazione. Pisa: Edizioni ETS. ISBN-13: 978-884671685-9.

Redmon Petrea (2011): From face-to-face teaching to online teaching: pedagogical transitions. In: G. Williams, P. Statham, N. Brown & B. Cleland (eds.): *Changing demands, changing directions,* Proceedings of ASCLITE 2011 (Australasian Society for Computers in Learning in Tertiary Education). Hobart: University of Tasmania, 1050–1060. ISBN Proceedings USB: 978-1-86295-644-5.

Richey Rita C. (2008): Reflections on the 2008 AECT definitions of the field. *TechTrends,* 52(1), 24–25.

Rizzo Rosalba (2009): *Multimodal and multimedia aspects of English language teaching and studies in Italian universities. An e-learning approach*. Como: Ibis. ISBN: 978-88-7164-315-1.

Roberts Gregory R. (2005): Technology and learning expectations of the Net Generation. In: D.G. Oblinger & J.L. Oblinger (eds.): *Educating the Net Generation*, EDUCAUSE e-book, 3, 1–7. ISBN: 0-9672853-2-1.

Roblyer Margaret D. & Edwards Jack (2000): *Integrating educational technology into teaching*. New Jersey: Merrill Prentice Hall, Upper Saddle River.

Rosenberg Marc Jeffrey (2001): *E-Learning: strategies for delivering knowledge in the digital age*. NewYork: McGraw-Hill, ISBN-13: 978-0071362689.

Rosenberg Marc Jeffrey (2006): *Beyond e-learning - approaches and technologies to enhance organizational knowledge, learning, and performance.* San Francisco: Pfeiffer. ISBN-13: 978-0-7879-7757-3. <http://www.scribd.com/doc/2151559/Beyond-Elearning-eBook> [Accessed February 2013].

Rotta Mario (2002): Il tutor online: tipologie. *FORM@RE, Newsletter per la formazione in rete*. Erickson Portale Internet n° 8 febbraio 2002. <http://formare.erickson.it/wordpress/it/2002/il-tutor-online-tipologie-2/> [Accessed |February 2013].

Rubens Wilfred, Emans Bruno, Leininen Teemu, Gomez Skarmeta Antonio & Simons Robert-Jan (2005): Design of web-based collaborative learning environments. Translating the pedagogical learning principles of human computer interface. *Computers and Education*, Elsevier 45(2005), 276–294. DOI: 10.1016/j.compedu.2005.04.008.

Rummel Nikol & Spada Hans (2007): Can people learn computer-mediated collaboration by following a script? In: F. Fischer, H. Mandl, J. Haake & I. Kollar (eds.): *Computer-Supported Collaborative Learning Series*. New York: Springer, 3, 39–55.

Rummel Nikol, Deiglmayr Anne, Spada Hans, Kahrimanis George & Avouris Nikolaos (2011): Analyzing collaborative interactions across domains and settings: an adaptable rating scheme. In: S. Puntambekar, G. Erkens & C.E. Hmelo-Silver (eds.): *Analyzing Interactions in CSCL: Methods, Approaches and Issues. Computer-Supported Collaborative Learning*. Springer, 12(3), 367–390.

Russell Daniel M., Stefik Mark I., Pirolli Peter & Card Stuart K. (1993): The cost structure of sensemaking. In: *Proceedings of the INTERCHI* and CHI '93 *Conference on Human Factors in Computing Systems*. Amsterdam, The Netherlands: ACM, 269–76.

Salomon Gray (1998): Novel constructivist learning environments and novel technologies: some issues to be concerned with. *Research Dialogue in Learning and Instruction*, 1(1): 1–12.

Salomon Gavriel (2000): *It's not just the tool, but the educational rationale that counts*. Invited keynote address to the World Conference on Educational Media, Hypermedia, and Telecommunication (*Ed-Media 2000)*. Montreal, June, 2000.

Scanlon Eileen, Tosunoglu Canan, Jones Ann, Butcher Philip, Ross Shelagh, Greenberg Joel, Taylor John & Murphy Peter (1998): Learning with computers: experiences of evaluation. *Computers and Education,* Elsevier Science, 30(1/2), 9–14.

Scanlon Eileen (2011): Analyzing productive interactions in CSCL: collaborations, computers and contradictions. In: S. Puntambekar, G. Erkens & C.E. Hmelo-Silver (eds.): *Analyzing Interactions in CSCL: Methods, Approaches and Issues. Computer-Supported Collaborative Learning*. Springer, 12(3), 319–339.

Schuitemaker-King Jenny (2013): Giving corrective feedback in CLIL and EFL classes. *Levende Talen Tijdschrift* Jaargang 14, 2, 3–10.

Sharples Mike, McAndrew Patrick, Weller Martin, Ferguson Rebecca, Fitz Gerald Elizabeth, Hirst Tony & Gaved Mark (2013): Innovating Pedagogy 2013 - Exploring new forms of teaching, learning and assessment, to guide educators and policy makers. *Open University Innovation Report 2.* UK: The Open University, 2013. ISBN 978-1-78007-937-0. <http://www.open.ac.uk/personalpages/mike.sharples/Reports/Innovating_Pedagogy_ report_2013.pdf> [Accessed September 2013].

Shneiderman Ben (1997): Foreword. In: R. Debski, J. Gassin & M. Smith (eds.): *Language learning through social computing.* Melbourne: Applied Linguistics Association of Australia and The Horwood Language Center, v–viii.

Shneiderman Ben & Plaisant Catherine (2010): *Designing the user interface. Strategies for effective human-computer interaction.* (5th edition). Boston, MA: Pearson. ISBN-13: 978-0-321-60148-3.

Siemens George (2005): Connectivism: a learning theory for the digital age. *International Journal of Instructional Technology and Distance Learning,* 2(1). <http://www.itdl.org/Journal/Jan_05/article01.htm>[Accessed August 2013].

Siemens George & Gasevic Dragan (2012): Guest Editorial - Learning and Knowledge Analytics. *Journal of Educational Technology & Society,* 15(3), 1–2.

Skinner Burrhus Frederic (1954): The science of learning and the art of teaching. *Harvard Educational Review,* 24, 86–97.

Skinner Burrhus Frederic (1968): *The technology of teaching.* Englewood Cliffs, N.J. Prentice-Hall.

Stahl Gerry (2004): Building collaborative knowing: elements of a social theory of CSCL. In: J.W. Strijbos, P. Kirschner & R. Martens (eds.): *What we know about CSCL: And implementing it in higher education.* Boston, MA: Kluwer Academic Publishers, 53–86.

Stahl Gerry, Koschmann Timothy & Suthers Dan (2006): Computer-Supported Collaborative Learning: an historical perspective. In: R.K. Sawyer (ed.): *Cambridge handbook of the learning sciences.* Cambridge, UK: Cambridge University Press, 409–26. <http://gerrystahl.net/cscl/CSCL_English.pdf> [Accessed August 2013].

Summer Theresa (2010): Learner autonomy. *Profil 2,* 7–10. ISSN 1869-3334. <http://opus.bibliothek.uni-wuerzburg.de/volltexte/2010/4977/pdf/Summer_Learner_Autonomy_Profil2.pdf> [Accessed August 2013]

Suthers Dan (2007): Roles of computational scripts. In: Fischer Frank, Kollar Ingo, Haake Jörg M. & Mandl Heinz (eds.): *Scripting Computer-Supported Collaborative Learning: cognitive, computational and educational perspectives.* New York: Springer, 177–185.

Swain Merrill (1993): The Output Hypothesis. Just speaking and writing aren't enough. *The Canadian Modern Languages Review,* 50(1), 158–164.

Szewkis Eyal, Nussbaum Miguel, Denardin Fernanda, Abalos Jose Pedro, Rosen Tal, Caballero Daniela, Tagle Arturo & Alcoholado Cristian (2011): Collaboration between large groups in the classroom. *International Journal of Computer Supported Collaborative Learning,* 6, 561–575. DOI 10.1007/s11412-011-9123-y. <http://dcc.puc.cl/system/files/MN47-Collab+in+large+groups.pdf> [Accessed August 2013].

Thang Minh Dang, Dimitrova Vania & Djemame Karim (2007): Personalised mashups: opportunities and challenges for user modeling. In: C. Conati, K. McCoy & G. Paliouras (eds.): *UM 2007. Lecture Notes in Computer Science* (LNCS)(LNAI). Heidelberg: Springer, 4511, 415–419.

Thompson John (2007): *Is Education 1.0 ready for Web 2.0 students*? <http://www.innovateonline.info/pdf/vol3_issue4/Is_Education_1.0_Ready_for_Web_2.0_Students_.pdf> [Accessed February 2013].

Tull Susan (2012): On Trak: first steps in learning analytics. *Educause Review* online (Published on Wednesday, July 18, 2012) <http://www.educause.edu/ero/article/trak-first-stepslearning- analytics> [Accessed August 2013]

Tyler Ralph W. (1949): *Basic principles of curriculum and instruction.* Chicago: University of Chicago Press.

Ullrich Carsten, Borau Kerstin, Luo Heng, Tan Xiaohong, Shen Liping & Shen Ruimin (2008): Why Web 2.0 is good for learning and for research: principles and prototypes. In: *Proceedings of 17th International World Wide Web Conference (WWW*2008). Beijing, China, 705-714. ACM 978-1-60558-085-2/08/04.

UNESCO (2002): *What are Open Educational Resources (OERs)*? <http://www.unesco.org/new/en/communication-and-information/access-to-knowledge/open-educational-resources/what-are-open-educational-resources-oers/> [Accessed August 2013].

Vaill Peter B. (1996): *Learning as a way of being.* San Francisco, CA: Jossey-Blass Inc.

Van Heertum Rich & Share Jeff (2006): A new direction for multiliteracy education. *McGill Journal of Education,* 41(3), 249–265.

Vasquez Vivian, Harste Jerome C. & Albers Peggy (2010): From the personal to the Worldwide Web. Moving teachers into positions of critical interrogation. In: Elisabeth A. Baker (ed.): *The New Literacies. Multiple Perspectives on Research and Practice.* New York: The Guildford Press, 265–284.

Vygotsky Lev Semenovič, Cole Michael, John-Steiner Vera, Scribner Sylvia & Souberman Ellen (1978): *Mind in society: the development of higher psychological processes*. Cambridge, Massachusetts: Harvard University Press.

Wang Feng & Hannafin Michael J. (2005): *Design-based research and Technology-Enhanced Learning environments*. ETR&D, Wilson, 53(4), 5–23. ISSN 1042-629.

Warschauer Mark & Healey Deborah (1998): Computers and language learning: an overview. *Language Teaching*, 31, 57–71. DOI: 10.1017/S0261444800012970.

Warschauer Mark (2001): Millennialism and media: language, literacy, and technology in the 21st century. In: D. Graddol (ed.): *Applied Linguistics for the 21st century. AILA Review*, 14, 49–59. <http://www.aila.info/download/publications/review/AILA14.pdf> [Accessed August 2013].

Warschauer Mark *(2012): The digital divide and social inclusion. America's Quarterly*, 6(2), 130–135.

Wesiak Gudrun, Al-Smadi Mohammad, Margit Höfler & Christian Gütl (2013): Assessment for complex learning resources: development and validation of an integrated model. *International Journal of Emerging Technologies in Learning (iJET)*, 8(S1), 52–61.

Wolff Dieter (2002): Content and language integrated learning: an evaluation of the German approach. In: D.W.C. So & G.M. Jones (eds.): *Education and Society in Plurilingual Contexts*. Brüssel: VUB Brussels University Press, 56–74.

Wolff Dieter (2003): Content and language integrated learning: a framework for the development of learner autonomy. In: D. Little, J. Ridley & E. Ushioda (eds.): *Learner Autonomy in the Foreign Language Classroom: Teacher, Learner, Curriculum and Assessment*. Dublin: Authentik, 211–222.

Wood Terry, Cobb Paul & Yackel Erna (1995): Reflections on learning and teaching mathematics in elementary school. In: L.P. Steffe & J. Gale (eds.): *Constructivism in education*. Hillsdale, New Jersey: Lawrence Erlbaum, 401–422.

Yelland Nicola & Masters Jennifer (2007): Rethinking scaffolding in the information age. *Computers and Education*, 48, 362–382.

Yelland Nicola, Cope Bill & Kalantzis Mary (2008): Learning by Design: creating pedagogical frameworks for knowledge building in the twenty-first century. *Asia-Pacific Journal of Teacher Education*, 36(3), 197–213.

Zerr Sergej, Bischoff Kerstin & Chernov Sergey (2011): GuideMe! The world of sights in your pocket. In: *Proceedings of the IEEE 27th International Conference on Data Engineering (ICDE 2011)*, 1348-1351. ISBN: 978-1-4244-8959-6. DOI: 10.1109/ICDE.2011.5767953. <http://www.l3s.de/~chernov/GuideMe.pdf> [Accessed August 2013].

Zydatiß Wolfgang (2007): Bilingualer Fachunterricht in Deutschland: eine Bilanz. *Fremdsprachen Lehren und Lernen,* 36, 8–25.

Fremdsprachendidaktik / Foreign Language Pedagogy
inhalts- und lernerorientiert / content- and learner-oriented

Herausgegeben von / Edited by Gabriele Blell und Rita Kupetz
Mitbegründet von / Co-founded by Karlheinz Hellwig

Band 1 Gabriele Blell / Karlheinz Hellwig (Hrsg.): Bildende Kunst und Musik im Fremdsprachenunterricht. 1996.

Band 2 Jennifer Ridley: Reflection and strategies in foreign language learning. A study of four university-level *ab initio* learners of German. 1997.

Band 3 Rita Kupetz (Hrsg.): Vom gelenkten zum freien Schreiben im Fremdsprachenunterricht. Freiräume sprachlichen Handelns. 1997.

Band 4 Sylke Schmidt: Wortschatzerwerb beim Fernsehen. Eine Untersuchung mit fortgeschrittenen Lernern des Englischen. 1998.

Band 5 Karlheinz Hellwig: Anfänge englischen Literaturunterrichts. Entwicklung, Grundlagen, Praxis. Primarstufe – Jahrgangsstufe 11. 2000.

Band 6 Olaf Jäkel: Sokratisches Textgespräch. Ein Modell zur schülerorientierten Gedichtinterpretation im Englischunterricht mit Fortgeschrittenen. 2001.

Band 7 Rita Kupetz (ed.): Empowerment of the Learner. Changes and Challenges. 2002.

Band 8 Christiane Lütge: Syntagmen und Fremdsprachenerwerb. Ein Lernersprachenproblem. 2002.

Band 9 Gabriele Blell / Rita Kupetz (Hrsg.): Bilingualer Sachfachunterricht und Lehrerausbildung für den bilingualen Unterricht. Forschung und Praxisberichte. 2005.

Band 10 Karlheinz Hellwig: Bildung durch Literatur. Individuelles Sinnverstehen fremdsprachiger Texte. Eine literaturdidaktische *Tour d'Horizon*. 2005.

Band 11 Gabriele Blell / Rita Kupetz (Hrsg.): Fremdsprachenlernen zwischen *Medienverwahrlosung* und Medienkompetenz. Beiträge zu einer kritisch-reflektierenden Mediendidaktik. 2005.

Band 12 Camilla Badstübner-Kizik: Bild- und Musikkunst im Fremdsprachenunterricht. Zwischenbilanz und Handreichungen für die Praxis. 2007.

Band 13 Anne Ingrid Kollenrott: Sichtweisen auf deutsch-englisch bilingualen Geschichtsunterricht. Eine empirische Studie mit Fokus auf interkulturelles Lernen. 2008.

Band 14 Gabriele Blell / Rita Kupetz (Hrsg.): Fremdsprachenlehren und -lernen. Prozesse und Reformen. 2008.

Band 15 Andreas Müller-Hartmann / Marita Schocker-v. Ditfurth (Hrsg.): Aufgabenorientiertes Lernen und Lehren mit Medien. Ansätze, Erfahrungen, Perspektiven in der Fremdsprachendidaktik. 2008.

Band 16 Christiane Lütge / Anne Ingrid Kollenrott / Birgit Ziegenmeyer / Gabriela Fellmann (Hrsg.): Empirische Fremdsprachenforschung – Konzepte und Perspektiven. 2009.

Band 17 Gabriele Blell / Rita Kupetz (Hrsg.): Der Einsatz von Musik und die Entwicklung von *Audio Literacy* im Fremdsprachenunterricht. 2010.

Band 18 Christiane M. Bongartz / Jutta Rymarczyk (Hrsg.): *Languages Across the Curriculum*. Ein multiperspektivischer Zugang. 2010.

Band 19 Stéfanie Witzigmann: Bildende Kunst in der Zielsprache Französisch als Einstieg ins bilinguale Lehren und Lernen. Explorative Studie in einer fünften Realschulklasse. 2011.

Band 20 Marcus Reinfried / Laurenz Volkmann (Hrsg.): Medien im neokommunikativen Fremdsprachenunterricht. Einsatzformen, Inhalte, Lernerkompetenzen. Beiträge zum IX. Mediendidaktischen Kolloquium an der Friedrich-Schiller-Universität Jena (18.-20.09.2008). 2012.

Band 21 Friedrich Lenz (Hrsg.): Bilinguales Lernen. Unterrichtskonzepte zur Förderung sachfachbezogener und interkultureller Kompetenz. 2012.

Band 22 Anke Stöver-Blahak: Sprechen und Vortragen lernen im Fremdsprachenunterricht. Interpretativ, kreativ und ganzheitlich mit Gedichten. 2012.

Band 23 Joanna Pfingsthorn: Variability in Learner Errors as a Reflection of the CLT Paradigm Shift. 2013.

Band 24 Sylke Bakker: Fragen des Assessments aus Sicht von Englischlehrkräften. Empirische Annäherungen durch qualitative Inhaltsanalysen. 2013.

Band 25 Carmen Becker: Portfolio als Baustein einer neuen Lernkultur. Eine empirische Studie zur Implementierung des Europäischen Portfolios der Sprachen. 2013.

Band 26 Rita Kupetz / Carmen Becker (eds): Content and Language Integrated Learning by Interaction. 2014.

Band 27 Hannah Ruhm: Narrative Kompetenz in der Fremdsprache Englisch. Eine empirische Studie zur Ausprägung mündlicher Erzählfertigkeiten am Ende der Sekundarstufe I. 2014.

Band 28 Ivana Marenzi: Multiliteracies and e-learning2.0. 2014.

www.peterlang.com